Building a Culture of Inclusivity

Effective internal communication for diversity, equity and inclusion

Priya Bates and Advita Patel

KoganPage

Publisher's note
Every possible effort has been made to ensure that the information contained in this book is accurate at the time of going to press, and the publishers and authors cannot accept responsibility for any errors or omissions, however caused. No responsibility for loss or damage occasioned to any person acting, or refraining from action, as a result of the material in this publication can be accepted by the editor, the publisher or the author.

First published in Great Britain and the United States in 2023 by Kogan Page Limited

2nd Floor, 45 Gee Street
London
EC1V 3RS
United Kingdom
www.koganpage.com

8 W 38th Street, Suite 902
New York, NY 10018
USA

4737/23 Ansari Road
Daryaganj
New Delhi 110002
India

Kogan Page books are printed on paper from sustainable forests.

ISBNs

Hardback   978 1 3986 1041 5
Paperback   978 1 3986 1039 2
Ebook   978 1 3986 1040 8

British Library Cataloguing-in-Publication Data

A CIP record for this book is available from the British Library.

Library of Congress Control Number
2023011295

Typeset by Integra Software Services, Pondicherry
Print production managed by Jellyfish
Printed and bound by CPI Group (UK) Ltd, Croydon, CR0 4YY

PRAISE FOR *BUILDING A CULTURE OF INCLUSIVITY*

This new book is a must-read for anyone working in internal communications. It highlights the need for effective communication around DEI efforts in order to make them stick and yield results. In particular, the authors argue that DEI initiatives will fail without good communication, as employees won't know how to get involved or what behaviour is expected of them in order to be inclusive. This book is packed full of practical advice and guidance to help communicators enable, engage and empower colleagues to deliver on DEI programmes. Particularly useful are the questions dotted throughout the book to help you reflect on your work and your organization, to help you plan how to take action. This book includes a comprehensive and fascinating history of internal communication, and lays bare a compelling argument for why DEI is essential for organizational survival. I highly recommend this book to anyone working in internal comms – it's the kind of book you'll underline, scribble in the margins and come back to for reference time and time again.
Joanna Parsons, Director of Colleague Experience, Bentley Systems

A lot has been done in the last couple of years to raise awareness regarding DEI. What I really like about this book is that it takes it beyond awareness, towards a concrete roadmap for practical change within businesses. One can feel the passion of the authors. Their principle 'progress not perfect' encourages you to keep going step by step towards a future where DEI is no longer a concept or goal but an everyday normality.
Karen Lange, Member of the Board for Human Resources, Bentley Motors

Building a Culture of Inclusivity has been an excellent companion to me whilst I have travelled for work. It has been a journey of learning, self-reflection and conscience pricking but, most importantly, a spur to continue to act in the many ways I can, as a leader, to create a more inclusive organization. The true test for me has been how many times I have already referred to something I have read in the book as well as thinking about the people I will buy it for as a gift to help to encourage them as leaders, communicators and colleagues. I love the structure of the book. The clear lines of thoughtful opportunities to learn something new/embed some things I already know

(and perhaps have forgotten!), supported by some pretty impressive references. The handy checklists have also helped me reflect on how I personally perform (progress not perfect!) and in the organization I support. A must read for anyone interested in building inclusive cultures.
Tricia Williams, Chief Operating Officer, Northern Trains

This is not your next-door book on inclusion. It's a power-packed playbook that is insightful, practical, enlightening and easy to read! Advita and Priya offer practical applications of DEI strategies with effective frameworks to address key challenges that continue in organizations: psychological safety, leadership capability to impact cultural change, growth mindset and perceived lack of empathy and trust. Supported by robust data, insights and case studies, the readers are reminded about how 'real work in DEI forces us to look in the mirror and come to terms with uncomfortable truths about ourselves. If you're passionate about change, this should be the first stop on your journey.
Shalini Gupta, Senior Internal Communications Manager, Arup

How we communicate plays a critical role in building a culture of inclusion in our organizations. Advita and Priya's combined expertise as strategic business communicators have resulted in the creation of practical DEI frameworks and models to help leaders be more intentionally inclusive. This brilliant book is a must-read resource for every leader seeking to understand how they can bring positive, meaningful and long-lasting change to their working environment.
Ruchika Tulshyan, author, *Inclusion on Purpose*

Building a Culture of Inclusivity is a brilliant book for anyone looking to develop a diverse organization, foster collaboration and promote creativity. Not only does it pose important questions for leaders and management teams, it also provides a roadmap to ensure good intentions convert into genuine, positive and lasting change. Patel and Bates have moved beyond the theory and created an essential guide which will change businesses for the better.
Anna Russell, Internal Communications Director, FTSE 100 business

What I really appreciate about *Building a Culture of Inclusivity* is that authors, Priya Bates and Advita Patel, have written a comprehensive and well-researched book on DEI that provides context and explains *why* DEI is so critical to an organization's strategic operations. It further details the important role of internal communications and provides best practices and a roadmap for successfully embedding DEI in organizations. *Building A Culture of Inclusivity* should be a required resource for those pursuing careers in communications and anyone seeking greater understanding of DEI.

John G. Clemons, College Professor, University of North Carolina Charlotte and Loyola University New Orleans

I cannot recommend *Building a Culture of Inclusivity* enough. This book is a must-read for not only internal communication professionals, but for any leader, HR professional, or individual who wants to understand how to effectively build and communicate a strategy on diversity, equity, and inclusion within their organization. Priya Bates and Advita Patel bring a lifetime of experience and expertise to the table, providing invaluable insights into what DE&I truly means and why it is crucial for the survival of any organization in our world today. As a communication leader, this book challenged my personal biases and emphasized the importance of constantly questioning my own thinking in a world where accurate and truthful information can be difficult to access. The authors provide a practical and easy-to-follow set of tips and techniques to help readers build a more equitable workplace, develop a solid DE&I strategy, and effectively lead and manage the change required to achieve your DE&I goals. Perhaps most importantly, *Building a Culture of Inclusivity* emphasizes the critical role of effective internal communication in achieving DE&I goals. The authors make a compelling case for why and how we need to lead DE&I through communication, and provide actionable advice for achieving excellence in this area. Overall, I have no doubt that this book will become your go-to guide for DE&I excellence. If you're looking to build a more inclusive and equitable organization, *Building a Culture of Inclusivity* is the book for you.

Adrian Cropley OAM, communication strategist and Founder of the Centre for Strategic Communication Excellence

We know from our research that internal communication is one of the most critical elements of an effective DEI effort. I applaud Priya and Advita for writing *Building a Culture of Inclusivity* that so aptly guides those involved with communication and DEI on a great number of how-to tips and informative context. This book is a significant contribution to the literature and I highly recommend reading it.

Julie O'Mara, Past Director of Marketing Communications, Whirlpool Corporation

Building a Culture of Inclusivity delivers on so many crucial levels with the right balance of rightly researched facts, useful frameworks and seamlessly integrated storytelling. Priya Bates and Advita Patel do a fine job of providing the building blocks for moving an organization towards a more inclusive environment. If you are a newly hired Human Resources or DE&I professional, an internal communicator or just a C-Suite executive who's been tasked with moving the DE&I needle, please consider adding this resource to your library.

Derrick Larane, Chief Operating Officer, pocstock

Priya Bates and Advita Patel have crafted the definitive roadmap for shaping organizational culture to embrace inclusivity. While DEI is under assault in some quarters, Bates and Patel eschew politics and focus squarely on what matters to any company's stakeholders: the business case. Thoroughly documented with meaningful data and case studies, *Building a Culture of Inclusivity* is as well-researched as any work I have seen on this vitally important topic. What sets it apart, though, is the authors' evidence-supported argument that trust - a core driver of culture - is the foundation for any effective DEI effort. While it is geared toward internal communicators, any business leader would do well to absorb and act upon the lessons in this important work.

Shel Holtz, SCMP, Webcor

There are a number of excellent workplace guides to DEI on the marketplace, however, *Building a Culture of Inclusivity* stands out for several reasons. The first is that it includes both fundamentals, the why and the how of creating a truly inclusive and strategic DEI approach. Advita Patel and Priya Bates teach us about the importance of respect, trust, and dignity and that true change starts with believing in the why, however, the takeaways and reflective questions in each chapter serve as a guiding hand on the next steps to take. The book shares necessary truths, but never preaches. Divided into two parts – the foundations that need to be built and the frameworks and models required to ensure a meaningful approach is taken – Patel and Bates continually stress their 'progress not perfect' approach which can still lead to performance over performative action. *Building a Culture of Inclusivity* is also a must have for internal communications professionals, as the book includes a substantial section on the role of communications professionals in truly representing their audiences by guiding a safe space, building leadership capability and connecting the dots between DEI strategy and employee delivery. I came away from reading with a much clearer and truer understanding of how to create an inclusive DEI engagement plan.

Naomi Jones, Corporate Affairs Director, Mars Wrigley UK

CONTENTS

About the authors ix
Acknowledgements xi

Introduction 1

PART ONE
DEI foundations 5

01 Why diversity, equity and inclusion are integral
to organizational survival 7

02 Why trust matters when cultivating an inclusive culture 34

03 Building leadership capability to impact and influence
cultural change 59

04 Understanding biases – the benefits and the pitfalls 80

05 The role of the internal communication professional in
DEI 102

PART TWO
Frameworks and models 135

06 The 4A Framework to move DEI from performative to
performing 137

07 Change and the Diversity Continuum 161

08 Focusing on the conversation versus the campaign 186

09 The intersectional approach for communicators 205

10 Why using inclusive language is essential in the
    workplace 223

11 How to build an inclusive engagement plan for DEI 249

12 Best practices to develop and communicate your DEI
    strategy 274

    Index 295

ABOUT THE AUTHORS

Priya Bates

Priya is an award-winning professional communicator with a passion for building strength from the inside out. As president and owner of Inner Strength Communication, Priya builds strategic internal communication, engagement, branding and transformational change plans that enable, engage and empower employees to deliver business results. Her clients include organizations and leaders across technology, retail, financial, healthcare, government, mining and manufacturing sectors looking to build strategic internal communication expertise.

As co-founder of A Leader Like Me, Priya creates an empowered community driving global diversity, inclusion, equity and belonging through conversation, courage and confidence.

Priya is an Accredited Business Communicator (ABC) and was proud to become one of the first certified Strategic Communication Management Professionals (SCMP) in the world. In 2010, she received the Master Communicator (MC) designation, the highest honour bestowed upon a communication professional, from IABC Canada. In 2016, she was recognized as an IABC Fellow, a global lifetime achievement award for her contribution to the profession. Priya is also a passionate volunteer with the International Association of Business Communicators (IABC), and is proud to have led the organization's successful global rebranding effort.

Advita Patel

Advita has worked with organizations for over 20 years helping them understand how internal communication can make a difference to the world of work. She helps business leaders understand how they can cultivate inclusive cultures through effective communications so all colleagues can belong and thrive in their work.

She is the founder of CommsRebel, an internal communication and employee experience consultancy, the co-founder of A Leader Like Me, a global membership programme which helps underrepresented women of colour succeed further in their career and the co-founder of CalmEdgedRebels, a coaching retreat for professionals who want to live up to their potential. She is also a qualified confidence coach and works with teams and individuals to help them achieve their goals with confidence.

Advita is an established leader in the communication industry. As well as co-hosting two podcasts (the award-winning *CalmEdgedRebels* and *Amplifying Diverse Voices – A Leader Like Me*), she has spoken at various events and podcasts, internationally, where she discusses internal communications, measurement, inclusion and confidence.

For eight years she volunteered for the Chartered Institute of Public Relations where she chaired the Internal Communications committee and was a Board member for two years supporting them through the Covid-19 pandemic. She is a chartered PR practitioner, and a fellow of the Chartered Institute of Public Relations. In 2022 she was named on the Northern Asian Power list and was the judges' choice for the Emerging Leader Award.

Advita believes that everyone has the right to belong at work and that communication can play a significant role in helping organizations understand how they can build an inclusive culture.

ACKNOWLEDGEMENTS

Priya Bates

Thank you to my husband Glenn and daughters Lita and Mary for keeping me grounded. Being a mixed-race couple and having biracial children who have British and Indian roots help me understand perspectives and privileges. It's for them that I dream of a future where everyone belongs.

Thank you to Canada and Toronto for giving me the opportunity to grow up in diverse communities where challenges and opportunities formed my ideas, opinions and beliefs that we are stronger together.

Thank you to the International Association of Business Communicators (IABC), and to so many colleagues who have become mentors and friends, for developing my love for internal communication and its role in driving change.

And of course, thank you to Advita for talking me into writing a book and challenging me to try new things and take risks. We have different approaches yet similar visions and values that put people in the centre of creating change.

Advita Patel

I want to dedicate this book to my parents, Bena and Pankaj, who sacrificed a lot so that my sister and I could live the life we do today. They fought hard, alongside others, to ensure we didn't have to endure the adversities they first faced when they entered the workforce in the UK. Their unwavering support and belief in me is the reason why I was able to write this book. Thank you to my sister Dharini for being my champion from day one. She's been my constant rock, giving me the motivation and confidence to keep going, even when I didn't think I could.

To my friends, Olivia Clayton, Jenni Field, Trudy Lewis and Manisha Sanyal, thank you for always being by my side and for sending me words of encouragement when I needed it the most. I'm beyond grateful to have friends like you in my life.

I'd also like to thank those of you who tirelessly push for better inclusion in your workplaces. It's not easy work, but your tenacity, support and determination will help change the world of work for the better.

Finally, thank you to Priya for being a fabulous co-author and business partner – I wouldn't have wanted to write this book with anyone else.

Introduction

This book is for internal communication professionals, diversity, equity and inclusion (DEI) leaders, human resource professionals and all leaders interested in building inclusive cultures. We are internal communication professionals who have collectively worked in the industry for more than 30 years across various industries, internally and within our consultancies. In the last few years, we recognized a gap in the knowledge within our profession on how internal communication can influence inclusive cultures. Our story of how we became business partners is an unusual one. We met briefly in Vancouver, Canada, for 10 minutes during the International Association of Business Communicators World Conference in 2019. We'd been connected via LinkedIn for several years, but until then, we had not spoken verbally. As soon as we met, there was an instant connection, as we shared similar experiences of being South Asian women in an industry where we don't often see leaders like ourselves.

At the beginning of 2020, before Covid-19, Advita connected with Priya to ask if she'd consider being her informal mentor to help her navigate the consultancy world. During these conversations, we discussed the challenges facing underrepresented people in various organizations. In March 2020, as the pandemic slowed down our client work, it allowed us to explore how we could support underrepresented women of colour in organizations looking for progression. We recognized the lack of representation in senior roles, and from our experiences, when you don't see people like you, you don't think you belong. This led us to create A Leader Like Me, a membership to help women of colour build confidence and courage to drive career progression.

As we were developing this training programme, a video went viral on social media in May 2020 showing a police officer in the USA with his knee on a Black man's neck, subsequently causing his death. The man who was murdered was named George Floyd. The murder of George Floyd shocked people across the globe and highlighted the horrific treatment of Black people in the United States and other countries. At this point, our clients and other organizations contacted us to help them navigate responses to avoid negativity reputationally, internally and externally. The statements that organizations shared demonstrated good intent but limited action. We knew that as internal communication professionals, there was much work we could do to support leaders who wanted to make a difference with DEI in their organization. During this time, we were also approached by our industry peers, who sought advice after the mandate was given to them for communicating DEI initiatives across their organization. Most people felt overwhelmed and anxious at the responsibility and struggled to understand where to start. We knew we had to do something to help.

Over the last three years, we have been advising and guiding organizations to create robust internal communication plans and strategies to address their DEI challenges. These plans have led to building inclusive cultures where colleagues can thrive and recognize the value they bring to the organization. We know that to change the world of work, so that it becomes more inclusive, we need to cultivate a community of leaders interested in using strategic communications to build inclusive cultures. We wanted to write a book where we could share our knowledge and expertise on how others can build inclusion with intention using effective communication methods. It was after reading Ruchika Tulshyan's book, *Inclusion on Purpose*, that we were inspired to approach Kogan Page with our book idea. We know that there are a limited number of books about internal communication (and probably broader) written by people of colour, particularly women of colour. In fact, when we did some research, we didn't come across one internal communication book written by a woman of colour. We wanted to bring our expertise to the market and show what the power of representation can do.

The ALLMe 4A Framework

This book covers our combined experience, expertise, learnings and mistakes to help you learn and make a difference in your organization. However, we specifically wanted to mention our ALLMe 4A Framework, as we believe this is the first stage of you becoming an inclusion advocate. We cover this framework in more detail in Chapter 5. We developed this framework to help people understand how to address challenges and barriers in the pursuit of being inclusive. The first step of the framework is to **acknowledge** where your gaps are in your learning. You can't learn or move forward if you don't first acknowledge there's a problem or a challenge. Once you've acknowledged what the problem or barrier is, you need to be **aware** of the present state. Do the research, understand the numbers and identify the disconnects. Following this step, you can then take appropriate **action**. Action is the plan to solve the problem or challenges. It sets real goals that are measurable. The final stage is **accountability**. It helps you measure success (or failure) to help you correct mistakes and determine next steps. Throughout this book we frequently state progress not perfect – this is incredibly important. Learning and unlearning habits, behaviours and bias can take time and mistakes will be made. However, taking accountability and ensuring that you're continuously learning is vital if you want to be fair and equitable in your workplace.

A few final notes

It's important to note a few things before you delve in: first, we are strategic business communication experts applying our diversity, equity and inclusion knowledge. Over the years, we have worked hard to educate ourselves and build our communities to strengthen our learning. As part of this learning, we've also had to unlearn some of our own biases and myths based on our lived experiences, and this is an ongoing process which means there may be parts of the book that we may not have got perfect. We are huge advocates of progress not perfect to continue moving forward and encouraging others to make changes. There will be words we've used that you may disagree with, phrases that cause some uncomfortableness and stories we've shared that are no longer relevant or are out of date because the world of inclusion moves fast. We also want to clarify some terms we've used. With both of us working across two continents with their nuances of language, we've used words and phrases that we hope describes the most common terminology in plain English.

The abbreviation we use is DEI: diversity, equity, inclusion. We purposely chose to use equity rather than equality because we believe that not everyone starts at the same point in their lives. To level the playing field, we need to provide equitable opportunities to those who may not have the same privileges as others. We realize that other terms are used across different countries and organizations, such as EDI (equality/equity, diversity, inclusion), DEIB (diversity, equity, inclusion, belonging), IDEA/AIDE (inclusion, diversity, equity, accessibility) and JEDI (justice, equity, diversity, inclusion). Ultimately, it's essential to find the abbreviation that aligns with your strategy and objectives, and each organization will have its preference.

We understand that there's no preferred term to describe groups of people who belong to one specific characteristic, and we recognize these groups are not homogenous. When possible, we do try to refer to specific identities. However, there are instances in the book when we specifically refer to the discrimination facing underrepresented people from racial or ethnic backgrounds. Our preferred term is to reference this group as people of colour, as that's how we both identify.

In most instances, we've used people first language as that's our preferred way, but we recognize some people prefer identity first. We share our thoughts on this in Chapter 10.

This book is intended to be used as a guide, and we recommend you start from Chapter 1 and work your way through. Part One will give you insight into why DEI is essential, and the second part will take you through some of our preferred approaches, models and frameworks. We've provided you with the latest thinking, practical advice and useful information which will help you build confidence and make an impact in this work.

This work can't happen in isolation and must be a partnership with leaders in the business, otherwise it will be difficult to build a truly inclusive organization. Thank you for taking the first step to making a difference in the world of work, building an inclusive culture and helping people to belong.

Priya and Advita

PART ONE

DEI foundations

01 Why diversity, equity and inclusion are integral to organizational survival

02 Why trust matters when cultivating an inclusive culture

03 Building leadership capability to impact and influence cultural change

04 Understanding biases – the benefits and the pitfalls

05 The role of the internal communication professional in DEI

01

Why diversity, equity and inclusion are integral to organizational survival

This chapter explores the why for diversity, equity and inclusion (DEI). Although we start with demographic trends coupled with global opportunities and challenges, it's important to note that even though the business case can be inspired by external information, it's critical to understand what your why is for your organization through both a professional and personal lens. As Simon Sinek (2009) says, 'If you don't know why, you can't know how.'

As strategic internal communication professionals working with a variety of global organizations over the past 20 to 30 years, we've always encouraged all our employers and clients to begin every project, programme and change initiative with the question 'why?':

- Organizations need to understand why they need to invest time, resources and effort.
- Leaders need to understand why they need to motivate to create alignment and momentum.
- Colleagues need to understand why to trust that they are moving in the right direction.

Making progress in DEI and creating positive cultures has to be a team effort. And with every team effort we have options: we can demand and threaten to drive action; we can manipulate people to do what we need; or we can inspire them to work together towards a common goal.

As we've worked with organizations in North America and the UK through our consulting businesses, we've had the opportunity to guide, and more importantly observe, the efforts of corporations, government, educational institutions and non-profits as they navigate the world of DEI with good intent yet trepidation as they step into an unknown that is constantly changing, often with limited resources.

That's why it's integral for us to start by explaining why inclusive cultures driven by DEI are vital to organizations. We also want to provide you with guidance that will help you ask the right questions to uncover what DEI means professionally and personally. Let's be honest, DEI is an incredibly personal conversation that involves, at its core, a personal effort by everyone involved including those who are responsible for communicating.

Dignity and worth

At the centre of 'why' is a conversation about dignity and worth. At a conference several years ago, we started hearing rumblings that the focus of DEI was evolving to a focus on belonging, dignity and justice.

Often, the focus on organizational DEI benchmarks is from a top-down point of view. Is the organization focused on diversity or is everyone we see and subsequently every decision we make coming from a unilateral point of view? Is the organization, its leaders and people, trying to create an equitable environment by being aware of processes, systems and biases that may favour some at the expense of others? Is the organization doing what it can to create a culture of inclusion where it proactively invites various individuals, experiences and opinions to the table?

Belonging, dignity and justice, on the other hand, are from a people point of view – from the bottom up. Do I feel like I belong? Am I respected and treated with dignity? Are decisions fair and just? Does the organization believe in me enough to make an investment in my development?

Throughout this book, we will continue to refer to DEI, yet you will read elements that refer to belonging, dignity and justice. This is our why… to change the world of work; to help organizations move past performative gestures and genuinely deliver results in the DEI space; and at the end of the day inspire employees to support good intentions to drive change that creates cultures where everyone feels included and worthy.

We will also focus on the integral role of internal communication to help connect the dots between aspirational goals and leader and colleague action. As business leaders, with strategic internal communication expertise, our focus is: to turn words into actions, values into behaviours, strategy into results, brand promises into colleague and customer experiences.

DEI history

Let's start with a little walk through the history of human rights. Although it feels to some like conversations around DEI are fairly recent since the murder of George Floyd in 2020, the truth is that that this conversation has been happening over centuries. Almost like a dam getting ready to burst, many are still reacting to keep the waters at bay, while others realize they need to prepare themselves for a changing future.

In reality, the world has been talking about human rights for hundreds of years. In the 1200s, the Magna Carta (The Great Charter) laid out the principle that everybody, including royalty, was subject to the law. Future documents like the English Bill of Rights (1689) and the Bill of Rights in the US Constitution (1791) affirmed rights such as free elections, freedom of speech and freedom from 'cruel and unusual punishment' (STTP Canada, 2022).

Although these documents typically excluded the rights of women, people of colour, Indigenous peoples and many social, religious and political groups, they set out basic principles that should apply to everyone.

After World War II, the world was horrified by the atrocities perpetrated by Nazi Germany that targeted Jews and other marginalized groups. The scale of human tragedy led to the global recognition that such crimes against humanity must be prevented from ever happening again. Governments around the globe committed to establishing the United Nations (UN), dedicated to fostering peace and preventing conflict:

> We the peoples of the United Nations (are) determined… to reaffirm faith in fundamental human rights, in the dignity and worth of the human person, in the equal rights of men and women and of nations large and small. (United Nations, 2022)

Member states of the United Nations pledged to promote respect for the human rights of all. To advance this goal, the UN established an international Commission on Human Rights led by Eleanor Roosevelt, a well-known human rights advocate. A major objective for the Commission was to create a document that, for the first time in history, would set out **human rights for every person**. The draft penned by John Humphrey, a Canadian lawyer and human rights expert, in 1948 became the foundation for the Universal Declaration of Human Rights (UDHR). The Declaration contained 30 articles that defined fundamental rights and freedoms for every human being on earth.

The preamble in the UDHR says that 'Recognition of the inherent dignity and of the equal and inalienable rights of all members of the human family is the foundation of freedom, justice, and peace in the world.'

Since passing the International Bill of Human Rights, the United Nations has adopted many additional legal instruments that protect women's rights, children's rights, Indigenous rights and the rights of persons with disabilities, to name a few.

The UDHR is one of the most important documents of the 20th century. Its principles have inspired hundreds of laws and conventions protecting human rights. These new measures are the result of collective and individual efforts by people all over the world.

The 20th century witnessed the beginning of the modern human rights movement. Since then, the world has seen profound social changes. The struggles for women's rights, civil rights and the resistance to apartheid in South Africa are examples of local and global activism that have made significant progress.

Much remains to be done with regard to many other issues. These include protecting the rights of Indigenous peoples, persons with disabilities and persons of diverse sexual orientations and gender identities. Relatively new issues like the right to privacy in an internet age and prevention of cyber bullying are now entering public awareness.

Around the world, the principles expressed in the UDHR continue to foster constant dialogue and action. There is global agreement among nations that every person is entitled to human rights. How to make them a reality for all is part of our ever-evolving human rights conversation.

Flashlights, mirrors, beacons

As we start talking about why, we also want you to pay attention to your own emotions, thoughts and fears. It's not unusual for us, two women of colour on two different continents, to work with communication, human resources and executive teams where we are the only people of colour in the room (live or virtual). In these engagements, we often spend time with diverse employees, who are passionate about driving or resisting change from all levels. There have been patterns of behaviour and reactions that we've noticed while developing DEI communication and engagement strategies and plans. By understanding these behaviours and reactions, we will be able to recognize them in others and, more importantly, in ourselves.

Flashlights

Everyone looks for themselves in the strategy, initiatives and actions. When they see themselves reflected, they are comforted. When they don't see themselves, they get angry, scared, or resist and shut down. We often think that our audience is the group we're trying to impact but when we don't plan communication for all, it leaves individuals feeling left out – the opposite of inclusion and belonging.

If you can't find yourself, instead of saying 'If it's not about me, it's not for me', reflect instead on why you are not present and why others need to be included. Also reflect on the role you play and contributions you can make to progress.

Mirrors

Real work in DEI forces us to look in the mirror and come to terms with uncomfortable truths about ourselves. Our systems, our privileges, our biases, our myths, our upbringing, our families, our lack of action, etc. This applies to everyone. That's why sometimes we reflect and other times we deflect by closing our eyes or becoming defensive. Acknowledging this impact and helping leaders and colleagues through these realizations, without driving guilt, is something we're all trying to figure out.

When you look in the mirror, the question for you is whether you will choose to turn away and ignore what you see, or look closer and reflect on why with curiosity instead of judgement.

Beacons

Individuals, leaders and professionals have emerged as beacons. Remember that beacons can serve as both warning and guiding lights who are trying to educate and change the future. These beacons paint a picture of the future – some a hopeful picture (think Martin Luther King and 'I have a dream') while others can create doomsday scenarios (think White Supremacy movements or Make America Great Again). We've learned to listen to both so that we can identify what is real and based on fact to help us be the change we want to see in the world.

The question to ask yourself is whether you will choose hope over fear. We think there is greater opportunity in hope.

TABLE 1.1 Flashlights, mirrors, beacons

Flashlights	Mirrors	Beacons
• Looking for yourself	• Looking at yourself	• Looking for direction
• Feeling included or excluded based on what you find	• Liking or not liking what you see	• Guiding light or warning light?
• Will you keep searching to find your role and share the spotlight?	• Feeling attacked or uncomfortable	• Will you choose hope or fear?
	• Will you look closer and reflect or turn away?	• Will you choose the past, present or future?

Created by authors for the purpose of the book

Know that regardless of who you are, or where you came from, you and those you communicate with will experience each of these scenarios at some point depending on the conversation and its impact. We believe that being aware is an important part of progress. That's why when we talk about 'why', we need to look at the big picture along with the personal picture to help acknowledge feelings in order to understand and support change.

How we react is human and our goal when observing ourselves is to observe with curiosity not judgement in order to ask ourselves why we feel the way we do.

We also challenge you to be a **worker** versus a **warrior**.

Part of our why for writing this book is the acknowledgment that real progress is a group effort. We were introduced to this analogy through a story told by Deepak Kashyap, Director of EDI and Corporate Wellness at Lotus Mindfulness Centre, on a podcast called 'Uncovering Belonging' hosted by Jade Pichette and Erin Davis (Pride at Work Canada, 2022). Deepak explained:

> The moment you are in the warrior mentality you have to choose sides and you have to look at the other side as a monolith to be attacked. But a worker has to passionately work with everybody. The worker doesn't have to choose sides. It has to be on the side of values and not identities.

We loved this analogy. We would probably also admit that as two women of colour, we probably started our work with a bit of a warrior mentality. As we ourselves learn about what is required to succeed, and our experience working with organizations with good intent, we realize that we will benefit from a worker mentality where everyone wins. At the end of the day, what we're looking for is respect and fair treatment that creates a culture of inclusion and belonging for everyone. We realize that we will have to do the hard work over the long term to truly change the world of work for the good of everyone.

Internal communication is an integral enabler of business success and the central role is to help colleagues be **aware** of the facts, **understand** decisions and directions, **do** what is expected and needed, and **believe** in the cause. By starting with answering the why, we help set the foundation for all of the work to come that will help enable, engage and empower colleagues to manage change and deliver results. And let's be honest, the work in diversity, equity and inclusion is a major long-term change effort that impacts each one of us not only professionally but personally as well.

Do we need to justify DEI efforts?

Recently, when talking about DEI, a discussion has emerged about not having to prove the **why**. That DEI is simply the right thing to do and we shouldn't have to prove its value to organizations and leaders. That it unfairly puts marginalized groups in a position to have to prove their worthiness. In a recent article, UK disability advocate and PR professional Sara Thornhurst (2022) says:

> Phrases like 'it makes good business sense', 'it's good for the bottom line' or 'more diverse businesses make more profit', are meant to encourage change but what they really do is uphold systems which can ultimately cause harm to marginalised voices and fail to cause change where it matters – in the beliefs, attitudes and actions of people with power.

While we agree that bottom-line driven arguments should not be the primary argument, they are important to **include** versus **ignore**. It's an important part of the **why** along with other elements that should be considered for organizations on any project, programme or paradigm shift. For good or for worse, creating connection to business numbers is the language of leaders and as long as they are ignored, it is difficult to get the attention of those whom make the decisions that determine investment and attention.

Demographics – the global reality

So many of the whys that resonate with leaders revolve around demographics and demographic trends. Leaders around the world start with data before making meaningful decisions for the business when identifying marketing opportunities around product, price, packaging and promotion. These conversation around data are starting to look inside organizations and starting to ask important questions.

Note that when looking at DEI, organizations are actively starting to explore a variety of traits including: age, disability, gender, race, religion and sexual orientation (listed in alphabetical order). Although other factors may emerge, these tend to be the primary categories today. As we explore global data to give you a sense of trends, it's important for you to understand data as it relates to your organization, community and customers in order to inform decisions.

Age

According to the United National World Population Prospects 2019, we have a rapidly aging global population. In 1950, people over 70 accounted for only 0.05 per cent of the population. Today, those over 80 represent 2 per cent (Rice, 2021).

We also have five generations in the workplace impacting on everything including benefits that will resonate and ways to communicate with each generation successfully to drive engagement. In fact, according to David Rice of the HR Exchange Network, by 2025, it is expected that Millennials will make up 75 per cent of the global workforce. This is the generation that has high expectations in terms of social issues including climate change, income inequality, public health, and diversity and inclusion.

TABLE 1.2 The world by age group

Age range (years)	Percentage of world population
< 20	33.2%
20–39	29.9%
40–49	23.1%
60–79	11.8%
80–99	1.9%
100+	0.01%

SOURCE Ang, 2021

- Traditionalists – born 1927 to 1946
- Baby Boomers – born 1947 to 1964
- Generation X – born 1965 to 1980
- Millennials – born 1981 to 2000
- Generation Z – born 2001 to 2020

Disability

According to the World Health Organization, about 16 per cent of the world's population lives with some form of significant disability (WHO, 2022). The global estimate for disability is on the rise due to population aging and the rapid spread of chronic diseases, as well as improvements in the methodologies used to measure disability (United Nations Department of Economic and Social Affairs, 2021).

- Around 16 per cent of the world's population, or an estimated 1.3 billion people, experience significant disability today. They are the world's largest minority (WHO, 2022).
- This figure is increasing through population growth, medical advances and the aging process, says the World Health Organization (WHO, 2022).
- In countries with life expectancies over 70 years, individuals spend on average about eight years, or 11.5 per cent of their life span, living with disabilities (Disabled World, 2022).
- 80 per cent of persons with disabilities live in developing countries, according to the UN Development Programme (Disabled World, 2022).

#WETHE15

Of note is the #WeThe15 campaign launched at the Tokyo 2020 Paralympic Games, which is a global movement publicly campaigning for disability visibility, inclusion and accessibility. #WeThe15 will build greater knowledge of the barriers and discrimination persons with disabilities face on a daily basis at all levels of society. The focus of the campaign is to ensure that persons with disabilities are not seen as special, but ordinary, contributing citizens and functioning members of society that want to be included.

SOURCE WeThe15, 2020

Gender

When looking at gender, data tends to fall close to 50/50 when it comes to binary individuals. Based on limited data, studies conducted in the US estimate that gender-diverse persons represent 0.1 to 2 per cent of the population (Spizzirri, 2021). In its latest 2021 Census of Population, Canada identified that 0.33 per cent of Canadians age 15 or older self-identified as non-binary (Statistics Canada, 2021). While studies conducted exclusively with the LGBTQ+ community in the UK discovered that 6.9 per cent of those surveyed identified as non-binary (Government Equities Office, 2019).

Although male at birth today hold a slight lead – 50.5 per cent compared to 49.5 per cent female at birth – for the most part, the data has remained largely the same and is not expected to change drastically in the next few years. In countries where there are larger discrepancies in male versus female proportions, they can be explained by historical events. The majority of countries and regions in the world have more females than males. But the top two populous countries, China and India, have a higher male population; therefore, there are slightly more males than females globally (Statistics Times, 2021).

Much research based on gender focuses on gender gaps especially as the impacts of the Covid-19 pandemic continue to be felt. Many countries have also created requirements for employers with more than 250 employees to publish annual gender pay gap reports. And there is a movement in some locations to publish salary ranges proactively to help diminish discrepancies.

TABLE 1.3 Share of global population

Rank	Region	Share of global population (%)
1	Asia	60
2	Africa	16
3	Europe	10
4	North America	7
5	South America	6
6	Central America	1
7	Oceania	1

SOURCE Desjardins, 2019

Race

When it comes to the global population, the majority of people in the world live in Asia, followed by Africa. In fact, they represent 76 per cent of the world's population. For global companies, they realize that growth opportunities are higher the wider their reach.

FIGURE 1.1 Share of population changes in various countries around the world

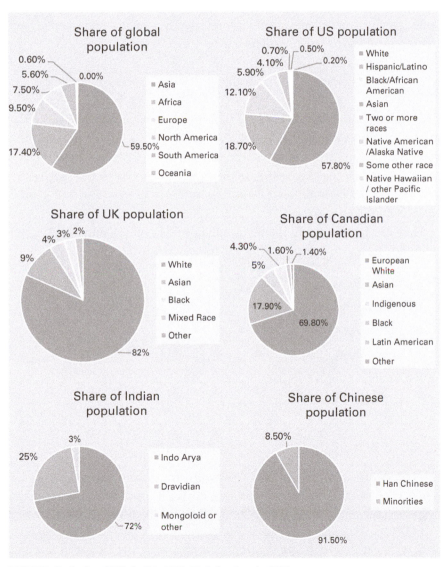

SOURCES Desjardins, 2019; Garlick, 2022; Statistics Canada, 2022

Conversations around race have escalated and evolved since the murder of George Floyd and the Black Lives Matter movement. Throughout the last few years, there has been increased attention on hate crimes that impact various racial groups and a focus on Indigenous communities due to the mass graves found in residential schools in Canada.

Various countries measure race differently. Take a look at Figure 1.1 to see an example.

It is important to note that organizations in colonized countries are starting to collect race and ethnicity statistics through self-identification. Because colleagues are worried about how information is going to be used, many are hesitant to answer these questions due to a lack of trust.

Religion

Although organizations do not tend to measure or ask about religious affiliations, we do see organizations who know that there is diversity amongst staff and customers; recognize commemorative religious observances throughout the year; have programmes and rules to combat antisemitism and Islamophobia; and create employee resource groups that bring folks together based on religion.

Here is a breakdown of the world's major religions (Deshmukh, 2022):

- 31.0% Christians
- 25.0% Muslims
- 15.6% unaffiliated
- 15.2% Hindus
- 6.6% Buddhists
- 5.6 % Folk
- 0.2% Jewish

Sexual orientation

By conservative estimates, LGBTQ+ individuals make up approximately 4.5 per cent of the US population, but account for 8 per cent of the country's disposable income, according to a 2020 report from Kearney (Petrock, 2021).

LGBTQ+ consumers are also more likely than members of other groups to seek out brands that represent and include them, to reward those that show sustained support of LGBTQ+ friendly media and causes, and to remain loyal to brands that are loyal to them (Varrella, 2021).

Please note that we have chosen the term LGBTQ+ since they are the common elements of the various abbreviations used globally. We acknowledge that in some organizations and regions, the letters IA are added to identify intersexual and asexual, along with 2S to identify two-spirit used by Indigenous populations.

As we reflect on the demographics in this chapter, did anything surprise you? One of the biggest 'ahas' for us was the fact that as more timely data became available, the numbers changed, in most cases grew when it came to identification of characteristics. This could have been explained by actual organic growth, new questions on characteristics being asked in census surveys and more comfort with self-identification.

As you look at the data, ensure you understand what is relevant to your own organization. Working with a global company may require a different focus than a local one. Data may simply not be available or accurate in a region or organization that doesn't ask the questions or where colleagues don't trust sharing.

DEI – why?

As we start looking at our why for DEI, we'll cover six Rs: rights, representation, retention, recruitment, reputation and results. They are intended to start a conversation and link the why to business objectives. Your role is to identify the ones that will resonate with leaders and colleagues to drive connection and investment.

Rights

We focus on DEI because it is the right thing to do.

Let's start by simply stating that focusing on creating workplaces in which people are able to thrive, contribute and belong is simply the right thing to do. We all want to be treated fairly. We all want to belong. We all want to feel respected. We all want to contribute.

DEI is focused on human rights. It's about equality – people being treated equally; equity when there is a correction to fix former systems that created inequities that purposely or inadvertently held certain people back. It's about justice and fairness. It's also about respect. We believe that equity has the edge on equality to drive fairness since until we ask ourselves the right questions, we may not realize that what we believe is equal treatment unnecessarily puts many groups at a disadvantage.

ADVICE

Ask yourself the following questions:

- Does your organization treat everyone fairly?
- Do you trust your organization to make decisions consistent with our values?

Representation

We focus on DEI to represent our publics accurately and realistically.

Representation means that individuals, leaders and organizations accurately represent their publics. These include colleagues and people who work for the organization, customers who buy from the organization and the communities in which the organization is located.

If all things are equal, the numbers and percentages we see at the frontline of an organization should be reflected as you move up in management levels. A recent focus on data has told us that this is simply not the case.

Leadership teams in Western and colonized cultures remain mostly white and male, and while some progress has been made on women entering leadership ranks, they still seem to favour a particular race. Now think of the impact of a lack of representation.

From a professional perspective, it's difficult for leaders, managers and employees to make the right decisions if their thinking and experience are uniform. What did Albert Einstein say? The definition of insanity is doing the same thing over and over again and expecting a different result.

ADVICE

For your organization, ask yourself the following:

- What are the demographics of your colleagues base?
- What are the demographics of the customers and communities you serve?
- What are the demographics in the part of the world you serve?
- What are the demographics of the communities in which you operate?
- When you look at your leaders and communication team, are they representative of your publics?
- When you look at your communication – marketing, advertising and stories (internal and external) – do the images and experiences reflect your publics?

Retention

We focus on DEI to retain our best workers.

In May 2021, we started hearing the term 'The Great Resignation' enter our vocabulary. It was coined by management professor Anthony Klotz, a professor of management at University College London's School of Management. During the Covid pandemic, we heard of colleagues re-evaluating their lives and lifestyles, prioritizing family, pursuing dreams, focusing on mental and physical health, and ultimately choosing how they wanted to work and live.

In 2022, around the world, a lack of staff meant noticeable impacts to customer and patient service. Not enough retail colleagues to open cash registers, not enough servers at restaurants, not enough baggage handlers at airports.

Every time someone quits, additional pressure is put on remaining team members, leading to burnout and risk where employees are concerned.

According to a study by Momentive (Matsumoto, 2022) conducted in June of 2021 in the US, the majority of the workforce (78 per cent) says it's important to work for an organization that prioritizes diversity and inclusion, including 58 per cent who say it's 'very important'.

In fact, they claim that colleagues' perception of their company's DEI efforts has a major impact on their job satisfaction. In the same study, workers who said their company is not doing enough work on DEI had lower scores for every component of employee experience factors including happiness, opportunities to advance and satisfaction with pay.

In a 2022 HR Trends report published by McLean & Company, organizations that are not focusing on DEI are experiencing 1.6 times more voluntary turnover than those that are focused on it (McLean & Company, 2022). They believe that this is caused by both:

- increased employee expectations regarding the organization's commitment to DEI, and
- increased likelihood that employees experiencing inequities, lack of inclusion and other DEI challenges will leave.

One study from Deloitte found that companies with inclusive cultures had higher employee retention rates (Deloitte, 2018).

Even with our work with women of colour in A Leader Like Me, our organization created to increase courage and confidence, we saw a lot of movement in our members since 2020. Some were happy to stay with organizations where they felt a profound sense of purpose and felt valued. Others saw a market that had opened up and opportunities become available and landed in external roles that now not only promised career progression but also exponential increases in salaries as organizations paid attention to payroll parity.

ADVICE

For your organization, ask yourself the following:

- Is your organization facing a retention challenge?
- Is retention a factor or focus in the organization's future strategy?
- Are marginalized groups quitting faster?
- Are you checking boxes and hiring for diversity only to have them leave within a year?

Recruitment

We focus on DEI to both attract and grow talent within our organization.

As organizations face challenges retaining, there is more of a focus on recruitment. The war on talent is big and a focus on DEI presents both opportunities and challenges.

Organizations are getting more strategic in hiring practices in order to create a more diverse workforce. That's why there are trends to use candidate evaluation tools designed to get rid of bias from recruiting and hiring (Friedman, 2022).

Recently, in HR circles, we've heard leaders talk about hiring for culture add versus culture fit. Culture fit involves hiring people who are similar in their thinking and experience to everyone else. On the other hand, culture add means that those hired are aligned on values and purpose but have something additional to offer in terms of perspectives and experience. They add skills, experience and perspective that the team or organization can benefit from.

ADVICE

For your organization, ask yourself the following:

- Is your organization facing recruitment challenges?

- Is recruitment a factor or focus in the organization's future strategy?
- Is your organization looking for culture fit or culture add?
- How would a DEI strategy and communication benefit the organization's recruitment efforts?

Reputation

We focus on DEI because our reputation matters.

In our age of social media and high expectations for organizations to do the right thing from a global perspective, decisions and actions have the potential to impact the reputations of organizations. Media attention and coverage of companies' DEI efforts have truly been under a microscope, especially when things go wrong.

In recent years, we have seen organizations that have had to take a good look at who they are and what they stand for.

Starbucks responded to an in-store incident in 2018 where two Black men in a Philadelphia Starbucks store were wrongfully arrested while having a business meeting. CEO Kevin Johnson apologized immediately, met with the men involved and closed stores down to train employees about systemic bias and racial profiling. He could have simply reacted to the local incident, but instead chose to be proactive to ensure incidents like this were avoided.

Our brand is who we are and how we deliver. Organizations invest in DEI efforts to be proactive about making the right decisions and encouraging the right behaviours.

ADVICE

For your organization, ask yourself the following:

- Does the organization's history, founding story or previous incidents related to DEI pose a risk to its reputation?
- Do you have a proactive strategy to train employees and leaders on your expectations when it comes bringing your values to life?
- What are your values? How do they come to life through your behaviours through employee and customer experiences?
- Do you have a plan ready to react if you are in a crisis situation?

Results

We focus on DEI because it is linked to better business results.

McKinsey has been investigating the business case for diversity since 2015 (Hunt, 2015). The data and findings have been consistent over the years. In fact, they say that the most diverse companies are now more likely than ever to outperform non-diverse companies on profitability.

In its 2019 analysis (Dixon-Fyle, 2020), they found that companies in the top quartile of gender diversity on executive teams were 25 per cent more likely to experience above-average profitability than peer companies in the fourth quartile. Companies with more than 30 per cent women on their executive team are significantly likely to outperform those with fewer or no women executives.

In the case of ethnic and cultural diversity, they found that companies in the top quartile outperformed those in the fourth quartile by 36 per cent. Moreover, McKinsey identified a widening gap between winners and laggards: those who were seen as leading in DEI practices outperformed by wider margins in every study compared to those who were yet to embrace diversity practices.

ADVICE
For your organization, ask yourself the following:

- Will your results be impacted by more focus and investment in DEI efforts?

- Will creating an inclusive culture where everyone feels they belong lead to better employee and customer experiences?

- Do your customers and communities choose your organization because of your DEI efforts?

- Will added DEI efforts lead to more customers choosing your products and services?

CASE STUDY
PepsiCo

PepsiCo began its DEI journey many years ago. A historical timeline made available and published regularly in its diversity reports (PepsiCo, 2022) lay claim to some important milestones. They were the first major company to grant a franchise to people of colour and hire African Americans and professionals. In the 1950s they were the first company to feature a typical African American family in their print advertising campaigns. In the 1990s they formed their first Ethnic Advisory Board. At that time, we assume that PepsiCo centred a business case around its why that was connected to their global expansion and bottom-line results.

Early in the 21st century, Steven S. Reinemund became CEO. In an article close to his retirement (Ethix, 2007), he said that, as a CEO, he spent a lot of time on diversity. He said, 'It's a business opportunity and the right thing to do. Diversity, for a consumer-products company, is obvious to me. We can't grow as a company if we don't represent our consumers from the frontline to the boardroom.'

In its published diversity reports (PepsiCo, 2022), it outlines its goals and highlights in the following areas.

Representation: It sets goals and shares progress for their 2025 target of 50 per cent women and 10 per cent each of Black and Hispanic managerial representation. They've said that their goal is to achieve representation that mirrors the communities where they work, build inclusive leaders across the organization and help uplift people from underserved communities globally.

Recruitment: They are partnering with diversity organizations, minority search firms and schools to ensure they have a diverse slate of qualified candidates and interview panels.

Retention: They have introduced mentoring, coaching and development programmes throughout career stages to retain diverse talent.

Reputation: They have received recognition publicly for their work and have been featured as 'CR Magazines 100 Best Corporate Citizens'; and named 'Best Place to Work for LGBTQ Equality' and 'Best Place to Work for Disability Inclusion.'

Results: Under Reinemund's leadership, revenue grew by $9 billion, net income increased by 70 per cent, earnings per share increased by 80 per cent. The share price grew from about $48 to over $60 (Forbes, 2006).

When Reinemund left PepsiCo, he and his board selected Indra Nooyi, an Indian-born woman, to succeed him saying that not only was she incredibly qualified but that she would make different decisions because of her knowledge of the global world.

How about colleagues?

Our DEI – why for organizations were outlined in the last section, but how about the **why** for employees?

Simon Sinek talks about the Golden Circle. It moves from the outside in from the what to the how to the why. Sinek says: 'If you don't know why, you can't know how' (Sinek, 2009).

As internal communication professionals and consultants, we notice that organizations and leaders are quick to tell employees about the decision that have been made, what will happen and when, yet they often forget to answer why.

Let's talk about explaining the why to employees through purpose, progress, performance, people and personal.

Purpose

When working with organizations, we always start with an organization purpose which can include a purpose statement, its mission, its vision and its values. A purpose asks who are we and what we stand for.

Messaging on why when it comes to DEI has to start with values. How many organizations include values like **respect** and **diversity**? When looking at employee messaging and making the case for DEI (or any other initiative or change), we would benefit from taking a value-based lens to our efforts.

We challenge you to look at your vision, mission, values, purpose and investigate the relationships to DEI. Are there connections you can explore? Are their potential disconnects?

How does your DEI strategy or efforts help drive actions, decision and behaviours that bring these elements of purpose to life in employee and customer interactions? We've done exercises with organizations that clearly articulate what a value looks like and what it doesn't look like.

Organizational values are a big opportunity to inspire others. Is there alignment? Do we believe? Can we internalize who we are and what we stand for to create pride in our organization, our work and ourselves?

Here are some purpose statements from organizations. Can you see how they can be used to identify opportunities and connections to DEI?

LinkedIn: To connect the world's professionals to make them more productive and successful.

Asana: To help humanity thrive by enabling all teams to work together effortlessly.

Nike: To bring inspiration and innovation to every athlete in the world.

Jet Blue: To inspire humanity – both in the air and on the ground.

Coca-Cola: Refresh the world. Make a difference.

AT&T: Inspire human progress through the power of communication and entertainment.

Coty: To celebrate and liberate the diversity of your beauty.

Expedia: To bring the world within reach.

Intel: To create world-changing technology that enriches the lives of every person on earth.

Mastercard: We work to connect and power an inclusive digital economy that benefits everyone, everywhere by making transactions safe, simple, smart and accessible. Connecting everyone to Priceless possibilities.

Pfizer: Working together for a healthier world.

United Airlines: Connecting people. Uniting the world.

Ask yourself about how you use purpose to explain the why for DEI.

Progress

Employees, especially Millennials and Generation Z, are looking for companies who are progressive, versus those that feel like dinosaurs. Employees also want to work for organizations that are stable, innovative and can survive changes.

When talking to colleagues, it's important to help them understand how business, political and competitive environments are changing and the role that DEI plays in addressing these changes.

Organizations may choose to lead progress or follow. In the case of leading, there is an opportunity to build pride and develop a case for why your organization wants to be first and will benefit from a leadership position. When choosing to follow competitors or other organizations, there needs to be a case made about the risks of not progressing.

Companies like Nike know what they stand for and are ready to push the envelope and take a public stand on DEI issues with inspiring messages that tell us 'You can't stop us', and that tell women to 'Never settle'.

If you can tie your **why** to progress and evolution and have honest and transparent conversation about changes, it will go a long way in helping to align your people.

Performance

Colleagues want to understand how the organization and themselves are performing. And if DEI efforts are connecting to future performance or can be linked to past performance, there is an opportunity to reinforce messages by providing proof of impact.

Here's what we don't want. We don't want to create a DEI strategy that simply checks a box to say we have one and is then shoved away in a drawer hoping that changes will happen magically because we've shared it during a town hall, road show or a strategy launch session.

When it comes to the why on performance, we need to articulate what success looks like and why it's important to the things that matter to employees including stability of the business and impact on employee incentives.

People

Employees respond to holistic impacts on their peers and colleagues. No one wants to see unfairness or a lack of justice. Many organizations identify the why by demonstrating and sharing the impacts on people.

Everyone loves to see people, especially the ones they care about, prevail. They also want proof that anyone can contribute, make a difference and succeed. Many organizations use people stories to educate and help employees understand the experiences and challenges faced by marginalized groups. By leading with empathy, stories help drive connection and build relationships. One thing you should be aware of is that when we are asking members of marginalized groups to share their trauma and experiences in order to influence the why, we need to ask permission and ensure they want to share rather than feeling forced to share.

We also need to make the case that focus on opening doors through equity, justice and accessibility leads to inclusion for everyone. For example, for many years, the focus on making spaces and facilities accessible at face value seemed good for the 15 per cent who are disabled. Is it worth the investment? Here is the reality... even non-disabled individuals require ramps when they are pushing strollers or have suffered from a physical injury. Many of us will see a level of deterioration in our eyesight, hearing and physical ability as we age.

Ask yourself what stories you can share about your people to help demonstrate the why. Help all employees realize that inclusion for the most marginalized usually results in benefits for all.

Personal

We've said a few times that DEI is extremely personal. During DEI change efforts, it's important to make the why personal. Acknowledge feelings.

In her Oscars acceptance speech, Chloé Zhao said that 'People at birth are inherently good.' What if we acknowledged that most people were doing their best based on what they were taught. That every one of us has an opportunity to rewrite the myths we thought were true.

Rachel Parnes (2021), in a LinkedIn Learning blog about Defining Diversity, says: 'To be a good employee, coworker and citizen in a professional world that is rapidly growing for diverse and fluid across identity traits, it's vital to be open, understanding, and respectful toward all.'

The most compelling example of DEI made personal appears in Martin Luther King's famous 'I have a dream' speech (History.com, 2017), where he talks about a day when his children will live in a nation where 'they will not be judged by the colour of their skin but the content of their character, everyone could see themselves in his vision of the future'.

Ask yourself how you can make the case for DEI personal so that it resonates with a future everyone wants for themselves and the next generation.

More importantly, think about your personal feelings about DEI. At a recent conference, Advita was asked what the bare minimum a communication professional can do to step into the DEI space because they really didn't have time for the effort. Advita told them to simply not bother. The truth is that if DEI is simply a check-box exercise and you don't believe in a case for why it is important, don't expect to convince others of anything different. Change starts with you believing in the why.

KEY TAKEAWAYS

- Conversations about human rights have been going on for centuries, not just the last few years.

- Be a worker not a warrior. During DEI efforts, you will sometimes find yourself being a flashlight (looking for yourself, including in initiatives); a mirror (reflecting on your own biases and behaviours or deflecting or becoming defensive when you are not comfortable with what you see or hear); or a beacon (leading the way or warning others about impacts).

- Although DEI should simply be the right thing to do, we believe that it is important to include rather than ignore the business case for it.

- Demographics and the global reality provide data that can help us understand the opportunities that exist within our changing publics.

- Although there are many traits to take into consideration for diversity programmes, most start with age, gender, disability, race, religion and sexual orientation.

- To answer the DEI – why for organizations, consider rights, representation, recruitment, retention, reputation and results.

- To answer the DEI – why for employees, consider purpose, progress, performance, people and personal.

REFLECTIVE QUESTIONS

- How do I really feel about DEI initiatives? Am I passionate about change or do I simply want to check boxes?

- Can I make a compelling case for DEI professionally and personally?

- Do I need to hear perspectives from others in order to build a case?

Bibliography

Ang, C (2021, 16 June) Visualizing the world's population by age group, Visual Capitalist, visualcapitalist.com/the-worlds-population-2020-by-age/ (archived at https://perma.cc/857S-G33T)

Deloitte (2018) Inclusive Mobility: How mobilizing a diverse workforce can drive business performance. London, Deloitte Development LLC

Deshmukh, A (2022, 11 February) Mapped: The world's major religions, Visual Capitalist, visualcapitalist.com/mapped-major-religions-of-the-world/#:~: text=Around%2031%25%20of%20the%20world's,the%20world%20 identifying%20as%20Jewish (archived at https://perma.cc/CU43-M3WZ)

Desjardins, J (2019, 28 March) The world's 7.5 billion people, in one chart, Visual Capitalist, visualcapitalist.com/worlds-7-5-billion-people-chart/ (archived at https://perma.cc/5VKK-8VE6)

Disabled World (2022, 6 April) Disability statistics: Information, charts, graphs and tables, disabled-world.com/disability/statistics/#:~:text=In%20countries%20 with%20life%20expectancies,disability%20creates%20a%20vicious%20circle (archived at https://perma.cc/WP7N-X77A)

Dixon-Fyle, S D (2020, 19 May) Diversity wins: How inclusion matters, McKinsey & Company, mckinsey.com/featured-insights/diversity-and-inclusion/diversity-wins-how-inclusion-matters (archived at https://perma.cc/E57P-6U9X)

Ethix (2007, 1 April) Steven S. Reinemund: Leadership for a 21st-century multinational corporation, ethix.org/2007/04/01/leadership-for-a-21st-century-multinational-corporation (archived at https://perma.cc/457Q-BG5S)

Forbes (2006, 14 August) PepsiCo: Soda king Reinemund to step down, forbes.com/2006/08/14/reinemund-pepsi-ceo-cx_cn_0814autofacescan03.html?sh=783908d72d65 (archived at https://perma.cc/8YSB-9L7N)

Friedman, E (2022, 15 February) Hiring and recruitment trends to expect in 2022, Forbes, forbes.com/sites/forbeshumanresourcescouncil/2022/02/15/hiring-and-recruitment-trends-to-expect-in-2022/?sh=1e4608cc279e (archived at https://perma.cc/A7C9-RVPP)

Garlick, S (2022, 29 November) Ethnic group, England and Wales: Census 2021, Office for National Statistics, ons.gov.uk/peoplepopulationandcommunity/culturalidentity/ethnicity/bulletins/ethnicgroupenglandandwales/census2021#:~:text=In%202021%2C%2081.7%25%20(48.7,million)%20in%20the%202011%20Census (archived at https://perma.cc/2G6F-5J6D)

Government Equities Office (2019, 7 February) National LGBT Survey: Summary report, GOV.UK, gov.uk/government/publications/national-lgbt-survey-summary-report (archived at https://perma.cc/MY4B-6K44)

History.com (2017, 30 November) 'I Have a Dream' Speech, history.com/topics/civil-rights-movement/i-have-a-dream-speech (archived at https://perma.cc/XFP7-BY4B)

Hunt, Dame V, Layton, D and Prince, S (2015, 1 January) Why diversity matters, McKinsey & Company, mckinsey.com/capabilities/people-and-organizational-performance/our-insights/why-diversity-matters (archived at https://perma.cc/2A58-UFRK)

Matsumoto, A (2022, 21 January) Data shows that prioritizing DEI may be the key to retaining employees, momentive, momentive.ai/en/blog/dei-key-to-retaining-employees/ (archived at https://perma.cc/6BTX-CYW3)

McLean & Company (2022) 2022 HR Trends Report. London; Ontario, McLean and Company.

Parnes, R (2021, October). Defining diversity, equity and inclusion in the workplace, and how to practice it, LinkedIn, linkedin.com/business/learning/blog/conversations-for-change/inclusion-in-the-workplace-making-dei-personal-priority (archived at https://perma.cc/Q3VJ-W9GD)

PepsiCo (2022, 5 December) Diversity Reports & Progress at PepsiCo, pepsico.com/our-impact/diversity/diversity-report (archived at https://perma.cc/MF6P-GJKJ)

Petrock, V (2021, 4 January) LGBTQ+ consumers value brand support beyond Pride Month, Insider Intelligence, insiderintelligence.com/content/lgbtq-consumers-value-brand-support-beyond-pride-month (archived at https://perma.cc/S959-W7PP)

Pride at Work Canada (2022, 17 May) The Uncovering Belonging Podcast, prideatwork.ca/ub-podcast/ (archived at https://perma.cc/555S-2VFQ)

Rice, D (2021, 28 January) Generations in the workplace, HR Exchange Network, hrexchangenetwork.com/employee-engagement/articles/generations-in-the-workplace (archived at https://perma.cc/5PM2-LQ4T)

Sakpal, M (2019, Sept 20). Diversity and Inclusion Build High-Performance Teams. Retrieved from Gartner.com: https://www.gartner.com/smarterwithgartner/diversity-and-inclusion-build-high-performance-teams (archived at https://perma.cc/L9BN-XVMX)

Sinek, S (2009) Start with Why, p. 70. In S. Sinek, *Start with Why*. New York, Penguin Group

Spizzirri, G E (2021, 26 January) Proportion of people identified as transgender and non-binary gender in Brazil, Nature, nature.com/articles/s41598-021-81411-4 (archived at https://perma.cc/M7QF-SESW)

Statistics Canada (2021, 15 June) A statistical portrait of Canada's diverse LGBTQ2+ communities, www150.statcan.gc.ca/n1/daily-quotidien/210615/dq210615a-eng.htm (archived at https://perma.cc/BXG2-939F)

Statistics Canada (2022, 26 October) Visible Minority and Population Group Reference Guide, Census of Population, 2021, www12.statcan.gc.ca/census-recensement/2021/ref/98-500/006/98-500-x2021006-eng.cfm (archived at https://perma.cc/FBA5-WVVC)

Statistics Times (2021, 26 August) Gender ratio in the world, statisticstimes.com/demographics/world-sex-ratio.php#:~:text=Gender%20ratio%20in%20the%20World&text=The%20population%20of%20females%20in,101.68%20males%20per%20100%20females (archived at https://perma.cc/3Q3D-CYUY)

STTP Canada (2022) A short history of human rights, Speak Truth to Power Canada, sttpcanada.ctf-fce.ca/human-rights/history/ (archived at https://perma.cc/6842-CSNT)

Thornhurst, S (2022, 11 August) Time to close the business case for diversity, Influence Online, influenceonline.co.uk/2022/08/11/time-to-close-the-business-case-for-diversity (archived at https://perma.cc/ZA9C-8WHL)

United Nations (2022, 12 December) United Nations Charter: Preamble, un.org/en/about-us/un-charter/preamble (archived at https://perma.cc/DTB3-2N95)

United Nations Department of Economic and Social Affairs (2021) Factsheet on Persons with Disabilities, un.org/development/desa/disabilities/resources/factsheet-on-persons-with-disabilities.html (archived at https://perma.cc/5J4U-42L2)

Varrella, S (2021) Distribution of sexual attraction worldwide 2021, Statista, statista.com/statistics/1270134/distribution-sexual-attraction-worldwide/ (archived at https://perma.cc/TG8P-TSK9)

WeThe15 (2020) #WeThe15, wethe15.org/ (archived at https://perma.cc/K3A5-YWGQ)

WHO (World Health Organization) (2011, 1 January) World Report on Disability Summary, who.int/publications/i/item/WHO-NMH-VIP-11.01 (archived at https://perma.cc/N23V-E4JC)

WHO (World Health Organization) (2022, 2 December) Disability, who.int/en/news-room/fact-sheets/detail/disability-and-health (archived at https://perma.cc/WTD8-JCW7)

World Population Review (2022a, 1 July) China Population 2022 (Live), worldpopulationreview.com/countries/china-population (archived at https://perma.cc/2RDW-E64B)

World Population Review (2022b, 1 July) India Population 2022 (Live), worldpopulationreview.com/countries/india-population (archived at https://perma.cc/L4EB-7GWN)

02

Why trust matters when cultivating an inclusive culture

The power of trust

We can't stress enough the importance of trust when you are building an inclusive culture. Without trust diversity, equity and inclusion (DEI) initiatives will fail. Think about your behaviour when you have to work with someone you don't trust. Do you open up and share how you're feeling? Do feel motivated and inspired by them? Do you outperform and share innovative ideas? Probably not.

Understanding our responsibilities to cultivate trust and inclusion will allow us to add much greater value to this vital area of work. Trust *is* subjective, but it's fundamental to almost every action we take daily. It can be the difference between success and failure, and it's not something we can build overnight without considering where the trust gaps are and what we need to do to earn and maintain trust with others. Cultivating inclusive cultures can't work on just desire, hope and want alone – we need to be intentional, focused, committed and aspirational in building high-trust cultures that are inclusive to everyone's needs.

Stephen Covey (2006), one of the leading experts in trust and the author of the bestselling book *The Speed of Trust*, once said:

> Trust is the glue of life. It's the essential ingredient in effective communication. It's the foundational principle that holds all relationships. When the trust account is high, communication is easy, instant, and effective.

When we were developing our chapters for this book, we knew that it would be impossible to cultivate inclusive cultures without talking about trust and the role internal communication can play in helping enable trust across the organization. In Chapter 1, we shared why inclusive cultures are essential and the benefits it can bring to organizations.

In this chapter we will:

- Delve into trust, which is a necessary attribute for any leader who is serious about cultivating a culture of inclusion.
- Discuss what trust means at an individual and organizational level.
- Explore the role internal communication can play to help build and maintain trust and the frameworks you can use to support leaders in your organization.

Without trust, you can't cultivate inclusive cultures. There is no exception. Trust is a fundamental part of our existence, underpinning almost every relationship, from personal to professional. Cultivating trust isn't only about how trustworthy we are but it's also how we trust other people. Your team may think you're extremely trustworthy, but if you don't reciprocate and trust them to deliver against the expectations set, then it's impossible to build a trusted relationship. It must work both ways.

Trust is something we experience nearly every minute of the day, from decisions we make about what brand of beans to buy or the partner we choose to spend our life with to trusting that we receive the correct medication from the doctor. For a leader, trust is the most powerful characteristic they can nourish as it can help them create teams who feel supported and empowered. With empowered teams, leaders will witness greater performance, lower sickness and higher team morale. But what exactly is trust? There are thousands of books and papers written by experts on defining trust, but in its simplest form we both believe that:

> trust is when we have confidence that our expectations of someone will meet the desired outcomes.

Think about a person and a brand that you really trust. What is it about them that makes them trustworthy? Why do you trust them? These are important questions to think about as you work through this chapter as it'll help you identify what trust means to you and how you can help others be trusted. Before we explore how internal communication can contribute to helping leaders in organizations gain trust, we must understand the overall concept of trust and what the current landscape tells us.

The trust shift

Since the pandemic, we've seen a shift in how people want to work. The world of work is becoming increasingly competitive, and it's changing. Colleagues work from different locations and expect flexibility, choices and autonomy to do their job. Leaders also have to deal with post-pandemic fatigue, political unrest and the cost-of-living crisis. These challenges can be complex when building a culture that fosters trust.

Before the digital age and the ability to work from any location, trust was built and earned through physical human connections. If you needed a favour or had a question to ask you'd head over to that person and chat about the help you needed. You were able to sit next to a colleague at work and spend time getting to know them, not only in a work context but personally as well. From these informal exchanges you could judge whether or not they were credible, reliable, empathetic and cared for others. We build trusted relationships through connection, and it's harder to do this when you don't spend time with people and get to know them. Even if you do, how often are you intentional about getting to know each other? With the pace of work and 24/7 access, people are under increasing pressure to deliver outcomes continuously – which can lead to toxic productivity, a breakdown in relationships, burnout and general dissatisfaction at work.

In 2022, a Gallup workplace report shared that most colleagues worldwide don't find their work meaningful or rewarding. They estimate that low engagement will cost the global economy $7.8 trillion, accounting for 11 per cent of the world's gross domestic product (GDP). Stress was one of the highest factors contributing to disengagement, with 44 per cent of employees experiencing it daily (Gallup, 2022). The lack of trust between colleagues and their leaders can cause low engagement. When colleagues don't feel they can trust their leader and their psychological safety is compromised, they will leave, stop performing or worse, cause reputational damage.

A survey carried out by The Institute of Leadership & Management (2014) found that where there was a low level of internal trust, the organization was also not trusted by the public. It's important to remember that what often happens inside the organization will always impact the reputation externally.

BrewDog, a global craft beer organization based in the UK, has been involved in several controversies during its 10+ years in business. They are known for their bold behaviour and unapologetic brand. But in 2021, 61 former colleagues wrote an open letter exposing the business of perpetrating a 'toxic attitude' and using 'lies, hypocrisy, and deceit' because their main focus was to generate positive PR, despite what it took to do that. Colleagues shared that the brand frequently cut corners and did not live up to its values, leading to some colleagues' mental health issues. According to a report published in *Marketing Week*, BrewDog's consumer impression dropped from a peak score of 28.5 to 0.4 in over a week. Its reputation also fell from a score of 19.1 to 1.6, and the likelihood of recommending the brand fell from 19.8 to 4.6 (Jefferson, 2021). The founders of BrewDog apologized and admitted some failings, but reputationally it could be viewed that the damage to the brand is irreversible.

The trust landscape

Over the past few decades, the way we earn trust from others has changed significantly. From listening to experts or authorities to being influenced by family, friends, peers and strangers we've never met. With the shift to digital, this change has meant we've seen trust and influence evolve over the years. There are now three distinct chapters, described by Rachel Botsman (2017), a leading authority on trust in the modern world: *local, institutional* and *distributed*.

Local trust was formed when we used to live in smaller communities. We trusted our neighbours to give sound advice. We supported each other within the boundaries we had. *Institutional trust* is the confidence we feel toward a particular organization. These were influential organizations that centralized messages, but often with bias. Communication took a one-to-many approach, broadcasting messages one way through traditional mediums without asking for feedback or thoughts. As the access to technology opened up, CEOs who depended on loyalty from their workforce and those who operated behind closed doors recognized they were no longer as influential as they once were.

As trust started to deplete in these organizations, we saw the trend move towards influencer trust. When aligned more with local trust, these influencers were relatable, and most of us savoured every word. Many of us diligently followed their advice until it became apparent that we may have been victims of dishonest behaviour (Brenner, 2021).

Now trust has evolved to *distributed trust*, and we've moved on from listening to a single source, to help us form an opinion on products or services. This distributed trust is now on a global scale, led by the power of many-to-many, through comments, reviews and thoughts from sites like TikTok, Reddit and TripAdvisor. Organizations such as Airbnb, Etsy, eBay, and Facebook Marketplace depend heavily on peer-to-peer reviews, and some even reward consumers for leaving feedback. All these organizations are trusted through peer review systems and have encouraged people to trust the product or service based on a stranger's experience. How many times have you purchased something after purely reading the reviews?

Organizations have to compete against distributed trust as colleagues have access to technology more than they've ever had before. Colleagues will find out information about the organization through consumer reviews and potential applicants will read reviews about organizations on sites like Glassdoor before they apply for opportunities. They search for customer feedback or look for hashtags on social media sites such as LinkedIn, Twitter and now TikTok before they consider accepting a new role.

The Edelman Trust Barometer (Edelman Trust Barometer, 2022) is a global survey measuring people's trust levels in institutions such as government, media and businesses. The Barometer reports annually how trust has shifted over the past 12 months and how the results can help organizations plan, make decisions and take action. The headline for 2022 was 'Cycle of Distrust'. The report showed that almost two-thirds of people distrust organizations. Trust in government has reached an all-time low, with only 42 per cent of respondents saying they trust the government to do what is right. But 61 per cent of people said businesses are one of the most trusted institutions, ahead of non-government organizations and the media. The survey showed that 'my employer' is now the most trusted at 77 per cent, and workers expect CEOs to be the 'face of change'.

The Barometer also found that leaderless movements were rising globally as people increasingly looked to their peers for guidance and support. This aligns strongly with distributed trust behaviour. This insight has important implications for leaders, who need to be aware of the changing landscape of trust and adjust their strategy accordingly. It's an opportunity to build stronger trusted relationships with their colleagues and bring some balance between institutional and distributed trust.

However, if businesses don't take advantage of this trust shift, Edelman (2022) state that four fundamental forces could stop progress in tackling societal and environmental matters such as Covid-19, racism and climate challenges:

1 Government–media distrust

2 Excessive reliance on business

3 Mass class divide

4 Failure of leadership

The distrust between the government and the media has continued growing, causing significant friction as people see these two institutions as an out of touch dividing force. With misinformation and disinformation rife across various social channels and media people are relying excessively on business leaders to take ownership of the communication. They also want them to take more prominent roles in topics where people want to see clear direction and support, such as climate change, social injustice, workforce reskilling and tackling inequities. To be an influential, trusted voice in some of these crucial areas, leaders will need to upskill. They will need to understand the importance of communication and how it can help them gain the trust of their workforce. They must also be prepared to understand some of their trust shortfalls and adapt if they want to build a culture of inclusivity and help people thrive.

Characteristics of a trustworthy person

From our conversations with leaders, they often ask 'How quickly can we build trust in this organization?' But gaining trust can't be done overnight; it must be built slowly and steadily over time, and most importantly, you need to **earn** the trust of your team and colleagues, you can't expect them to trust you automatically because of your job title or role. And there are different factors for leaders to consider if they want a high-trust culture. Covey says: 'Trust is a function of two things: character and competence. Character includes your integrity, your motive, and your intent with people. Competence includes your capabilities, skills, results, and track record. And both are vital' (Covey, 2006).

In 2000, Trusted Advisor consultants David Maister, Charles H Green and Robert M Galford developed the Trustworthiness Equation (TrustedAdvisor, 2021). The trio believe that trustworthiness equals the sum of credibility, reliability and intimacy divided by a person's self-orientation:

Trustworthiness = Credibility + Reliability + Intimacy / Self-orientation

TABLE 2.1 Trustworthiness behaviours based on the Trustworthiness Equation

Factor	What it means	Descriptive behaviours	How to improve	Can it be measured
Credibility	Your words and how believable you are	Am I competent, capable and have relevant credentials? Am I a subject matter expert? Do I give confidence? Do I tell the truth?	Invest in continuing professional development Be open to what you know and don't know Ask curious questions so you can understand the need to help build knowledge	Yes – qualifications, engagement scores and HR data
Reliability	Your actions and how much people can depend on you	Do I do what I say I'm going to do? Do I have a good track record of delivering work when I promised? Am I consistent? Do I understand the frame of reference, so I deliver against expectations?	Don't over promise and under deliver, nor under promise and over deliver – just deliver what you promised Build a good track record of doing what you said you would do	Yes – engagement scores, performance data, deliverables and KPIs
Intimacy	Your emotions and how safe people feel sharing information with you	Do I create a safe environment? Do I keep information confidential about others? Am I empathetic? Do I show vulnerability?	Be curious about other people and who they are Be vulnerable enough to admit your fears and concerns Listen properly to what people are sharing	Difficult to measure as it's subjective but engagement scores, colleague retention and absence figures can indicate leadership intimacy
Self-orientation	Your motives and how you focus on others rather than yourself	Am I only in it for myself and do I only care about my outcomes? Can I be self-obsessed? Do I only worry about me?	Be transparent and engaging Don't take over conversations, and make sure you're allowing others to speak Check in frequently to see if your approach works for your team/client	Difficult to measure as it's subjective but can use data from focus groups, pulse checks and HR data such as performance, absence and retention

SOURCE TrustedAdvisor, 2021

Maister et al shared that most people rely on credibility and reliability when they want to earn the trust of others. These two qualities are often viewed as 'rational' and are easier to measure (Maister et al, 2002). However, to truly gain trust, you can't ignore the two emotional elements of trustworthiness – intimacy and self-orientation. Often in workplaces, these are the two factors seen as 'soft skills' that some people feel are unnecessary in organizations. These factors are harder to measure but can help cultivate a high-trust culture which can help more people feel included, contribute to conversations and belong.

Leadership traits

Now we've explored the key components of trust, we need to reflect and review what trust looks like at an individual level. What type of behaviours does a trusted leader display? We asked you at the start of this chapter to think about someone you trust. Consider:

- What is it about that person that you trust?
- What do you trust them with and why?
- Think about why people trust you?
- What do people often trust you with?

Exploring these questions about ourselves and others is a key component of understanding trust. There will be some situations where you will trust other people very easily with limited proof that they are trustworthy but, in some instances, people will need to earn your trust by displaying behaviours that lead to trustworthiness. How you choose to trust someone will be dependent on the risk you believe they will bring to your safety. Let's put this theory into a work context.

Raj has been made redundant several times in his career. He has been lied to by his previous managers, so he has put up defensive mechanisms in his current role. Raj doesn't trust his boss Michelle as in his view Michelle doesn't ask him questions in meetings, is dismissive of his ideas, takes other people out for coffee and rarely engages in conversation. But Michelle has reacted to Raj's behaviour and has retreated. She doesn't trust Raj and finds him aloof and disengaging. Because Raj had some challenges in previous roles, he decided to keep his distance until Michelle could prove she was trustworthy. Michelle believes she's a trustworthy leader but failed to recognize that not everyone in her team will have had positive experiences with trust.

Leaders need to recognize that their role is to empower others to succeed. They need to use their communication skills to influence and inspire their teams so they can continue to deliver great work, even in their absence. In this situation, as the leader of the team, Michelle must take the first steps to build and cultivate trust with Raj. His experience with Michelle has left him feeling excluded and isolated. He doesn't feel like he belongs and dislikes coming to work. Communication between them is almost non-existent so Michelle needs to demonstrate trust traits that will help Raj connect with her and bridge the trust gap. In his book *The Speed of Trust*, Covey shares 13 leadership behaviours to help leaders like Michelle earn trust from colleagues like Raj.

1 Be direct: Michelle needs to talk straight and remove ambiguity from any conversations with Raj. It's important for her to tell him how she feels and to ask him what he needs from her for him to do his job well. It's important for Raj to reciprocate and share openly with Michelle on the support he requires to succeed in his role. This conversation should happen on neutral ground, away from distractions and other colleagues.

2 Demonstrate respect: Michelle needs to show genuine care for Raj. Asking him what he needs from her to help him thrive, being curious about his day/work, inviting him to relevant meetings, not cancelling one-to-one check-in meetings and keeping communication lines open will help build respect.

3 Create transparency: Michelle needs to be open with Raj and demonstrate some vulnerability. Share learnings and mistakes, invite questions and set up regular catch-up sessions. It's important that Michelle can show him traits that he can verify with others (e.g. credible, reliable, supportive).

4 Right wrongs: As a leader, Michelle has to take the first steps and make things right with Raj. Having a conversation about what needs to be better next time, apologizing quickly and not making excuses can help build strong trust relationships.

5 Show loyalty: Acknowledging Raj in meetings and giving him credit for work he's been responsible for will show loyalty from Michelle, especially if this happens when Raj isn't there to represent himself.

6 Deliver results: As a leader it's important the team see you delivering great results and how you demonstrate impact. This will help them understand that you're a team player and they can trust you to make the right decisions. In Michelle's case, Raj will see that Michelle is credible and can be trusted to make the right decisions.

7 Get better: Continuously improving and acting on feedback will help Michelle show her team that she does listen and is willing to improve.

8 Confront reality: Rather than passive aggressive behaviours or micromanaging it's important that Michelle addresses tough stuff directly, no matter how uncomfortable it might be. If she keeps burying her head in the sand, relationships will become difficult to maintain.

9 Clarify expectations: It's important for Michelle to clarify what she expects from her team, in an open forum where everyone is invited. Give everyone an opportunity to discuss and validate their feedback. This behaviour will also help build safe spaces where people can speak openly without the fear of retaliation.

10 Practice accountability: Michelle needs to hold herself accountable and others in her team for any poor behaviour they may have demonstrated towards Raj. Take responsibility for results. Be clear on how you communicate how you're doing and how others are doing.

11 Listen first: Allowing Raj to share his thoughts first will help Michelle understand some of the issues Raj has faced. It's important to listen before you speak and not to presume you have all the answers – or the questions.

12 Keep commitments: If Michelle shares with Raj that they will have weekly catch-ups then she must do what she said she was going to do. Over committing to something that you can't deliver will cause further mistrust.

13 Extend trust: To avoid future situations like this with other colleagues, Michelle needs to drop her armour first. Extend trust abundantly to those who have earned your trust. Don't withhold trust because there is risk involved.

SOURCE Adapted from Covey, 2006

Vulnerability and trust

When we work with leaders, especially emerging leaders, one of their greatest fears is being 'too nice' and not being respected. These perceptions and assumptions can cause unnecessary trust pitfalls, leading to poor behaviours. Being nice isn't a prerequisite to being a leader but demonstrating vulnerability is much more compelling. Vulnerability is a critical factor of trustworthiness and trust. Brené Brown, a renowned shame, vulnerability and empathy researcher based in Texas, USA, defines vulnerability as:

> ... uncertainty, risk, and emotional exposure. But vulnerability is not weakness; it's our most accurate measure of courage. (Brown, 2015)

Vulnerability, like trust, is a risk, and it can be uncomfortable, which is why it takes courage to demonstrate it. Many theorists believe that vulnerability plays a significant role in interpersonal trust and that we need a certain degree of vulnerability to trust another person. In the business world, leaders can resist showing vulnerability as they fear it may open them up to criticism if they admit to making a mistake or expose their weaknesses if they show any emotion. But research shows that when leaders show vulnerability, the impact on the team can be powerful. Leaders are more influential, it can help build connections and elevate performance. To be influential and to inspire teams it's not about grand gestures. In her *Dare To Lead* book, Brown talks about small moments of trust (Brown, 2018).

Creating a safe space doesn't require vast amounts of investment of time or budget. These micro behaviours demonstrate more trust, empathy and kindness and can create big trust waves across the organization. These gestures are often subtle like remembering someone's birthday, sending someone a handwritten note or remembering the names of their loved ones. It demonstrates an element of vulnerability and can build greater connections between leaders and colleagues. The leaders who lead with vulnerability, such as admitting when they were wrong, showing interest in their colleagues through curious questions, responding positively to questions or doubts, are the leaders who will create a thriving, trusted, inclusive culture. To understand how to create these small moments of trust, Brown shares her BRAVING framework to support leaders. These mini statements are also a great starting point for internal communication professionals.

- **Boundaries**: What are your limits? What's ok and what isn't ok? This will help set expectations and allow people to understand what is needed from them.

- **Reliability**: Like the trustworthiness equation, reliability is about doing what you say you will do.

- **Accountability**: Do you own your mistakes and appreciate people for what they do? Taking responsibility for your actions is essential to building small moments of trust.

- **Vault**: Keeping information that people share with you secret. Often people connect through meaningless gossip, but this demonstrates that you can't be trusted with information, which can hinder growing safe environments.

- **Integrity**: Choosing to do the right thing over being fast, fun or easy.

- **Non-judgment**: Share what you need and want without judging anyone else. Don't lie or make up stories about what that other person feels.

- **Generosity**: It's essential to be compassionate and make generous assumptions of someone else's words, beliefs and behaviours if you feel they have betrayed your trust.

SOURCE Brown, 2022

Internal communication's role in supporting trust

As Covey's quote at the start of this chapter implied, effective communication is one of the cornerstones of building trust in an organization. From our research and work with our clients, we know the most significant barrier to progression when cultivating inclusive cultures is the disconnect and sometimes distrust colleagues have with their leaders. This is often due to poor communication and limited opportunities for connections. We've witnessed first-hand the impact low trust in organizations can cause which includes fear, frustration, annoyance and resentment. It can stop the progression of good work and can impact overall performance, leading to poor experiences for colleagues and customers. And as internal communication professionals and those responsible for communicating internally, we have a significant role to play in helping leaders become trusted communicators who can influence and deliver with impact.

As internal communication professionals we often have an umbrella view of the organization. Depending on the trust we've built across the organization (more on this later in the chapter), we would normally hear the rumblings and speculation before it reaches leadership. Alongside this information and data from various audits, surveys and pulse checks we may conduct, we can often provide robust support and guidance to our leaders by advising them where there are gaps in the communication and how they can address these gaps. Research from a decade-long study on the neuroscience of trust led by Paul J Zak showed that colleagues in high-trust organizations perform better, have more energy, collaborate with their peers and are loyal, compared to those from low-trust companies (Zak, 2017).

Throughout our careers, we've been privileged to witness incredible leaders who have high trust, inspire and motivate their teams. We've also worked with leaders who have low trust and they often struggle to make an impact, leading to poor behaviours. The leaders who had high trust were incredible communicators. They were open, honest, reliable, vulnerable, authentic and supportive. They never claimed to know something they didn't, and they always created an environment that encouraged their team to share openly about the challenges they were facing. They also had a great relationship with the communication team. They always asked for feedback after a town hall or similar session they'd delivered: 'How did I do?', 'What could I do better?', 'Did that message come across alright?'

Low-trust leaders were often defensive, complex, not dependable and often led through fear. They didn't care for feedback or have any desire to improve. Their teams were scared to make mistakes or made plenty of errors as they were worried about asking for support. Their engagement scores were low, they often couldn't retain talent and stress-related sickness was rife. The environment was toxic, and people were surviving, not thriving.

A few years ago, Advita supported an organization undergoing significant restructuring. Initially, the project team were told that there would be no job losses and that everyone who wanted a job would have one. The communication plan was developed with key messages about the future and how they will become even stronger together. However, things changed overnight, and the organization realized they needed to make further cuts, and a redundancy programme was initiated. This change led to secret conversations behind closed doors, which excluded some initially involved people. Communication was one of the teams excluded. After a week of speculation and gossip, a senior director approached a junior communication officer and asked them to send out an email announcing the redundancy programme. The junior officer attempted to challenge the director but was told:

> If I wanted to hear your opinion, I would have asked. I don't have time to discuss this further, just do what I'm telling you to do.

The director stood over the communication officer until they sent out the note. Fast-forward two weeks, the organization made regional and national news about the redundancy programme, especially as the executive team had received significant bonuses that year. Trust was instantly broken across the organization. Colleagues were angry and upset, and people who weren't on the redundancy list suffered survivor's guilt and found new opportunities. To earn the trust back, it took a change in leadership.

When leaders pull rank, it can be difficult to challenge with impact. We can't change their behaviour, but we can work on our trustworthiness with key stakeholders. In the case of the communication officer, they didn't know the leader well. They were intimidated by the leader's behaviour but didn't know how to manage the situation. Regardless of what level we are in organizations, our role is to ensure we are managing, creating and implementing communication strategies and channels that inform and engage colleagues. To do this efficiently and effectively we need to know the people we are talking with and the people responsible for influencing cultural change, e.g. leaders. Challenging with confidence comes down to how much trust we've built with leaders. As internal communication professionals, we need to earn the trust of leaders so we can influence and share advice. Here are three simple steps you can take to build your confidence and challenge:

1 Get to know your leaders and spend some time earning their trust. Understanding their behaviour patterns will give you a framework to follow to help you see how you can support them. If it's not easy for you to get face time with them, then speak to others who work with them. Create a stakeholder analysis document where you can log helpful information, which will help you keep track of your conversations.

2 Understand your organization, inside and out. Conduct a SWOT (strengths, weaknesses, opportunities and threats) analysis or a PESTLE (political, economic, sociological, technological, legal and environmental) analysis. You should also know information like annual turnover, customer and colleague base demographics, key competitors and risks.

3 Demonstrate your capability through effective measurement. Show leaders how considered and planned good communication can deliver outstanding results. Keep a dashboard of your results so they can see the impact and ensure you report on monthly successes.

We discuss more frameworks and models in Chapter 6, which will help you cultivate trust further.

We have seen from working in various organizations how low trust can create a culture of uncertainty and low morale. No matter how much investment is made in training, if the basic leadership capabilities are not there to cultivate trust, then it's a complete waste of time. When we conduct our inclusive audits and investigate deeper why there's low trust, the top comment shared is often inefficient and irregular communication from leaders. Zak, during his study, confirmed that only 40 per cent of colleagues reported being well informed about their company's goals, strategies and tactics. This uncertainty led to chronic stress, which according to Zak, 'inhibits the release of oxytocin and undermines teamwork'.

We have a set of five questions that we use to understand how leaders communicate to their teams and if their colleagues trust them. As you read through the questions, think about yourself or another leader in your organization:

1 Is the leader transparent with their communication, and do they admit that they don't know the answer?

2 Is the leader supported by their team when they communicate changes?

3 Is the leader open and direct with their team?

4 In team meetings is the leader challenged? Do colleagues ask questions and share their ideas freely?

5 Does the leader deliver on the promises they make to their team?

A few years ago, Priya supported an organization going through a merger and acquisition. However, a six-month proxy battle caused distress and uncertainty among colleagues. Rather than shy away from difficult questions, a senior director ensured they frequently communicated with colleagues, so they knew what was happening. They were **transparent** and **honest** with their answers; if they couldn't answer due to privacy, they told colleagues the truth. If they didn't know the answer, they shared they didn't know but would find out. They spent time answering difficult questions with the workforce and were brilliant at putting things in perspective.

Colleagues trusted them implicitly because they demonstrated **credibility, were reliable, fostered connections and intimacy** and **cared about others.** The outcome of this behaviour led to the organization achieving its best first and fourth quarters in history. This wasn't an overnight success. The communications team spent 12 months with the leader before the merger and acquisition, building their profile and ensuring colleagues connected with them through various channels. How we build relationships during the good times is crucial, as when crisis hits, the trust leaders have gained will be hugely beneficial.

High-trust cultures and psychological safety

A psychologically safe team must be able to have healthy conflict and allow for productive disagreement. When leaders and managers are too polite and support ideas that are not viable, they will lower their credibility and people will question their experience.

The most successful organizations have a psychologically safe environment where they hear from colleagues who are understood, cared for and supported. When people feel safe and reassured, they begin to trust more. Studies have shown that organizations with a high-trust culture can outperform low-trust companies by 300 per cent.

Internal communication can't fix a poor trust culture alone. That's also not the role of the function. However, we can undoubtedly guide, inspire, motivate, engage and support leaders to do the right thing and help them build a psychologically safe space. In our experience we know that most leaders have good intent but when they don't have communication support to showcase their trust, then people will automatically make assumptions about their character.

Psychological safety is the foundation of enabling a trusted culture. But it's important to note that psychological safety and trust are different. Amy Edmondson, author of *The Fearless Organization* (2018), outlines that psychological safety is a shared belief that the team space is safe for people to take risks and trust is relevant to interactions between either two individuals or two parties. However, Edmondson acknowledges that trust and psychological safety require people to be more vulnerable, which is essential if we want colleagues to contribute to conversations without the fear of retribution.

Creating a safe environment is paramount when cultivating a culture of inclusivity. When colleagues don't feel safe, they won't speak up; when they can't speak up, they will become disengaged and disconnected from the organization. A research study undertaken by Google in 2015 demonstrated that those in teams with higher psychological safety are less likely to leave and will often bring in more revenue than those who don't feel safe (re:Work, 2019).

Table 2.2 describes what psychological safety feels like and explains the behaviours that need to be displayed for a psychological safe environment.

Building a psychologically safe environment requires time, patience and energy. Leaders may be pivotal in building safe spaces, but every colleague should also take ownership and accountability to create safer environments,

TABLE 2.2 What does psychological safety feel like in a workplace environment?

High psychological safety	Low psychological safety
No blame culture. The ability to solve problems quickly and efficiently without fear	Finger pointing and looking for scapegoats
Everyone focused on delivering and accomplishing organizational objectives without land grabbing	Putting their priorities first and focusing on things that make themselves look great. Taking glory for work that was a team effort
Efficient communication where leaders are open about organizational issues and business conditions	Inefficient communication that's broadcast heavy, with lots of gossip and speculation
Passion for their work which leads to innovation and high performance	Apathy for their work leads to poor performance and low engagement
Can raise issues/concerns without retribution	Scared to speak up
Autonomy and support to do the right thing	Lots of micromanagement and passive-aggressive behaviour
Opportunities to grow and develop lead to promotions and progress	Limited developmental opportunities, no training or support to progress
Asks difficult questions	Asks no questions
Colleagues enjoy coming to work and are generally fulfilled	Dislike work and their role, feel miserable and constantly watch the clock
Positive reinforcement which is sincere and well executed	Support is fake or manipulative
Offers solutions to problems	Shares problems but no solutions
Admits errors	Hides mistakes
Will ask for help	Frightened to ask for support
Challenges status quo	Does what's asked without question

including internal communication professionals. A poll, shared by Advita on LinkedIn, asked if building trust was part of the internal communication team's responsibility – 97 per cent answered yes (out of 120+ responses). But how do we help cultivate trust within the remit we have? As well as ensuring we are continuously earning trust from our stakeholders, we also need to review how we use our channels to cultivate high trust. The channels need to be open and transparent and encourage two-way communication. Colleagues should be able to ask questions and be reassured that they are being heard through effective feedback mechanisms and action.

Closing the trust gap

Now you understand the characteristics of trustworthiness, it's essential to understand where the trust gaps are in your organization. We know trust is earned when a leader is reliable, open, accepts different viewpoints and is congruent between their words and actions. But how can strategic communicators help close the 'say-do' gap and help leaders understand how they can minimize the trust gaps? As communication professionals, we need to ensure that our communication strategies, the channels we use and the data we review are as inclusive and trustworthy as possible. The communication strategy should be aligned with the values of the organization and the corporate objective, goals and aims. Without values, organizations will struggle to identify their trust gap and how behaviours are aligned (or not aligned in some cases).

Values

Organizational values are integral to building trust. They provide a shared understanding of what is important and what is acceptable so colleagues can be empowered to make the right decisions on behalf of the organization. When colleagues share common values, it can create a sense of belonging, helping to foster trust further. Values can also guide leaders when they have to make decisions in the organization's best interest. By demonstrating the behaviours linked to the organizational values, leaders signal that they can be trusted to do what they say they will do.

Values can also be powerful during change. They can create a cohesive culture and prove a sense of stability within an organization helping everyone work towards the same goal. However, we know from the work we do that when values are meaningless, and are often just stickers on walls or screen saver images, there will likely be confusion, poor behaviours, low trust and potentially chaos. Without values or meaningful values, it's difficult to address poor behaviour or keep people accountable. For example, if one of your organizational values is 'we will always treat everyone with respect and dignity' but the culture is toxic and peppered with poor behaviour, it demonstrates that the organizational values have no impact whatsoever, creating mistrust and disengagement. If values in your organization are performative, work needs to happen to make them purposeful. Otherwise, it will be challenging to build a genuine culture of inclusivity.

Listen, learn and lean in

As communication professionals, we need to advise and guide leaders to be more accessible, transparent and open with their communication. Listen, learn and lean in are three steps that can help you close the trust gap and help leaders identify where their individual and team trust gaps are.

Listening is part and parcel of being a leader, but continuous active listening (which we cover in more detail in Chapter 5) is something people tend to struggle with. As communication professionals, we can help leaders establish channels like monthly roadshows, regular walk-the-floors and drop-in sessions so leaders can listen and, importantly, respond. One of the biggest criticisms of leaders and a pitfall of poor trust is not actioning colleagues' issues. Observation should also be a crucial part of listening. Make notes of people dominating meetings, those who haven't spoken for a while, people who continuously keep their camera switched off and folks who are interrupted more times than others – these observations can help leaders understand where they need to step in and support. Listening can also help you identify patterns of behaviours, particularly behaviour towards any underrepresented groups.

Learning about the team and what makes them thrive is crucial when closing the trust gap. Regular one-to-one check-in sessions, taking regular interest in what's happening outside of work (if they are comfortable sharing – never force anyone to share if they don't want to), asking them what they need to do their job well and what do they want in terms of development demonstrates that leaders care and have interest. The trust equation, described earlier in this chapter, is a good starting point when you use the four attributes of trust: credibility, reliability, intimacy and self-orientation. To understand more, leaders could send out mini pulse checks to gauge feelings, or focus groups could be held with their team to identify trust gaps.

Leaning in and addressing the challenges and issues you have observed during your time with the leader is imperative. As a trusted advisor to the leader and an independent voice, you can help them identify the trust gaps and how they can diagnose mistrust. Sharing your thoughts and observations, especially if the feedback isn't positive, can be challenging. This is why it's important to contract with the leader right at the start of your relationship. Tell them what you are there to do and ask them what they need from you. Regular updates from you on what you've observed (without spying or sharing identifying data) can be helpful. Keep a dashboard of performance data and track progress, this can help prove how small changes can have a big impact on culture.

Internal communication trust pitfalls

For internal communication, there are several pitfalls we should avoid if we want to build a psychological trusted, safe environment through effective communication:

- Not allowing an opportunity for feedback
- Irrelevant messaging
- Inaccurate and incorrect communication
- Making assumptions
- Limited representation within channels
- Lack of information
- Not coaching line managers in communication skills
- Inconsistency
- No time to respond to the information shared
- Lack of action fatigue

NOT ALLOWING AN OPPORTUNITY FOR FEEDBACK

Feeding back is a significant part of building a safe, high-trust culture and earning trust of colleagues. When you send out information or host sessions like town halls without any process for feeding back, you are telling colleagues you are not interested in their views. If people cannot contribute to conversations, ask curious questions or understand what is being asked of them, they will feel excluded and potentially disengage from the organization.

IRRELEVANT MESSAGING

Irrelevant messaging can cause more harm than intended. In a noisy world with more distractions than ever, our colleagues trust us to communicate relevant and accurate information to them. When we are inconsiderate of what we are sharing without thinking about the 'why', we demonstrate that we don't care about their time.

INACCURATE AND INCORRECT COMMUNICATION

As professional communicators we often have to-do lists that are never ending and due to our pace of work, we can sometimes send out information without double checking for mistakes. We also need to be mindful of incorrect or misinformation that hasn't been verified by a trusted source. Occasionally mistakes can happen and in those instances, we learn and move forward. But if you find errors frequently or are slow to rectify misinformation, you need to reset and review where the gaps are in your sign-off process. Colleagues will start to lose trust in your credibility and it won't help you establish strong trusted relationships.

MAKING ASSUMPTIONS

The person responsible for the channels should ask relevant questions to ensure that the distributed information is accurate without assumptions. Making assumptions without due diligence can cause confusion, gossip and speculation. You must have evidence and data to back up your sharing of information.

LIMITED REPRESENTATION WITHIN CHANNELS

We have a responsibility to ensure we are representing our workforce through our channels. We often conduct inclusive communication audits and the lack of representation in communication channels can cause marginalized groups to feel excluded (e.g. not captioning videos or not having transcripts available). Review your channels without bias and check against your demographics to ensure you are not unintentionally cutting people out or excluding them. Remember when you address the challenges facing the minority, the majority will always benefit.

LACK OF INFORMATION

Sending out vague messages or not explaining what colleagues need to do with the information shared can also lead to gossip and speculation. You're implying that colleagues can't be trusted and are not important enough to be told everything. Be mindful when you're asked to send messages without context, and don't fear asking relevant questions. Consider ethics if you have to communicate information that doesn't explain the whole story. It's okay to tell colleagues that you can't share information yet, this will be better received than lying or ignoring their question.

NOT COACHING MANAGERS

As we shared earlier in this chapter, it's not the role of only internal communication to build trust. Leaders play a significant part but need support through coaching and training. Robust communication skills can help leaders to understand how they can improve connections within their teams. As communication professionals, we must take ownership supporting leaders and upskilling them to be an effective communicator.

INCONSISTENCY

One of the biggest failures of trust and psychological safety is not delivering on your promises. If you say there will be weekly communications on a Monday at midday, then make sure you send a weekly communication on a Monday at midday. People trust you to keep them informed, even if you have nothing to say. Without explanation, missing the communication or sending it out on a different day/time can cause mistrust. If you're unable to commit to a day or time, then make sure you communicate that clearly. Also consider whether your actions match your behaviours – saying one thing and doing another will damage your credibility.

NO TIME TO RESPOND

We live in a fast-paced world where we are churning out information constantly. We must ensure that the information we share with the workforce is relevant and timely. We also need to allow colleagues time to absorb what we're sharing and give them opportunities to raise concerns or issues, because not allowing people time to understand the information will lead to mistrust and disengagement. To avoid information overload, we must be mindful of what communication is going out, when and to whom. The first step to understanding our communication process will be to undertake a channels audit, which is inclusive and supportive. The audit will give an understanding of how much information is being shared, how often and who the messages are going to. This will give you the foundation to plan your communication cycle, with time built in for questions and responses.

LACK OF ACTION FATIGUE

How many times have you heard people say that colleagues won't complete surveys as they have 'survey fatigue'? It's not survey fatigue, it's lack of action fatigue. If you ask for feedback but don't pay attention to it, you are at risk of causing distrust. Comments shared by colleagues should be acknowledged and addressed, whether the answer is positive or not. By doing this, you're showing that their voice is important, and you're demonstrating reliability, transparency, openness and vulnerability.

Trust isn't linear

Throughout this chapter, we've written about the characteristics of trust. But we need to understand that trust isn't linear. We're privileged to live in a world with people from different backgrounds and cultural experiences. When building and cultivating trust, we must be aware of the diversity of people we work with. Not everyone will have the same lived experience as you, and not everyone will follow the same trust patterns. That doesn't mean that they are less trustworthy or don't deserve your trust. Take time to get to know people for who they are, those who are not neurotypical, people who may be from different cultural backgrounds and folks who are socially anxious may have a different interpretation of trust. It's critically important to ask questions and build connections. Being curious and finding out patterns of what trust means to everyone will help create an inclusive environment where everyone can belong.

KEY TAKEAWAYS

- Trust is subjective, but four key components help to build trustworthiness: credibility, reliability, intimacy and self-orientation. Others may describe these as competence and character attributes.
- The lack of trust between colleagues and employers can cause low performance and disengagement. Consider the 13 trust attributes and understand what you think needs additional focus.

- Leaders need to understand their trust gap before earning and building trust. Being self-aware is critical.
- Psychological safety is essential in high-trust cultures. If people don't feel safe, they won't feel trusted or be able to trust anyone else.
- Vulnerability can help leaders break down barriers and help build stronger relationships with their team.
- Internal communication can help drive high-trust cultures through inclusive and engaging communication.
- Not everyone will follow the same trust pattern as we live in a diverse world, so it's important to be curious and get to know people's habits and behaviours.

REFLECTIVE QUESTIONS

- Where's the trust gap in your organization?
- What does trust mean to you?
- Overall, in your organization, do you think the colleague population trusts the leadership team?
- Who are your most trusted colleagues and what are their characteristics?
- What key channels do you need to help cultivate trust in your organization and how will it help build trusted relationships?
- Do you consider different characteristics and cultural backgrounds when you're building trust?

Bibliography

Botsman, R (2017) *Who Can You Trust*. 1 ed. New York, Hachette Book Group

Brenner, M (2021) The rise and fall of the social media influencer, Marketing Insider Group, marketinginsidergroup.com/influencer-marketing/the-rise-and-fall-of-the-social-media-influencer/ (archived at https://perma.cc/6J3X-N6LG)

Brown, B (2015) *Daring Greatly: How the courage to be vulnerable transforms the way we live, love, parent and lead*. 2 ed. London, Penguin Books

Brown, B (2022), The BRAVING Inventory, brenebrown.com/resources/the-braving-inventory/ (archived at https://perma.cc/M5A7-BHWV)

Charles, F (2021) *The Thin Book of Trust. An essential primer for building trust at work*. 2 ed. s.l., The Book Publishing Co.

Covey, S M (2006) *The Speed of Trust*. London, Simon & Schuster

Edelman Trust Barometer (2022) 2022 Edelman Trust Barometer, edelman.com/trust/2022-trust-barometer (archived at https://perma.cc/AMT9-R65V)

Edmondson, A (2019) *The Fearless Organization*. 1 ed. New Jersey: John Wiley & Sons

Frances, F X and Anne, M (2020) *Unleashed*. 1 ed. Boston, HBR

Frost, S and Alidina, R-K (2019) *Building an Inclusive Culture*. London, Kogan Page

Gallup (2022) State of the Global Workplace: 2022 Report, gallup.com/workplace/349484/state-of-the-global-workplace-2022-report.aspx (archived at https://perma.cc/2E9Y-2W3N)

Jefferson, M (2021) 'Lies, hypocrisy and deceit': BrewDog's brand health takes hit from allegations, MarketingWeek, marketingweek.com/brewdog-brand-health/ (archived at https://perma.cc/6V3L-YV9M)

Maister, D, Green, H C and Glaford, R (2002) *The Trusted Advisor*. 2 ed. London, Simon & Schuster

Nienaber, A-M, Hofeditz, M and Romeike, P D (2015) Vulnerability and trust in leader follower relationships, *Personnel Review*, 44, 567–91

Ott, B (2017) 3 reasons why performance development wins in the workplace, Gallup, gallup.com/workplace/231620/why-performance-development-wins-workplace.aspx? (archived at https://perma.cc/FL8A-RD8N)

PricewaterhouseCoopers (2016) *Redefining Business Success in a Changing World, CEO Survey*. London, PwC

PricewaterhouseCoopers (2022) Trust: the new currency for business, pwc.com/us/en/services/consulting/library/consumer-intelligence-series/trust-new-business-currency.html (archived at https://perma.cc/M74D-6RP5)

re:Work (2019) rework.withgoogle.com/print/guides/5721312655835136/ (archived at https://perma.cc/JWV4-H5FK)

The Institute of Leadership and Management (2014) Leadership Essentials: Building trust, institutelm.com/learning/leadership-framework/authenticity/building-trust/leadership-essentials-building-trust.html (archived at https://perma.cc/GEX4-NU7U)

TrustedAdvisor (2021) *The Trust Equation*, rustedadvisor.com/why-trust-matters/understanding-trust/understanding-the-trust-equation (archived at https://perma.cc/2ADJ-TKB8)

TrustedAdvisor (2022) About, trustedadvisor.com/about (archived at https://perma.cc/T62G-NUYS)

Zak, J P (2017) The neuroscience of trust, *Harvard Business Review*, hbr.org/2017/01/the-neuroscience-of-trust (archived at https://perma.cc/B45Z-SC2U)

03

Building leadership capability to impact and influence cultural change

In this chapter we talk about the various levels of leadership required to drive progress on DEI and the evolution organizations go through in their efforts. We finish with a focus on leading change. What we want to make clear is that DEI and building inclusive cultures is a team effort.

It should be no surprise that leadership is a central tenet influencing change. And in the DEI space, leadership at all levels is critical to **define** what success looks like; **guide** others into new ways of thinking, feeling, understanding and working; and explain and **showcase** best practices.

A former executive Priya once worked with often talked about the concept of evolutionary and revolutionary times for organizations. Evolutions were times where organizations grew in the same direction over time. Evolution signalled growth and continuous improvement. Revolutions, on the other hand, were times when changes in direction were needed quickly to adapt to new ways of working, whether it was technological advancements, changing competitive environments or crisis responses.

These different times required different types of leaders. Evolutionary leaders were brought in to keep the lights on while revolutionary leaders were brought in to drive change.

When it comes to DEI, although we've collectively and globally gone through an evolution over centuries that has slowly increased the focus on human rights, we're sure everyone will agree that we are in revolutionary times from a DEI perspective today. For some, changes feel too fast and too sudden. They seem too hard to accomplish results and change behaviours with many asking for more time. While for others, those who have been marginalized and are at a disadvantage, change feels too slow as generations fight for the next one to be treated fairly.

TABLE 3.1 Leadership types in DEI

C-Suite/Executive	Leader at the top of the organization
DEI Leader	Leader given the mandate for DEI in the organization
Communication Leader	Leader communicating changes to employees
People Manager	Leader who manages people
Influencer	Leader whose opinions matter and influence
Individual Contributor	Leader on the ground without title or seniority

When it comes to leadership, those leading the way to create inclusive cultures feel like this is more of a fight than simply growth. Remember that reference to warriors versus workers in Chapter 1? We're looking for a balance of leading courageously while helping people understand that this is an important step towards a future and the world of belonging, dignity and justice we all crave. What we're probably seeing is an acceleration of an evolution.

As we talk about leadership, we're going to look at the different levels of leadership required to move culture change forward. As internal communication professionals, we often work with leaders at various levels of our organization.

Why do we need leaders and hierarchies if everyone wants to be treated the same?

Before we go into details about the roles of various levels of leadership, let's begin by talking about why leadership is needed. Aren't hierarchical structures part of the problem? Wouldn't flatter structures and consensus cultures actually lead to more fairness?

Here's the reality: hierarchy is an important organizational property of many biological and social systems, ranging from neural, ecological, metabolic and genetic regulatory networks, to the organization of companies, cities, societies and the internet (Mengistu, 2016).

Hierarchies evolved in human history as populations grew and became organized into nations, states, militaries and corporations to wield the power of the collective to be both more efficient and effective to achieve positive results. The alternative is every person for themselves making

TABLE 3.2 Maslow's Hierarchy of Needs

Self-actualization	Worthiness, being your best
Esteem	Respect, status, recognition, strength, freedom
Love and belonging	Friendship, family, connection
Safety	Security, employment, health, wealth
Physiological	Air, water, food, shelter, sleep

(Saul McLeod, 2022)

decisions at random without larger ideals, guidance and direction. As Peter Turchin explains: 'societies that were larger and better organized out-competed smaller and more shambolic ones... It's a pipe dream to imagine that large-scale society can be organized in a non-hierarchical, horizontal way' (Turchin, 2014).

It is true that hierarchies and certain social networks can evolve for evil as well as good. Think of colonization that quickly eliminated Indigenous populations around the world, or slavery and the tenets of white supremacy that created a hierarchy that justified the treatment of Black people.

We believe hierarchies are human. We live with them in government structures, organizational structures, religious structures and in our own family structures. Even in personal structures, people often talk about Maslow's Hierarchy of Needs theory, which identifies personal growth journeys that evolve from physiological needs, to safety, to love and belonging, to esteem, and eventually self-actualization (Saul McLeod, 2022).

As we focus this chapter on leaders, we believe leadership is required at all levels of organizations and communities. We believe that from a DEI perspective leaders make the difference in staying where we are or moving forward. We believe leaders are required at all levels of an organization and that you don't need to have a title or role to be a leader. Finally, when it comes to personal journeys, everyone inside and outside our organizations have the potential to be their best and are worthy of respect, recognition, safety and security.

It's all about trust

Our last chapter revolved around trust and its importance in driving culture and especially our vision of inclusive cultures.

As discussed in Chapter 2, the recent Edelman Trust Barometer findings (Edelmen, 2022) have highlighted an opportunity when it comes to business, leadership and colleagues. While 61 per cent said that business is one of the most trustworthy institutions compared to government at 52 per cent and media at only 50 per cent, 77 per cent trust 'My employer'. In fact, 60 per cent of employees want their CEO to speak out on controversial issues they care about, while 80 per cent want CEOs to be personally visible on public policy and when discussing work they have done to benefit society. Behind scientists, 'My coworkers' were most trusted at 74 per cent followed closely by 'My CEO' at 66 per cent.

For us, this presents an incredible opportunity for all of the leaders we are focused on to drive both cultural change inside organizations and societal change in general.

Exploring leadership

As we focus on the role of leaders, let's explore the types of leaders we need to drive success. We're sure you're reading this book in order to lead the change you want to see, so we're hoping you will see yourself identified in one or several of the descriptions below. Know that every type of leader is needed to make real progress on DEI.

C-suite/executive

The c-suite or executive represents the leader or group of leaders at the top of an organization. It could be the CEO, president or owner and could include top management. These leaders set priorities, create business strategies and make decisions on investments including resources and budget for DEI efforts.

When it comes to the top leaders, actions speak louder than words. What colleagues see is more important than the words they hear or read. In fact, whenever we see a public statement on DEI by an organization, many of us search online for the make-up of the executive team and the progress they say they are making on DEI efforts. If there is a statement on International Women's Day and we see an all-white and male leadership team, it tends to make us question whether the commitment is superficial and performative.

The Edelman Trust Barometer tells us that the famous CEOs of global organizations from Mark Zuckerberg of Facebook to CEOs of big banks generally tend not to be trusted, yet people trust the CEOs of their own organizations. We believe there is an opportunity to leverage trust in organizational leaders to drive societal change.

As in any change effort, we need strategic, financial, moral and visible support from the leaders at the top in order to lend credibility to our organization's change efforts.

When it comes to DEI, CEOs/executives must:

- Be visible in support of DEI efforts.
- Ensure the business strategy has DEI objectives and key performance indicators (KPIs) embedded.
- Provide investment into resources and budget.
- Ensure actions and decisions match words and commitments.
- Be accessible to those leading the DEI efforts.
- Be accountable to and report on results.

DEI leader

A DEI leader has been given the DEI mandate for the organization. DEI is part of their job description and part of their accountability. In the past few years, we know that DEI has often been added to the job description of HR, IC or other business leaders with limited resources.

The DEI leader is responsible for working with executives and other organizational leaders to create the DEI strategy and move it forward in their organizations. Often, DEI leaders are passionate employees who have limited experience and training since the demand for DEI leaders seems to have outpaced the supply of experts.

What's also important is the realization that the DEI leader is not representative of everyone in marginalized communities. The DEI leader collaborates with others to build a DEI strategy and is connected to the business strategy, the people strategy and the communication strategy.

The DEI leader also helps advise executives on priorities and possibilities. If there are limited resources, the DEI leader makes the business case on what is needed to move the organization forward.

When it comes to DEI, the DEI leader must:

- Have access to the c-suite/executives.
- Be responsible for DEI strategy.

- Make the business case for investment needed for change.
- Identify obstacles to success.
- Set the plan and report on progress regularly.
- Listen to employees and their needs.
- Have a clear connection to employee resource groups.
- Work collaboratively with leaders, business operations and communication to drive change.

Communication leader

A communication leader connects the dots between the DEI strategy and employee delivery. Note that there are external communications like marketing, PR and customer/community relations that may be an important element of communicating DEI, yet for the purposes of this book, we will focus on the role on internal communication.

That being said, think about internal communication as having an impact from the inside out. We need to ensure employees are aware of strategy and goals; understand the reason why they are important to the organization; do what's expected through words, decisions and actions; and believe that the organization is going in the right direction for all.

Internal communication, when done right, helps translate values to behaviours; words to actions, strategies to results; and brand promises into employee and customer experiences. In an ideal world, communication has the power to bring DEI to life in every decision and interaction.

One thing to note, we're seeing a lot of organizations assign internal communication to individuals with passion but without training and experience, because everyone can communicate – right? The truth is there are experts trained to use communication solutions to solve real business problems yet there are simply not enough strategic practitioners out there to meet the need. However, here is an opportunity to build the skills necessary if the organization thinks beyond the newsletter, memos and speeches.

When it comes to DEI, the communication leader must:

- Work closely with the DEI leader.
- Have access to the CEO/executives to drive visibility and messages.
- Encourage employee input and feedback.
- Create and implement a communication plan that brings the DEI strategy to life.

- Keep people managers informed of messages to drive consistency.
- Own and operate the trusted tools and channels where employees receive information.
- Point out disconnects, if any, between DEI efforts and other organizational initiatives.

People manager

People managers supervise and manage the people in your organizations. For years, many studies found that employees prefer to receive information about the company from their managers. This is even more relevant in a hybrid workplace. The 2022 Gallagher State of the Sector Report, which reviews the state of internal communication globally, identified *Enhancing people manager communication* as the number three priority. The number one priority was *Engaging teams around purpose, strategy, values* (Gallagher, 2022).

> *'People join organizations and quit managers* – whoever said this originally certainly made a point that resonates with A LOT of employees. Whether that is still true in the context of the Great Resignation is anyone's guess, but it's hard to argue with the fact that people managers are one of the most significant influencers of the employee experience in any organization.' (Gallagher, 2022)

Whether we are on the shop floor, working in an office or interacting with hybrid or remote employees, the manager to employee relationship is critical to driving performance. Communication professionals need to leverage this essential group to unlock opportunities when it comes to communicating with and engaging employees.

When it comes to DEI, people managers must:

- Communicate regularly with their teams in groups and one on one.
- Understand the reasons and key messages around DEI.
- Be trained on what good looks like and how to manage fairly.
- Implement operational changes needed across the organization (e.g. policies and processes).
- Answer employee questions and listen to feedback.

- Manage performance.
- Call out inappropriate behaviour.
- Set an example.
- Create context to connect DEI to the role of the team or individual.
- Build relationships with and among team members in workplaces and in the virtual environment.
- Create psychologically safe environments for honest and open dialogue.

Influencer

An influencer is someone who is trusted and whose expertise or opinion can change the thinking or behaviour of others. Unlike other leaders, an influencer doesn't have a formal title and chooses to be an influencer without a job description. An influencer doesn't simply do what their organization tells them to do. They have their opinions and are not afraid to share it with others and rally people around them.

Influencers have the power to support your efforts or derail them and they can be disruptive. And keep in mind, those who are extremely good at creating a following inside your organization may not have leadership titles but can lead effectively.

The question is, do you know who the influencers in your organization are? They could be a popular leader, the union representative or an individual contributor who is simply passionate about their beliefs.

In our consulting work, we have often identified influencers and invited them to provide feedback. We also give them insights into the programmes that have been launched. Sometimes this helps to support initiatives, and at other times, it is with the intent of identifying their concerns so that we can be prepared to answer challenging questions.

When it comes to DEI, influencers may:

- Support or derail your efforts and narrative.
- Call out disconnects.
- Create hype or stoke fears that need to be addressed.
- Feed the rumour mill.
- If brought in early, can help influence messaging and Q&A.
- Become an extension of your team.

Individual contributors

Individual contributors are the colleagues in your organization who do the work, serve the customers and don't have any direct reporting relationships. They represent the masses yet leadership among these individuals is critical for DEI efforts to move forward. Individual contributors are often where diversity in your organization lies. They are the upcoming leaders, they are the face to your customers and other stakeholders, and they create the culture that lives in your organization which comes to life with everyday interactions. They are the owners of the employee and customer experience.

Individual contributors may also manage unofficially. In fact, many of them are leaders in the employee resource groups (ERGs) that your organization has set up. DEI efforts require people to create inclusive cultures where the right decisions are made without bias and where people feel like they belong.

There is also an opportunity to find individual contributors willing to help to drive progress in DEI goals.

When it comes to DEI, individual contributors must:

- Have the ability to provide feedback from the ground level of your organization.
- Be the source of metrics and data on representation in your organization.
- Have the opportunity to participate in feedback and review of strategies and change efforts.
- Know exactly what best-practice behaviour looks like to bring the DEI strategy to life.
- Care about the cause and believe it is the right thing to do for the organization.

We need leadership at all levels in the organization. As DEI and internal communication plans are built, leaders should be a proactive part of internal communication strategies and it's important to recognize each unique role in order to deliver a meaningful and actionable plan that targets the right information, to the right leader at the right time.

DEI E-volution

As we look at the role of leadership, let's also look at the evolution we have seen in leaders and organizations in the DEI space. It's important to understand exactly where all leaders are personally in order to plan the step to the next phase.

Although we've acknowledged that DEI recently feels like more of a revolution versus evolution, it is a mistake to assume that organizations and individuals will go from ZERO to HERO in the DEI space overnight. We're hoping these phases of our DEI E-volution will help you identify where you, your leaders and your organization are in the process so that you can plan your next step to move forward.

We've created six phases that individuals and organizations need to step through: Exist, Enter, Educate, Embrace, Engage and Embed. We hope you will see clearly and relate to each of these phases in your DEI journey.

Exist

When we're in the Exist Stage, we choose to stay exactly where we are. We do not want change in systems, processes or programmes and probably fight to keep things the same. This is often the 'we've always done it this way', phase where we resist change since we feel that what exists today is simply working for us. When we work for successful companies or we have personally benefited from current systems that exist which have often suppressed others, we resist a need to change, consciously or unconsciously. Perhaps as a leader, you feel forced to step into the unknown or into a future and work that seems complicated when things are going really well right now. Perhaps you are feeling forced to drive change when what is currently happening has served you well. Existing feels easier because you don't have to work that hard. Here's the truth: as long as there is a desire by leaders to exist, any work that is done will not lead to real results or movement towards change. And perhaps that is exactly where you want to be until a business case for change (refer to Chapter 1 on why) is made.

FIGURE 3.1 The DEI E-volution

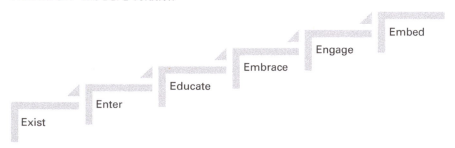

Positive: Everything seems to be working for you, the leaders or the organization at this time (e.g. results are good, you get opportunities and the organization is profitable).

Warning: If marginalized communities do exist, perhaps they are not high enough in the influence chain to express their concerns. This could lead to attrition or disengagement.

Fix: Understand your personal role and the role of leadership on how to make the case for change and stepping into the DEI space. Refer to our first chapter on why to identify the reason that change and a focus on DEI is needed for your organization.

Enter

When leaders and organizations are in the Enter Stage, it's usually because they acknowledge that change is needed. Perhaps they are worried about their reputation or they see others doing something about DEI and want to keep up or not feel left out. In the Enter Stage, we see organizations dipping their toes into DEI. Perhaps it's black boxes and rainbows? Maybe they are starting to acknowledge commemorative dates and events like International Women's Day or Black History Month. They may start sharing celebrations of a variety of religious holidays that are meaningful to their organizations. Entering is a first step of feeling included, which is a little ironic since it often feels like the organization wants to feel more included versus creating inclusive cultures for their colleagues. Still, it's progress even though not perfect.

At this stage, we may even see employee resource groups (ERG) emerge. A Women's Group, a Pride Group and a variety of groups that acknowledge a variety of religions and cultures. For the most part, ERGs are volunteer-led, and more and more we've seen an inordinate amount of work on top of these volunteers' own jobs which continues to put these individuals at a disadvantage. Be conscious of asking underrepresented individuals to do additional work on their own time while others receive career-building opportunities.

Positive: There is an acknowledgment that some change is needed and organizations are starting to recognize and value differences in their workforces. They also have good intent to begin their DEI journey.

Warning: Work in the Enter Stage may feel very performative and could further marginalize groups and individuals who are being asked to provide extra work on behalf of lower priority DEI initiatives versus projects that receive funding which could lead to promotions. In other words, while these leaders are working towards change, those with privilege are given funded assignments that provide exposure to senior leadership.

Fix: The role of leadership is to move from the outside in. As you look at public sentiment to your support of the DEI conversation, identify the risk of simply doing the promotional work without doing the internal work. Talk to your ERGs and leaders and identify their points of frustration. Also identify disconnects – what we say versus what we do that could hurt credibility. Look at your mission, vision, values and strategy and identify where DEI may play a role in helping drive results. Also make ERG leadership an opportunity to identify high potential candidates for career progression.

Educate

In this stage, individuals focus on learning through education, reading and training. According to recent research conducted by the HR Research Institute, about 75 per cent provide DEI-related training (HR Research Institute, 2022). The most common are:

1 Unconscious bias training about the automatic thoughts and assumptions that we have learned and that need to be questioned.

2 Inclusion awareness teaches how to notice when certain groups or individuals are included or excluded.

3 Conversations training supports discussions of uncomfortable issues.

4 Inclusive recruitment policies training which is often delivered to recruiters and hiring managers to increase diversity.

Other training includes conflict resolution, anti-racism and communication practices. What's interesting in the research is that only 40 per cent of organizations provide training to all colleagues.

Organizations in this stage also focus on listening exercises to learn about the experience of underrepresented colleagues. We've also seen organizations and individuals starting to read books and create book clubs to educate themselves.

Positive: A first real investment in driving change, creating empathy and understanding amongst leaders and employees. Organizations are investing in high-level training and individuals are taking personal accountability for learning.

Warning: Many initiatives and training feel reactive and tend to be one-time in nature or only provided to a limited number of colleagues. Organizations may feel like education is enough to drive changes in behaviour but it is important to treat education as the beginning of change, not simply a check-box exercise. For many colleagues and observers, it feels like training and codes of conduct seem to be driven by a legal strategy to protect organizations and say they did educate in case of liability versus actually driving change.

Fix: The role of leadership is to create maintainable and demonstrable change. Understand how training is driving behaviour change and improved outcomes. Involve your communication team to raise awareness and sustain the learnings from training. Is there improvement in customer satisfaction or employee engagement scores? Where in the employee life cycle does DEI matter? Make the case to drive people and programme investment beyond training.

Embrace

When organizations and leaders start to embrace DEI, we start to see real investment in ownership and leadership. At this point, we see investment in resources. Perhaps they have hired a DEI leader in the organization who will start creating a focused DEI strategy that will determine investments and plans moving forward. They also start measuring the present state of the organization in DEI, setting measurable goals for change and exploring processes and systems that may need to change.

In the organizations we have worked with, we've started seeing DEI plans come to life and many human resources, internal communication and other organizational leaders take on the DEI mandate officially as part of their job description or as a dedicated role for the organization.

The challenges occur when DEI is seen as separate from the business strategy and as a vacuum in itself. Also, if the DEI leader has limited access to leadership and a limited budget, it's seen as a nice-to-have versus a must-have by employees. Around the world, we have heard from HR and internal communication leaders who are feeling alone and stuck between leadership demands for change without resources and employee resistance or apathy. And if there is a lack of trust, it's difficult to get support to drive change forward.

It's often at this stage that we are brought in to organizations with leaders who have good intentions but are seeing limited progress on their goals.

Positive: A strategy and plan is in place. The organization has taken the first step in investing in resources to guide the DEI programme and identify KPIs that signal success. Organizations have also made the case for the why for DEI that ideally is tied to business imperatives.

Warning: Strategies and plans are aspirational yet when there isn't a plan to engage employees in the efforts and a lack of resources available to drive change, organizations can tend to give up, citing resistance and fear of failure.

Fix: The role of leadership is to move the needle and bring the DEI strategy to life through positive employee and customer experiences. Collaborate with internal communication expertise to identify what needs to be done to help employees be aware of the strategy; understand why it's important to the organization; do and say the right things; and believe in the cause and direction set by the organization.

Engage

When organizations and leaders focus on engagement, they are realizing that change involves everyone in the organization at all levels. The DEI strategy describes why it is important to the organization and where the organization should focus on driving the goals articulated. What tends to be missing is what leaders and employees need to do differently in everyday decisions and interactions to lead to the results. A great DEI strategy is essentially a change plan and we've often said that a change plan cannot be successful without a solid communication plan designed to engage employees in the change efforts.

Many successful organizations who are leading the way when it comes to DEI are in this stage. They have set strong goals. They have made commitments. They have trained their employees. They understand where they are and what they need to improve in order to be more inclusive. Although they may make some mistakes along the way, they are able to recover quickly and course correct.

They are actively measuring progress as they get to the ideal state where they feel they are representative of their publics and they are starting to reap rewards.

Positive: A communication and engagement plan that supports the DEI strategy is in place. The organization is investing in resources, measuring results and driving progress. It also recognizes that change is a collective effort from leadership to the frontline in order for goals to be met.

Warning: There is a fear that DEI is a temporary fix to a temporary problem. Organizations are hiring individuals but cultures and habits built over years are harder to change so they are seeing attrition. There is still resistance to change and they need to stay the course over time and provide a psychologically safe environment to keep conversations open when things go wrong.

Fix: The role of leadership is to understand that DEI is not just the job of a few key people provided with the mandate or the role of ERGs who are volunteering their time; it is the responsibility of everyone at every level in the organization. Encourage leaders to move to creating a sustainable plan that delivers action.

Embed

In this final stage, organizations and leaders who embed thinking and decision making in the life cycle and everyday operations of the organization are working towards a world where there is sustainable change when it comes to DEI. We all want a world that we feel is fair and just. A world where we are treated with dignity and respect. Where we all feel like we belong. We also want to strive toward a world where DEI is not an added project or programme, but just the way we live and work and organizations are centred around its values.

When DEI is embedded, it is incorporated into recruitment efforts, orientation of all new employees and retention and recognition programmes for existing employees. It also gets embedded into external reputation efforts from branding to advertising to supplier management and customer service. It becomes the way we do things around here.

DEI that is embedded is the ultimate when it comes to creating inclusive cultures. It eventually means clear expectations, fair treatment, a sense of belonging and an organization that employees are proud to work for and customers are proud to interact with.

Positive: DEI is not one person's job but embedded in the strategy, mission, vision, values and behaviours of an organization. The everyday actions demonstrate a commitment that does not need to be separated from who the organization is and how it delivers.

Warning: This is the hard work and takes time. Individuals whom have benefited from privilege in the past may feel like they are being discriminated against or silenced from saying and doing things the way they used to. It's the 'what about me?'.

Fix: The role of leadership is to keep communicating. Because DEI efforts take time and may evolve as we learn more, it's important to measure change and keep employees informed of efforts, milestones and key accomplishments against business objectives aligned to recruitment, retention, representation, reputation and results.

The bottom line is that DEI is not a one-time campaign; it involves organization change over time and a continued conversation about progress with individuals at all levels leading the way.

The DEI E-volution is a set of steps since each step is a movement forward. We believe understanding where you are personally from a leadership perspective and understanding where your organization is right now can help you choose the next steps you need to take to evolve and move forward.

CASE STUDY
The BlackNorth Initiative

In the summer of 2020, the BlackNorth Initiative was founded by Canadian entrepreneur and philanthropist Wes Hall to counter anti-Black racism in corporate Canada. He unveiled the CEO Pledge acknowledging that top leadership played an important role in driving change. In the first year, it garnered almost 500 signatures (Ayer, 2022).

Pledge goals included a commitment to implement unconscious bias and anti-racism training; creation of strategic inclusion and diversity plans; and goals to ensure 3.5 per cent of executive board and/or senior leadership roles based in Canada were held by Black or visible minority leaders and at least 5 per cent of their student workforce was from the Black community.

Although progress seems slow, Dahabo Ahmed-Omer, executive director of the initiative, reminds us that systemic changes do not happen overnight, and that's the reason for the five-year timeline in the pledge itself.

There has been some progress: one year later, 33 per cent of signatories had a current strategic diversity and inclusion plan with related KPIs, while another 46 per cent had one in progress. When it came to data collection, 30 per cent had platforms or systems in place while another 37 per cent were building one.

Leading change

In Chapter 7, we'll spend a lot more time talking about change management since we know that DEI is a large-scale change effort that requires organizations and their people to change their thinking and behaviours over time.

In this chapter, let's spend a little bit of time talking about the role of leadership in change. What is clear is that leaders must be involved strategically, actively and visibly in DEI efforts in order for real progress to be made.

According to Gallup, it's important that leaders practice what they preach. They must be actively involved, have a visible role in DEI efforts and set an example for colleagues to help sustain momentum. They have an opportunity to showcase their commitment through proactive communication and being actively involved in goal setting with their teams (Tschida, 2021).

Here are our ABCs of leading change.

Actively participate

All leaders must actively participate in DEI efforts. If DEI is treated as the job of HR, internal communication or the DEI manager or team, employees will simply not take it seriously.

How leaders can actively participate:

- Connect DEI to the business strategy and key tenets like the mission, vision, purpose and values.
- Commit budget for people resources, training and programmes.
- Identify executive sponsors and hold senior level and executive leaders accountable for results.
- Provide access to DEI, HR and communication leaders.
- Act as spokesperson for the change.
- Simply show up to trainings and meetings. If there is an expectation of the organization to attend training yet leaders don't show up to learn, employees are less likely to make training a priority.
- Set the example in everyday words, actions and behaviours including your communication.

Believe in the cause

Leaders simply must believe in the cause. In order for real progress, they need to believe in both the business and social case for change:

- Reflect on what DEI truly means for them personally and professionally.

- Acknowledge privilege that got them into the roles they are in today.
- Understand where the myths believed true in the past, may not be true today with increased education.
- Know the why: why is this important for the organization to move forward and succeed?
- Make sure that the messages being delivered feel credible versus forced.

Communicate often

Leaders must communicate regularly through the change process. We often tell communication professionals to identify key milestones in a change cycle. The beginnings, the celebrations, the struggles, the successes, the failures and the achievements. Remember that this is not a short-lived campaign, but a regular conversation with employees:

- Have a proactive communication plan for all levels of leadership.
- Keep people informed along the way – the good, the bad and the ugly – in order to build credibility and trust.
- Ensure all leaders have messages and the answers to any questions that may be asked to drive consistency.
- Incorporate DEI messaging into every day conversations – connecting the dots in key moments.
- Ensure communication is two-way and allows for listening and feedback.

Define the desired state

Leaders have to inspire others along the path to success, yet if what success looks like is not clearly defined or is vague at best, the result is often confusion and inaction:

- Define what success looks like.
- Have specific, measurable, achievable, realistic and time-bound (SMART) goals over at least a year and longer if possible.
- Talk aspirationally about the ideal state and set a plan for what improvements will be made over shorter milestones to showcase progress.

- Connect the desired state to the mission, vision and values of the organization. There is an opportunity to talk inspirationally about who you are and what you stand for.
- Use messaging that inspires people's heads (intellectually), hearts (emotionally) and hands (physically).

Enable action

Leaders create the conditions for success by investing in resources, clearly articulating expectations and opening the doors for progress to be possible.

- Invest time to dedicate to DEI progress.
- Invest in people resources to lead DEI efforts. If it's simply added to someone's already busy plate, the chances of success are limited.
- Invest in training.
- Invest in programmes.
- Identify metrics and KPIs by which success will be measured.

Follow up

Leaders need to showcase progress. We often use the phrase *progress not perfect* to describe the DEI change effort. It's full of complex emotions, doubts and barriers. The key to any long-term change effort is to inspire people to stay on course.

- Communicate regularly: you may want your plan to have an annual or quarterly report card to show progress on initiatives.
- Break down milestones into smaller chunks so that aspirational five-year goals can show movement on an annual basis.
- Hold leaders, executives and teams accountable for results. Keeping these initiatives front and centre through performance conversations or bonus-linked initiatives will make them more likely to be taken seriously.
- Talk about challenges and barriers. Identify solutions or update goals if necessary.
- Apologize or acknowledge when things go wrong or mistakes are made. Take action if necessary. You need a plan to help people fail and learn to improve in a psychologically safe environment but also have a plan to take corrective action when reputation is at risk.

KEY TAKEAWAYS

- Hierarchies are necessary to drive efficiencies and deliver effectively in large complex organizations.

- The Edelman Trust Barometer tells us that since societal leaders like media, government and global CEOS are not trusted, there is an opportunity for local CEOs and colleagues to drive societal change from the inside out.

- There are various levels of leadership needed to drive change. They include c-suite/executives, DEI leaders, internal communication leaders, people managers, influencers and individual contributors.

- Most organizations go through a DEI E-volution: Exist – Enter – Educate – Embrace – Engage – Embed. Identifying where you are personally and organizationally will help you decide on the steps needed to move forward.

- Leading change is needed: actively participate; believe in the cause; communicate often; define the desired state; enable action; and follow up to be successful.

REFLECTIVE QUESTIONS

- Who are the leaders in my organization?
- What is my leadership role?
- Where am I personally in the DEI E-volution?
- Where does my organization sit in the DEI E-volution?
- Are my leaders actively leading change?
- What is the risk if they choose not to lead?

Bibliography

Ayer, S (2022, 8 February) The BlackNorth Initiative: Learnings on advancing racial equity in Canada, Imagine Canada, imaginecanada.ca/en/360/blacknorth-initiative-learnings-advancing-racial-equity-canada (archived at https://perma.cc/N4FV-EWSR)

Dahlstrom, L (2018, 2 July) Beyond May 29: Lessons from Starbucks anti-bias training – and what's next, Starbucks Stories & News, stories.starbucks.com/stories/2018/beyond-may-29-lessons-from-starbucks-anti-bias-training-and-whats-next/ (archived at https://perma.cc/AF4T-XAVF)

Edelman (2022, 18 January) 2022 Edelman Trust Barometer, edelman.com/trust/2022-trust-barometer (archived at https://perma.cc/35UN-2JY7)

Gallagher (2022) State of the Sector 2022: Global internal communication and employee engagement insights and trends, ajg.com/employeeexperience/state-of-the-sector-2022/ (archived at https://perma.cc/W9WE-WW2D)

Gupta, S (2021, 19 August) Three characteristics of effective DEI leadership, Forbes, forbes.com/sites/forbescoachescouncil/2021/08/19/three-characteristics-of-effective-dei-leadership/?sh=321c5d8210dc (archived at https://perma.cc/FBH8-KZ7A)

HR Research Institute (2022) *The Future of Diversity, Equity and Inclusion,* hr.com/en/resources/free_research_white_papers/the-future-of-diversity-equity-and-inclusion-resea_l0wk79fe.html (archived at https://perma.cc/M9PK-WELZ)

Mengistu, H (2016, 9 June). The evolutionary origins of hierarchy, *PLOS Computational Biology*, p. 2(6): e1004829. doi: 10.1371/journal.pcbi.1004829. PMID: 27280881; PMCID: PMC4900613

Pei, W (2020, 20 April) The case for hierarchy, Princeton University Press, press.princeton.edu/ideas/the-case-for-hierarchy (archived at https://perma.cc/ZT29-QT4C)

Samson, D (2022, 18 January) The stabilizing force of business, Edelman, edelman.com/trust/2022-trust-barometer/stabilizing-force-business (archived at https://perma.cc/35UN-2JY7)

Saul McLeod, P (2022, 4 April) Maslow's Hierarchy of Needs, Simply Psychology, simplypsychology.org/maslow.html (archived at https://perma.cc/BB3D-N2B3)

Tschida, N J (2021, 27 April) 3 actions for leaders to improve DEI in the workplace, Gallup, gallup.com/workplace/348266/actions-leaders-improve-dei-workplace.aspx#:~:text=A%20leader%27s%20active%2C%20visible%20role%20in%20DEI%20efforts,communication%20and%20collaborative%20goal%20setting%20with%20their%20teams (archived at https://perma.cc/KM6K-7YS3)

Turchin, P (2014, 20 December) The Evolution of Hierarchy, peterturchin.com/cliodynamica/the-evolution-of-hierarchy/ (archived at https://perma.cc/JH36-CBCC)

04

Understanding biases – the benefits and the pitfalls

*The case for change and why bias plays
an integral part in the decisions we make*

Internal communicators are natural storytellers, but for us to reflect the world we live in and the publics that we support, we need to be open to experiencing different opinions. We have to be self-aware to understand where we fall short with our biases and unlearn some behaviours we've observed from irrational beliefs about certain groups and communities. Otherwise, we'll never be able to cultivate a truly inclusive culture.

In Chapter 2, we shared how you can build trustworthiness and why trust is essential in cultivating inclusive cultures. However, to understand our behaviours around trust, we need to take a step back and reflect on how bias plays a part in our decisions. You could argue that diversity, equity and inclusion (DEI) are much higher on senior leaders' agendas than ever before. Some organizations are now being held accountable for their actions around DEI; for example, Goldman Sachs refuses to take companies public if they have an all-male board (Elsesser, 2020). We know from many studies and reports that there's a strong correlation between diversity and financial performance. When organizations have a representative workforce, their financial performance is 25 per cent better than organizations that don't have representation (McKinsey & Company, 2020). So why do we still have to keep fighting the case for inclusion? Bias is a significant factor.

Research conducted by Yamagishi and Yamagishi (1994) concluded that trust is a form of cognitive bias which means how we make decisions about whether to trust is not wholly based on the information presented in front of us. An interesting study by researcher Lisa DeBruine (2002) showed that when people saw faces that looked similar to them, they tended to trust that person more. Studies (Quillian et al, 2017) have also demonstrated how implicit biases and assumptions can affect hiring, significantly reducing the chances of anyone with an ethnically sounding name being appointed. Considering these studies, we must recognize how internal communication professionals understand how biases can influence the organizations we support. How do our biases determine what stories to share and what not to share? How do we ensure that our biases don't affect our decision-making capabilities? How can you frequently check-in to ensure you're not making assumptions about certain groups?

We can't describe bias as right or wrong. It's something that exists in all of us. But it's important that we understand how we manage our bias, and in this chapter, we will be exploring how we can make fair decisions by tapping into our rational and logical thought processes.

In this chapter you will learn:

- What bias is.
- How unconscious and conscious bias can influence our decisions.
- How to build more curiosity into your role.
- Why intellectual humility is important.

What is bias?

To understand how bias can impact how we make decisions we're going to use the real-life story of Anna Sorokin. In late 2021 Netflix published a show called *Inventing Anna* based on Anna Sorokin, who pretended to be a wealthy German heiress (Carlin, 2022). Both of us were fascinated with how Anna had managed to scam countless wealthy socialites in New York with her ambition to create a private members' club called the Anna Delvey Foundation. Sorokin had managed to charter a private jet and stayed in countless five-star hotels without payment or arousing too much suspicion. It's evident by the amount of money she managed to extort ($275,000) from some of New York's top socialites that bias will have played a significant part in them trusting Anna. The New York elite that Anna tricked were intelligent, educated, high-powered people surrounded by various advisers and supporters. Considering the Trustworthiness Equation we discussed in Chapter 2, you could argue that Sorokin didn't follow any of the attributes needed to build trust. She had no credibility, she wasn't reliable and from what we know, little intimacy or empathy was shown for others. So how did she convince people to invest without accurate data or evidence about her experience?

Sorokin's example shows that regardless of the lack of information available about her credentials, people judged her on irrelevant characteristics such as how she dressed, looked and behaved. The New York elite made these decisions based on their personal biases from their lived experience of what a wealthy elite member of society portrays. They related with her. They saw themselves reflected in her behaviour and they believed everything she shared as they were convinced that she was 'one of them'.

As we said earlier in the chapter, biases are not good or bad, but they can become a problem when we make decisions based on concepts or personal opinions that may or may not be accurate. In its simplest form, bias is when we lean heavily towards one person or a group, either in favour or against them. Amos Tversky and Daniel Kahneman (1974) termed this type of bias 'cognitive bias'. Their studies established that cognitive biases '… stem from the reliance on judgmental heuristics'. In Kahneman's book *Thinking, Fast and Slow*, he defined heuristics as 'a simple procedure that helps find adequate, though often imperfect, answers to difficult questions'. Sorokin's life started to tumble when she couldn't keep up with her lies and her reputation for not paying hotel bills preceded her. It wasn't the wealthy New Yorkers who caught her out, but hotel managers across the city who realized that Sorokin was a con artist – the people who didn't allow bias to cloud their judgments.

How we make decisions

It's estimated that on average we make around 35,000 decisions every day (Hoomans, 2015) Most of these decisions are automatic and involuntary. Heuristic principles can help us get through our day and make quick decisions more efficiently, for example, which brand of coffee to buy. Daniel Kahneman would describe this as System 1 thinking (Kahneman, 2011). System 1 thinking allows our brain to create short cuts, so we don't over think every time we need to make a decision. We learn what short cuts to take through our lived experiences and learned behaviour. So, for example, over time we would learn that a particular brand of coffee tastes better than other brands. Using this intelligence, we walk into a store and automatically pick up the brand we like. We don't tend to think too deeply or spend the day understanding lots of data or information about coffee brands, unless something stops us in our tracks, for example a new coffee-tasting station, at the store, which requires our brains to slow down. Slowing our brain down to decipher new information and data is what Kahneman would call System 2 thinking. With System 2, we are more deliberate, conscious and controlled with self-awareness. We look for meaning or new information to help us understand how things can fit together.

But according to Kahneman we tend to spend 95 per cent of our time making decisions from the System 1 part of the brain. We don't often make the time, have the resources or pay attention to what's required to slow our thinking down, so our brain jumps to various conclusions and make assumptions based on our past experiences. And that's when problems arise as we end up filtering out useful and important information. These quick judgments are often flawed with inaccurate stereotypes and personal opinions, which can cause challenges in the organizations we support. Think back to a time where you've made a decision that didn't work out. Were you under time pressure? Did you consider all outcomes? Did you ask people who are different from you their thoughts? We know it's impossible to do this for every decision you have to make, because you'd never get anything done and you'd live in a world full of chaos and distraction. However, to ensure your decisions are well thought through it's important to connect with people who may think differently to you. It's also helpful to read blogs, listen to podcasts and watch talks that you normally wouldn't as this will help you understand a different point of view, whether you agree with that view or not.

How unconscious and conscious bias can influence our decisions

After the murder of George Floyd in May 2020, we received several emails and direct messages from internal communication professionals seeking advice on how they could ensure that their communication was fair, representative and free from bias. Freeing ourselves from bias isn't a task we can undertake in a few hours. In fact, it's virtually impossible to live a life without bias. If somehow we could, it's likely we'd spend our lives in a constant state of panic and uncertainty unable to make any sort of decision. To stop leaping to conclusions, believing in certain stereotypes and making assumptions without accurate facts, we need to understand how we manage our biases effectively and comprehend what we need to do to bring in some additional reflection time. Some issues and decisions will require a deeper review of why we made certain decisions over others. How we make these decisions can be broken down into conscious (explicit bias) and unconscious bias (implicit bias).

Explicit bias isn't unconscious. It occurs due to deliberate thought and ideologies we may have formed through the environment that surrounds us. We know and are aware of our prejudice and attitudes towards certain groups. We may also discriminate because we believe we're more superior to that group. Most explicit bias behaviours are overt – for example a male colleague refusing to report to a woman, a Millennial believing that older people are no good with technology or a non-disabled person saying that disabled people are unable to work. None of these attitudes are unconscious; they are deliberate conscious choices based on their clear beliefs and learnings. The challenge with explicit bias is that organizations confuse some of these beliefs as unconscious (implicit bias) and try to 'change' mindsets through unconscious bias training, which is often ineffective (Ashworth-Hayes, 2021). We know this because if it did make a difference, we'd see broader representation of different characteristics in senior management roles, there wouldn't be a gender-pay gap, people with disabilities would be able to access transport, office buildings and other venues with ease, and the persecution of the LGBTQ+ community wouldn't exist across the globe. Some may argue that these decisions are not always conscious, but we disagree. There's plenty of research, evidence and experts who have raised concerns about these types of behaviours over the years but yet we don't see as much progress as we should.

We all like to believe that we are fair and reasonable in our daily lives. But, being completely neutral is challenging as our social, familial and institutional environments will heavily influence our behaviours. Implicit bias (unconscious bias) are attitudes held subconsciously that affect how we think about others. We often believe we form decisions from rational thought, but more often it's from an irrational belief. From these beliefs, we create unconscious stereotypes against others which can affect the way we behave towards them – positively or negatively. As explained earlier, we make approximately 35,000 decisions daily, so we wire our brain to categorize information and make generalizations subject to past experiences, social constructs and our environment to create mental shortcuts. But these shortcuts can establish prejudices and stereotypes linked to particular groups and communities.

To identify some of your implicit biases, ask yourself what type of person you imagine when you think of a doctor, nurse, engineer, CEO or carer. Are you crossing the road when you see a group of young Black teenagers or holding your bag tighter when you walk past homeless people? What are your thoughts when you see someone in the office not contribute to the birthday fund or not participate in a team night out? Do you ask white people 'where they are **really** from'?

In 2022, there was a social media outcry when a royal aide questioned a guest about where they were 'really' from at a celebration event held at Buckingham Palace. Ngozi Fulani, founder of the charity Sistah Space, claimed that Susan Hussey (the late queen's lady-in-waiting) moved her hair to reveal her name badge and then persistently questioned her heritage, asking where her 'people' came from. Fulani shared this exchange on her Twitter account and the following day Lady Hussey resigned, with the Palace releasing a statement to say that 'racism has no place in our society' (Furness, 2022). Views on whether this exchange was blown out of proportion were discussed at length on various news items and opinion pieces. Some supporters of Lady Hussey argued that at 83 years old, she should have been forgiven for asking these questions (Wyatt, 2022) and others stated that asking someone where they are from is not offensive but rather about being curious. However, there's a vast difference in being curious and being persistent with a line of questioning that someone is uncomfortable answering. Asking people where they are 'really' from is a form of microaggression, especially during formal or work events. Microaggression is described as a comment or action that subtly undermines someone's identity by playing into stereotypes or historic biases. It implies that the person asking the question, especially if it's a person from the dominant culture, doesn't think you belong. It can be damaging and can cause people to feel excluded, even if the questioning isn't coming from a malicious intent. Raskshita Arni Ravishankar shared in *Harvard Business Review* (Ravishankar, 2020) three things we can do to ask better questions:

1 Check your biases – it's important to understand that we all make mistakes but being aware of these mistakes and rectifying them is critical. Consider if you'd ask that question to everyone, despite their background.

2 Understand your privilege. We all have privilege – understanding what our privilege is and recognizing our place in the world and the impact we can have is important. Consider kindness when you're being curious, get

to know people on a human level, find out what their interests are, what led them to do the work they do today, etc.

3 Don't persist. A key issue with Lady Hussey's line of questioning was her persistence and from the alleged exchange shared online it was clear that Ngozi Fulani was uncomfortable. If you ask something that you regret, apologize immediately and let it go. Avoid statements such as 'I'm only joking!' or 'Stop being sensitive.'

According to the Cognitive Bias Codex developed by John Manoogian III (JM3) based on the categorization by Buster Benson (Designhacks.co, 2016), there are more than 175 cognitive biases and heuristics, from anchoring bias, where we rely heavily on one piece of information, to observer effect, where we subconsciously influence participants in a focus group or an experiment. It's vital to consider, as internal communication professionals who often have to ask curious questions, how questions manifest under a range of different cognitive biases. Table 4.1 explores some of the most common cognitive biases that we may face.

How curiosity can help manage our biases

As internal communication professionals, we have to make quick decisions daily about how we communicate organizational updates and stories to our colleagues. Many of us work in busy, active roles with limited resources and time, so our biases will automatically filter out noise and information that we believe isn't relevant based on our beliefs and sometimes our 'gut feeling'. However, when we make these swift decisions, we create stories and assumptions to justify our choices. In our work we sometimes refer to this as the 'invisible army syndrome' which often accompanies confirmation bias. The invisible army appears when people try to influence others about their decision and when questioned they will bring in the 'invisible army' to further their cause. For example, a few years ago Advita supported a communications team struggling to gain engagement with some of their channels. During a focus group session with the team, Advita asked why they believed the workforce wasn't paying attention and what data did they have to back up that assumption. One participant shared that they heard that 'colleagues weren't happy' with the new intranet as they still felt it was 'clunky and unsuitable'. The organization had recently invested a significant budget in updating the intranet, so the team's director was concerned by the feedback.

TABLE 4.1 Examples of common types of cognitive biases

Common cognitive bias	Description	Examples of behaviours that impact decisions	How to manage the bias
Anchoring bias	The tendency to rely heavily on one piece of information and you 'anchoring' all your decisions on that first piece.	When we're creating campaigns or communication plans and we have information that shows colleagues prefer face-to-face communication, we interpret new information from the reference point of our anchor rather than review objectively.	Increase knowledge through research, consult with specialists, think of different reasons on why that first piece of information may not be accurate.
Availability heuristic	When we give excessive importance to the information that is available to us.	When you read information from one department on how they don't enjoy a certain channel. This information may come the quickest to mind when we have to make a decision on whether or not to retire the channel.	Stop and think about the information you have in front of you. Are you making a fair judgment? Have you considered other data points or information? Have you spoken to other teams?
Bandwagon effect / groupthink	When we adapt to a certain behaviour, style or attitude because other people are doing it, despite our own belief or views.	You're in a meeting and everyone agrees on Campaign A; even though you know it's flawed you will go along with the decision because everyone else has. It's a form of groupthink.	Think critically about why that decision was made, and ask curious questions: 'Have we thought about the consequences of Campaign A?'

(continued)

TABLE 4.1 (Continued)

Common cognitive bias	Description	Examples of behaviours that impact decisions	How to manage the bias
Cognitive dissonance	The state of internal discomfort caused when ideas, values, beliefs or practices are conflicted.	A leader confides in you that there will be some redundancies on the horizon and you need to be part of the project team. But you uncover that a good friend of yours is at risk and they are just about to re-mortgage their home for a kitchen extension. You're torn as you feel you need to tell them because of your friendship.	As difficult as it might be, you need to think about what's really within your control or influence. How ethical is it for you to share this information? Are you being unfair to others? Are you breaching confidentiality? Understand what's in your control and encourage leaders to ensure that communication is efficient, timely and accurate.
Confirmation bias	The tendency to search for, interpret and remember information that confirms our thoughts and ideas.	You want to introduce a new channel, but you only seek out information that confirms your belief that this new channel will work, so you automatically discredit anything that doesn't support your case for change.	Consider all the information available and seek out different perspectives and views, especially from those who have opposite thoughts. Be willing to change your mind, even if it means updating your current beliefs.
Halo effect	The tendency to have a positive impression of a person, company or brand based on their traits.	A leader who is charismatic, kind and generous is always featured in various internal and external publications. They have 'the face' and 'the charm' to represent the organization. We ignore or forgive other traits like them sharing incorrect information because we still believe they are best.	Slow down the decision-making factor and be clear on why this person has been chosen for the story or for representing the organization externally. Be honest with yourself and talk to others who are different from you to check if you are at risk of favouritism.

SOURCE Adapted from Cognitive bias cheat sheet (Benson, 2016)

When probed further, the participant struggled to recall who shared that information and it became apparent that the feedback was based on assumption rather than fact. They used their 'gut feeling' and created an invisible army to back up their assumption and case for change. This can be problematic when we don't use data to back up our challenge as it diminishes our credibility and trust if we get it wrong.

As leaders who are responsible for communicating, we must address our biases, assumptions and stereotypes before we can fight for inclusion in our workplace. It's not always helpful to our reputation or for building trust when we bring in an 'invisible army' or lead only with our 'gut feeling'. Gut feelings are a result of processing that can happen in our brain. It compares sensory information and current experiences against stored knowledge and past experiences, which will help us predict what comes next. However, this predication is often created through our lived experience and doesn't often consider cognitive biases. So whilst it's important to trust your instinct, you must familiarize yourself with biases that impact you so you can spot them before you make any assumptions. To do this we have to be curious and ask questions. Not only will this help us but it will encourage our stakeholders to identify their own biases and understand the gaps before any communication goes into the public domain. A part of understanding whether our gut feeling is accurate or not, it's important to adopt a curiosity mindset.

Curiosity is a powerful tool in our communication toolbox. It allows us to improve relationships, build connections and be more innovative in our thinking. We often think we make decisions objectively based on the information in front of us, but as discussed earlier in this chapter, we rarely do. Our mental shortcuts can lead us to avoid information that we find uncomfortable or don't like, so we see patterns that don't exist.

Research has shown that we often believe that our view of the world is shared by most people. This isn't always our fault. Innovative technology, like artificial intelligence, mimics our habits and shares the information we want to read and hear. Our social media channels recommend people to follow who have similar political interests, and our streaming services tell us what to watch based on our previous habits. With this bias, we often ignore inconsistent information that we disagree with and misinterpret certain situations so we can confirm what we already believe. In 2022, Queen Elizabeth II passed away at the age of 96. There was an outpouring of love and sympathy to the Royal Family from many celebrities, dignitaries, organizations, institutions and people from across the globe. However, when the news broke, some people spoke candidly about the British monarchy and its role in colonialism around the world. It's easy to dismiss this as historical events that are not relevant anymore but it's vital that you understand why there's been so much criticism because it helps to form a better understanding. The monarchy played a central role in the expansion of the transatlantic slave trade starting from 1500s. In 1660 Charles II formed the Royal African Company, led by the Duke of York. They extracted goods such as gold and ivory from the Gold Coast, and transported 5,000 African people annually to the Caribbean and Virginia. Many had 'DY' burned into their skin to signify they belonged to the Duke (History.com, 2018). Though some argued that this shouldn't be attributed to the modern monarchy, others debated that the current monarchy is still benefitting from the funds they gained whilst trading enslaved people of colour and profiting from stolen goods such as the Koh-i-Noor diamond from India and Pakistan. Supporters of the British monarchy argued that a constitutional monarchy can bring stability and can be economically more viable than forming a republic. The British monarchy contributes £1.155 billion into the economy and can have a significant impact on tourism and the fashion industry (Eleftheriou-Smith, 2015).

The assumption that everyone was saddened by the Queen's death was evident by the number of statements shared internally by organizations and brands externally who spoke on behalf of colleagues, some who were not in mourning. Whether you agree or not, ultimately people will have different viewpoints. The hurt and anger by some individuals was palpable which led to a war of words and tension and unkind words being shared by both sides (Monarchists and Republicans). As communication professionals, it's important to be aware of the complexities surrounding some key issues across the globe, which sometimes we will have to support our leaders in communicating. We can't allow our biases to assume that everyone will feel the same way about these issues from across the globe, e.g. Brexit, the war on Ukraine, the conflict between Palestine and Israel, etc. It's hard to understand where to start but curiosity can help us create an understanding from both sides, and lead us to productive disagreements which can allow us to question our opinions and viewpoints using our intellectual humility.

We must not confuse intellectual humility with uncertainty, timidness or lack of confidence. Intellectual humility allows us to recognize that our thinking, beliefs and opinions are fallible. People who are intellectually humble will be open to learning from others and approach discussions with curiosity, interest and vulnerability. They will always be actively interested in what others have to say and accept that their viewpoint may need to change based on their discovery. To understand if you have high humility, consider whether you agree or disagree with the following statements.

> 1 I always find new information and build knowledge to help evolve my thinking.
>
> 2 I know that my beliefs, views and opinions may be wrong.
>
> 3 I am open to changing my mind if I have enough data and evidence to prove me wrong.
>
> 4 I have friends/family/colleagues I work closely with in my life who are different to me (cognitively and visibly).
>
> 5 I respect and recognize the value of viewpoints that are different to my own.

If you agreed with the majority, then you are likely to have high humility. To continue to cultivate intellectual humility try introducing the following actions into your daily activities:

- Take time to really listen to what others are saying. Switch off your devices, move away from your distractions and listen with intention.
- Practice taking time for yourself and focus on the present. It's easy to keep busy and not pay attention to what's happening around you. Frequent reflections can help you unlearn and learn new ways of thinking.
- If you have a strong view about something, do take the time to find out information and beliefs from the opposing side. This can help form a balanced discussion.

The challenge we've witnessed with curiosity is the balance between being too intrusive and genuinely being interested in finding out information to inform your decisions.

There are steps you can follow to help build confidence in your curiosity – we call it the **SPARK** framework because it can help spark conversations and address biases:

- **Seek** out the information and find evidence that counter-argues your opinion or thoughts. This could be through following different voices, reading newspapers, listening to podcasts or watching videos you would never usually watch.
- **Powerful** questions can help you dig deeper into expanding your understanding of why you feel strongly about your point of view or opinion. Consider the following questions:
  - o Where have I got the evidence that backs up my thinking?

o Why am I feeling this way about this group/person/organization?

o Where did I hear this information, and were they a trusted source?

o Am I being fair with my assessment or am I basing my thinking on other people's opinions?

- **Adjusting** your mindset can be difficult. But once you get into the habit of asking yourself some exploratory questions, your brain will modify. It will create new neural pathways and alter existing ones as you continue learning further information, building knowledge, creating new memories and adapting to new experiences.

- **Revising** your thinking around your viewpoints and opinions frequently will ensure that you foster more positive interactions. Your willingness to continue to learn from others, and be open to new thoughts and ideas, will help you build stronger connections. As soon as you enter a conversation and say 'You're wrong' you will instantly cause friction which will lead to conflict and an unproductive discussion. Instead try saying 'Can you help me understand how you came to that decision?'

- **Kindness** is critical when exploring curiosity with confidence. There will be viewpoints you disagree with, and the evidence you uncover may not be enough to convince you to change your mind. If that happens, then it's essential to raise your thoughts respectfully, and embrace the principles of productive disagreement developed by Buster Benson (Donohue, 2020):

  1 Use respectful language and avoid using insults, or harmful words.

  2 Put yourself in their position and try to understand their point of view.

  3 Ask honest, open questions with permission, without judgment or accusations.

  4 Don't speak for other people or assume what that other person thinks, even if they have the same cultural background or characteristic – we're not a monolith.

  5 Ideally find middle ground that works for both sides but accept that sometimes you may need to respectfully agree to disagree.

How biases can impact internal communication messages

The communications profession isn't very diverse, according to research conducted by Diversity Alliance Action and the Chartered Institute of Public

Relations (CIPR) (Sogbanmu, 2022). Most PR and communication teams are white, cis-gendered women who are non-disabled and heterosexual. You could argue that this set-up of teams is common because our affinity bias will only allow us to connect with people who share similar qualities to ourselves. If we're not aware of this bias, then it's likely that our teams will look and feel the same. If you look around your team, do you have a range of voices from diverse backgrounds? Do you represent the publics that you serve? This can be an uncomfortable realization, but there are ways to tackle this bias by ensuring you put contingencies, methods and frameworks in place to help break the pattern of behaviour. For example, during recruitment who do you advertise job opportunities with; are you contacting different voices in the industry to share your opportunity; is your job advert inadvertently describing a culture where only one type of character would 'fit'?

Over the years, we've worked with clients where we have identified non-inclusive practices that teams have missed due to their bias and limited representation surrounding them. Some examples include stock images which misrepresent the diversity of the organization, no captioning or subtitling on videos, masculine language in communications (we share more on inclusive language in Chapter 11) and limited accessibility to rooms and offices. Covert examples would include asking that one person of colour to take part in your communication campaigns to show you're inclusive, or showcasing various awareness-raising months but your policies, processes and behaviours contradict the campaign messages. For example if you recognize International Women's Day but have a gender pay gap issue in your organization. This type of behaviour can be hard to spot when you are working at pace and don't have representation of voices from diverse backgrounds in your team.

A couple of years ago, Advita was working with a client who needed some support with identifying where their inclusion gaps were in their channel strategy. During the review, the client mentioned that they have limited engagement with underrepresented colleagues and asked for advice on how to build better relationships with all colleagues. As the client talked, Advita saw covers of their staff magazine proudly displayed on the wall in the office. She glanced over the 12 covers and realized that all the front covers showed what appeared to be all white colleagues. This organization's demographic audit showed that 22 per cent of their colleagues were non-white, and approximately 12 per cent of colleagues had declared a disability. Yet, the team who were advocates and inclusion champions failed to see this error. This pitfall demonstrates that even the most engaged team determined to cultivate inclusive cultures can miss glaringly obvious matters, even when it's staring them in the face.

Inclusion is a big part of belonging in organizations and when you feel ignored, it can cause disengagement, and talented people will leave. Exclusion can make you feel like you don't matter and that no one cares about you or what value you bring to the organization. To avoid falling into the pitfalls of exclusion and to be intentional with your work, the following advice will help you be more aware of how you make fair decisions in your organization.

1) Audit your communication plan

Effective communication is imperative to help create a productive workplace. We often develop our communication plans in isolation, which prevents us from understanding where the inclusion gaps are. And even if you complete the plan with your immediate team, it's essential to be aware of the representation you have around you, demographic representation and cognitive diversity. If you are the only person leading the communication function, build a diverse community around you so you can sense-check information and ensure you've not inadvertently missed anything. Avoid common mistakes like not having different choices for how people receive information, not considering the organization's demographics and understanding challenges some colleagues may face in accessing information (e.g. not providing films that are captioned).

2) Manage your stakeholders

A critical part of our work in organizations is being aware of who we are communicating with daily and being aware of their needs. Understanding this breakdown will help us identify our knowledge gaps and ensure we are identifying the biases we may have about some groups of people. We have worked with many communication teams who have no idea of the demographic set-up of their organization. Without knowing this, they will not be able to understand where the inclusion gaps are and what they need to do about them. Once we know the demographics of our colleagues, including where they are based, their educational background and how they like to receive their information, we can create more personalized, bespoke communication which can address bias and help improve inclusion.

3) The opposing argument

Some of our biases can be deep-rooted, and we must actively search for opposing evidence to our beliefs and assumptions to stop our mental short-cuts from taking over. Part of this will be about understanding your colleague base, but it's also vital to know who your customers are as these are the people our colleagues face every day. What are your customers saying about your organization? How much do you know about your organization? Not only in terms of internal knowledge but also external industry knowledge. Understanding the business's pressure points will help you confidently contribute to conversations.

4) Representative support

As we mentioned in the first point, if your team is not representative of your customer and colleague base, you need to create a community of people where you can sense-check things like campaigns, plans and messages. You're not expected to know absolutely everything, but you need to know when to ask for help, advice and support. Especially if you think you might have a bias in specific topics.

5) Speak up

Internal communication professionals often have an overview of the organization and hear information other leaders may not know. As well as ensuring we're addressing the bias in our communication team and the messages we send out, we have to hold other people accountable for their biases by asking curious questions (refer to the SPARK framework discussed earlier in this chapter). Being an active bystander and sharing our learning will help others take effective action to make the necessary changes.

The impact of cognitive diversity

In 2022, Liz Truss, then Prime Minister of the UK, appointed the most diverse senior cabinet the government had seen. For the first time in history, her top four positions – Deputy Prime Minister, Secretary of State for the Home Office, Chancellor of the Exchequer and Foreign Secretary – were allocated to women and people of colour. But this news was met with some scepticism by many across the UK. All four people in these top positions, even though diverse in terms of gender and ethnicity, had similar educational experiences. Some people argued that this meant they couldn't understand some of the challenges facing many across the UK, and were therefore unable to represent the views of the public effectively. After 44 days, Liz Truss stepped down as Prime Minister due to a series of errors and losing trust from the general public. The error often made by senior leaders, across various organizations and institutions, is mistaking diversity for inclusion. Both terms are often clumped together but they are not synonymous. Diversity equals representation, which can be measured through quantifiable data, which organizations often use as a mark of success. Inclusion on the other hand is **how we make people feel about their contributions and values**. Without inclusion you are at risk of creating an environment that isn't safe, doesn't consider participation, limits innovation and builds on groupthink. In the case of Prime Minister Truss, she may have created a representative cabinet, but how many of those voices can relate to the plight facing women and ethnic minorities across UK?

Some of the people we've spoken with in the past struggle to define the difference between diversity, inclusion, equity, equality and belonging. To support this we've developed a phrase, inspired by Verna Myers and Daniel Juday, to help people understand what these words mean in a workplace context:

> Diversity is being on the event guest list; equality is making sure everyone is invited to the event; equity is having access to suitable transport to bring you to the event; inclusion is being asked to choose the topics for the event; belonging is being a member of the event planning committee.

As we shared in Chapter 3, many leaders within organizations understand the benefits of hiring people from diverse backgrounds and know the financial benefits this can bring. However, in our experience, we have seen leaders conform to culture-fit rather than culture-add. Their biases can influence how they make decisions about people, and their System 1 brain can often shortcut decisions to make their lives easier. How often has your CEO or senior leader brought across people they've worked with previously? Some may argue that there's nothing wrong with this as their relationship has been developed through building and cultivating trust. That may be the case, but from the research conducted by Yamagishi and Yamagishi (1994), we know that trust is a bias, and we will often trust people who are very similar to us in behaviours. But to avoid confirmation bias and to bring more innovation into the team, especially if we have complex problems to solve, cognitive diversity can help us explore different mindsets.

Cognitive diversity includes people with different thought patterns, ideas, problem-solving methods and mental perspectives – some refer to this as 'diversity of thought.' In his book *Rebel Ideas*, Matthew Syed (2021) states:

> Building a collective intelligence cannot be reduced to a box-ticking exercise...
> people who start out diverse can gravitate towards the dominant assumptions of
> the group.

Syed argues that even if a leadership team is diverse in terms of demographic diversity, it doesn't mean they have cognitive diversity. Alison Reynolds and David Lewis (2017) have studied the subject for many years. They believe cognitive diversity has two critical impacts on an organization:

> First, it reduces the opportunity to strengthen the proposition with input from
> people who think differently. Second, it fails to represent the cognitive diversity
> of the employee population, reducing the impact of the initiatives.

Before we go further into our thoughts on this subject, we want to be clear that cognitive diversity must work in collaboration with demographic diversity. We have held many conversations with leaders who often hide behind cognitive diversity to cover the lack of diverse representation. Their biases have led them to believe that they have different thoughts around the table but after conducting inclusive communication audits, we have uncovered this is rarely true. We have witnessed groupthink, confirmation and authority bias from leaders, people struggle to recognize when a poor decision has been made and will often stay quiet or agree so they can 'fit in' with everyone else. When there is true cognitive diversity around the table, we see curious questions being asked, sometimes uncomfortable questions. There's productive disagreement, innovative thinking and several different ideas on how to address a complex problem. People often leave the table feeling energized, inspired and they don't worry about speaking up against the status quo.

To ensure cognitive diversity isn't stifled by poor leadership or behaviours, there are steps to follow to bring out different thoughts and opinions without compromising the organization's integrity.

Step one: Safe space. We've written about safe psychological teams in Chapter 2, but to allow for cognitive diversity, creating a safe space for people to explore their thinking is crucial. This space has to be judgment-free and open to all sorts of thinking/challenges. If people can't express their viewpoints honestly, they will retreat and may end up conforming to groupthink, especially if they believe that will get them further in the organization.

Step two: Allocate different roles to people. To avoid confirmation bias/groupthink, intentionally allocate dissimilar roles to team members. If you have a naturally upbeat colleague, ask them to think about what could go wrong in the project. If you have a colleague driven by data/insight, ask them to buddy up with someone creative. Shaking up our normal patterns of behaviour can allow everyone in the team to reframe the way they may think about challenges.

Step three: Mix things up with different teams in your organization. Invite colleagues from operations, HR, finance, legal, etc, and make sure you go to where they are. They will bring various perspectives and allow you to see things differently. If you have a complex challenge to solve, moving away from your current team set-up and allowing other colleagues from different teams to join will help you move away from groupthinking.

Addressing our biases and other people's bias can be uncomfortable and complicated. As leaders we must be vulnerable enough to know when we're being unfair, discriminatory and prejudiced against certain groups. To explore humility, we need to allow ourselves to be open to new information and listen, without judgment, to other people's experiences, especially when we are responsible for communicating information to help people perform and thrive, so our organizations can succeed.

KEY TAKEAWAYS

- Be aware of how your bias can impact how you build and cultivate trust with others. If you are trusting someone based on no evidence, then tread carefully and make sure you're not letting your beliefs cloud your judgments.

- We have two core systems that help us make decisions: System 1 creates mental shortcuts so we make decisions automatically and System 2 helps us slow down our thinking so we can make rational choices. We need to be more mindful of System 1 and ensure we're slowing down our thinking when we have to make decisions on more complex issues.

- Biases are neither good or bad, they exist so we can make quick decisions otherwise we wouldn't be able to move forward with anything. However, we need to continuously review why we feel the way we feel about certain stereotypes and characteristics.

- Curiosity can help remove biases we may have about other people. Using the SPARK framework will help you be curious with confidence and build stronger relationships with others.

- As well as being aware of our biases, we need to make sure we address biases in other people who are at risk of making decisions based on irrational thoughts and beliefs.

REFLECTIVE QUESTIONS

- How well do you know yourself and the biases you keep about certain groups of people? Write down how you feel and where that feeling came from.

- Is your communication plan inclusive, does it include the different demographics across your organization? Are you aware of the challenges facing the workforce? Does your bias influence what type of stories you share and what type of leaders we support?

- Do you speak up if someone has shared something that's not true and their opinion is based on their prejudice and bias?

Bibliography

Ashworth-Hayes, S (2021, 14 February) Why unconscious bias training doesn't work, *The Spectator*, spectator.co.uk/article/why-unconscious-bias-training-doesn-t-work (archived at https://perma.cc/Q87B-ZM27)

Benson, B (2016, 1 September) Cognitive bias cheat sheet, Better Humans, betterhumans.pub/cognitive-bias-cheat-sheet-55a472476b18 (archived at https://perma.cc/63GZ-A664)

Brown, B D (2018) *Dare to Lead*. 1 ed. London, Penguin Random House

Carlin, S (2022, 11 February) The true story about Netflix's *Inventing Anna*, *Time*, time.com/6147088/inventing-anna-true-story/ (archived at https://perma.cc/LFQ2-Q78Z)

DeBruine, M L (2002) Facial resemblance enhances trust, *Proceedings of the Royal Society B: Biological Sciences*, 269(10), 1307–312

Designhacks.co (2016) Cognitive Bias Codex, sog.unc.edu/sites/www.sog.unc.edu/files/course_materials/Cognitive%20Biases%20Codex.pdf (archived at https://perma.cc/KQ7B-3T93)

Donohue, B (2020, 20 February) Buster Benson on the art of productive disagreement, *Intercom*, intercom.com/blog/podcasts/buster-benson-on-the-art-of-productive-disagreement/ (archived at https://perma.cc/YCW5-LQRP)

Eleftheriou-Smith, L-M (2015, 8 September) The biggest myth about the Queen? Her contribution to the British economy, *The Independent*, independent.co.uk/news/people/the-biggest-myth-about-the-queen-her-contribution-to-the-british-economy-10491277.html (archived at https://perma.cc/4TFE-3Q8Y)

Elsesser, K (2020) Goldman Sachs won't take companies public if they have all-male corporate boards, Forbes, forbes.com/sites/kimelsesser/2020/01/23/goldman-sachs-wont-take-companies-public-if-they-have-all-male-corporate-boards/?sh=cfa65ac9475a (archived at https://perma.cc/4LQW-BJ22)

Furness, H (2022, 30 November) Queen Elizabeth's aide, Lady Susan Hussey, resigns amid racism row, *The Telegraph*, telegraph.co.uk/royal-family/2022/11/30/royal-household-member-resigns-unacceptable-deeply-regrettable/ (archived at https://perma.cc/S8P8-XFB5)

Graff, F (2021, 13 August) How many decisions do we make in one day? PBS North Carolina, pbsnc.org/blogs/science/how-many-decisions-do-we-make-in-one-day/ (archived at https://perma.cc/DPT8-XHZE)

History.com (2018, 22 August) What was the Royal African Company? history.com/news/what-was-the-royal-african-company (archived at https://perma.cc/A8G6-3RRF)

Hoomans, J D (2015, 20 March) 35,000 decisions: The great choices of strategic leaders, The Leading Edge, go.roberts.edu/leadingedge/the-great-choices-of-strategic-leaders (archived at https://perma.cc/7MKA-JKAL)

Hunt, V, Layton, D and Prince, S (2015, 1 January) Why diversity matters, McKinsey & Company, mckinsey.com/business-functions/people-and-organizational-performance/our-insights/why-diversity-matters (archived at https://perma.cc/S2WR-SDMT)

Kahneman, D (2011) *Thinking Fast and Slow*. 1 ed. London, Penguin

McKinsey & Company (2020) *Diversity wins – How inclusion matters*. London, McKinsey & Company

Quillian, L, Pager, D, Hexel, O and Midboen, H A (2017) Meta-analysis of field experiments shows no change in racial discrimination in hiring over time, *PNAS*, pnas.org/doi/10.1073/pnas.1706255114 (archived at https://perma.cc/3GGE-ATE4

Ravishankar, A R (2020, 22 October) What's wrong with asking "Where Are You From?", *Harvard Business Review*, hbr.org/2020/10/whats-wrong-with-asking-where-are-you-from (archived at https://perma.cc/V3QR-TWR7)

Reynolds, A and Lewis, D (2017, 30 March) Teams solve problems faster when they're more cognitively diverse, *Harvard Business Review*, hbr.org/2017/03/teams-solve-problems-faster-when-theyre-more-cognitively-diverse (archived at https://perma.cc/9QEG-7Y9C)

Sogbanmu, E (2022, 8 June) Time to turn diversity talk into action in the PR industry, PRovoke Media, provokemedia.com/latest/article/time-to-turn-diversity-talk-into-action-in-the-pr-industry (archived at https://perma.cc/G7CP-78BS)

Syed, M (2021) *Rebel Ideas*. 1 ed. London, John Murray

Tversky, A and Kahneman, D (1974) Judgment under uncertainty: Heuristics and biases, *Science*, 185(4157), 1124–31

Wyatt, P (2022, 1 December) In defence of Lady Susan Hussey, *The Spectator*, spectator.co.uk/article/in-defence-of-lady-susan-hussey/ (archived at https://perma.cc/K7MJ-HG5N)

Yamagishi, T and Yamagishi, M (1994) Trust and commitment in the United States and Japan, *Motivation and Emotion*, 18(2), 129–66

05

The role of the internal communication professional in DEI

Understanding how inclusive internal communication can contribute to building inclusive cultures and how we add value to the organizations we support is vital. Over the decades, our roles have evolved, and since the Covid-19 pandemic, some leaders have finally started to recognize the strategic value we can bring to the workplace. However, if we want to influence and lead by example, we must understand the importance of our role implicitly and build confidence in what we do. To be an effective inclusive communication professional, it's likely that you will face resistance, adversity and some challenge. People are uncomfortable with change and will fear leaving their comfort zone. It's our role to connect the dots, help leaders communicate better and ensure our colleagues relate to the organization's overall mission, vision and values.

In the previous chapters, we explored the attributes needed to understand the broader benefits of DEI. In this chapter, we will discuss:

- The history of internal communication and why it plays such a significant role in today's modern workplace.
- The role of an internal communications professional and the value we can bring.
- How we can influence culture shift within our organizations and the clients we support.
- The skills needed to be an inclusive internal communication professional.

We believe that internal communication is the backbone in any organization, large or small. It helps to build trust and understanding between leaders and colleagues, and it can be a powerful tool for promoting the values, the mission, the purpose and culture of an organization. One of the many challenges we often encounter is finding an agreed definition of internal communication and the key role of an internal communicator. Before we delve deeper into the purpose, we must understand the history of internal communication and how it's evolved into the profession it is today.

The history of internal communication

1840–1939

There's often a misconception that conversations around internal communication started in the mid-1940s. But one of the earliest examples of employee communication was a publication called the *Lowell Offering*, the first recorded company magazine. Young female workers wrote the magazine at the New England Lowell Cotton Mills between 1840 and 1844 (and revived again from 1848 to 1850 as the New England Offering). The mid-1800s was when industrial life in New England began, and women still didn't have the right to vote. The New England area was rural, and material for clothing was grown on farms around the community, spun and woven by women.

The only form of direct communication was through stagecoaches or boats. The news of the day was almost a week or so behind. Education was limited, and the community struggled to access the latest books and literature. However, the industrial age allowed young women to enter paid employment and contribute to the economy. Working at the mills helped them provide for their families and gain broader educational opportunities (The Gilder Lehrman Institute of American History, 2018). The young women who worked in these factories were eager to learn and contribute to the Industrial Revolution, so they attended 'improvement circles' across Massachusetts state. These circles encouraged women to learn and share experiences. One of the groups started to publish the *Lowell Offering* here so more people could access the knowledge shared by others. This publication shared short stories of women's lives at the mills, including poetry and interesting articles.

As demonstrated by the women of the mills, the impact of internal communication and the change it can bring is significant. The *Lowell Offering* helped bring a community together and brought different voices from mills across Massachusetts state. It soon became widespread, and people in the USA and Great Britain read it. It also attracted the attention of literary greats like Charles Dickens, who visited the mills in 1842 (Forgotten New England, 2019). However, despite the publication's popularity, it was peppered with controversy. Harriet Farley, one of the editors of the *Lowell Offering*, was criticized for not using the publication to highlight the poor conditions at the factories. She maintained that the publication wasn't a magazine for political commentary and claimed it was a literary magazine. Even with the criticisms, in 1843, Farley joined the Massachusetts Anti-Slavery Society and became an influential leader, using her power and privilege to raise awareness for the cause of abolitionism. But the magazine ceased publication in 1844 when protests about the poor working conditions increased, and Farley's popularity descended as she continued to defend the management by stating that conditions in the factory were not unjust (Library Company, 2012).

Challenges in how we fairly represent our colleagues are still a cause for concern for many internal communication professionals. We often try to balance corporate news and the representation of information our colleagues want to know. When we don't get it right and refuse to listen to what people are telling us, the workforce will eventually ignore all communication and disregard information shared with them.

1940–1950

In 1942 the first official book on internal communication was published by Alexander R Heron called *Sharing Information with Employees*, following a gathering of industrial relations specialists in Burlington, Vermont. Heron recognized that for organizations to thrive, line managers and leaders had to share information with their workers to understand what was happening across the organization. Heron's book could be seen as revolutionary for that era, as his thinking was incredibly contemporary. The book was written in the middle of World War II when women filled many of the roles traditionally held by men to produce goods to support the war effort. In early 1941, it became compulsory for women aged 18 to 60 to register for war work (IWM, 2019). Unmarried women aged between 20 and 30 could join the services or work in the industry. This shift changed the world of work and how we communicated with employees internally. People were no longer content with being told what to do and collecting a salary; they wanted equal rights and their voices heard. The women knew that some industries wouldn't function without them, so they demanded fair wages and better treatment.

Heron also acknowledged and recognized the many challenges faced by those of a different class or race. He shared that the fear complex we have against people different from us is often due to our lack of knowledge about that community. Heron also stated that leaders must be willing to share information freely and aggressively. He determined that when leaders are willing to intentionally share information with the workforce it can address fear and build more loyalty as people are likely to cooperate much more. When there was such political unrest, and things were changing rapidly, leaders needed to step up and work closely with their employees:

> The aggressive willingness to share information with the employee is practical because honestly and wisely followed through, it will induce a constructive cooperation which cannot be bought or forced (Heron, 1942).

ICI was an organization ahead of its time and understood the importance of information sharing and inclusion. In the 1940s, they produced a series of internal films called *Just Billingham* to bring more transparency to how work is completed, from long-service awards to how wages are paid. This would have been a considerable investment for the organization and demonstrates how some of the channels we believe are modern-day creations were developed almost eight decades ago (British Film Institute, 2012).

By 1949 many large organizations started to produce newsletters/magazines, then called 'house organs', aimed at frontline workers. The founders of the British Association of Industrial Editions (now known as the Institute of Internal Communication (IoIC)) described the house organs as 'cheerfully amateur' (Institute of Internal Communication, 2018). The Association was founded on 12 March 1949 to help raise the communication industry's standards. The 51 founders were keen to create a modern approach to industrial editing, so they conducted an in-depth analysis of 115 in-house magazines. By the late 1950s, the Association produced their publications and claimed that 10 million people read its journals. And by the 1960s, membership of the Association had reached 1,000 members (IoIC, 2019).

1960–1980

The notion of 'top-down' information sharing continued, and in the 1960s Douglas McGregor published *The Human Side of Enterprise*. McGregor's book evolved leadership behaviour into two core managerial styles: Theory X and Theory Y (see the box on page 106). His premise was about providing the right environment to motivate colleagues to be productive and engaged workers (McGregor, 1960).

Theory X (authoritative) was based on the theory that people are lazy and prefer to work as little as possible. Colleagues who fall under this category don't like responsibility, like to be told what to do, lack ambition and are seen as gullible. Based on these assumptions, structures within organizations changed to ensure goals were achieved, despite the passive and resistant workers. Managers were more pessimistic and micromanaged by taking away decision-making responsibilities. This limited motivation meant that performance was often linked to tangible results like product output or sales figures. Colleagues had no incentives and were tempted by rewards to achieve their goals. Though Theory X isn't as fashionable in the modern workplace, many larger organizations will still identify with some of these behaviours due to centralized control.

Theory Y (participative) proposed that if managers had a more optimistic view of their people, they were more trusting and gave more autonomy for work to be completed. Colleagues with managers who followed Theory Y principles took pride in their work and sought responsibility to help solve business problems. Environments felt safer and colleagues thrived in their roles, assisting organizations in performing much better.

As we discussed in Chapter 1, the mid-1960s saw the introduction of equal employment laws and affirmative action. In the UK the British economy was picking up and the need to fill vacancies increased for factories in London, the North and the Midlands. However, this increased immigration meant that the UK saw a rise in anti-immigrant politics and protests organized by anti-immigration groups. Fuelled by hostility often led by the press and some prominent influential figures, the National Front, who believed that all non-white immigrants should be banned from entering the country, undertook violent protests across the UK. These protests caused the second-generation migrants to retaliate through mass anti-racist demonstrations. These tensions led to the introduction of the Race Relations Act 1965, which made it illegal to discriminate against people's race (Ghosh, 2011). This change brought workplace diversity training and a shift in how communications were managed. Organizations that had previously excluded people of colour from applying for roles were no longer allowed to discriminate and were expected to provide equal opportunities. However, although the standard of living had improved for many white working-class workers, for people of colour the standard of living was dropping (Smith, 2011). Black people were twice as likely to be unemployed as white people, and many workers felt union officials were not looking out for their best interests. In 1965 Black and Asian workers at the Courtaulds Plant in Preston, UK, took unofficial strike action following a decision made by management to 'speed up' production, but this change only impacted workers of colour. The Transport and General Workers Union (TGWU) refused to support the strikers and stated that Indian and Pakistani workers rarely attended branch meetings (Hill, 2020). This mistrust of union representatives and management led to strikes and walk-outs. Communication was still very much top-down, directed and controlled by leaders with limited contributions from colleagues, leaving them isolated and excluded from conversations. Voices were not being heard, and people had no option but to petition and strike for their rights. Although the Courtaulds strike failed (though some reports state that a deal was struck, but that it was kept confidential), it exposed the discrimination between white workers and people of colour, including how they received communication.

1980–current

From the 1980s, we saw the industry transform again due to more political unrest and shifting societal values. Organizational leaders realized that workers needed more than top-down information and wanted to contribute to conversations. Workers demanded more answers from their leaders about corporate performance and more transparency. Internal communication became a much more significant role than just writing for internal organizational magazines. More listening took place, and employees started to have a voice in how they felt about executive decisions. In 1984, in the UK, the National Coal Board was one of the first organizations to support the representatives from the trade unions to be featured in a local newspaper (Institute of Internal Communication, 2019). Allowing the employee's voices to be heard during times of adversity and crisis is a powerful move, and for the Coal Board, it helped improve communications. At the time, the mineworker strikes were one of the biggest industrial disputes, and tensions were high.

By the 1990s, the recession had hit, and the danger of redundancy, freezes on pay and damage to colleague engagement posed significant challenges for leaders. As discussed in Chapter 2, fear breeds distrust which can inhibit how colleagues perform. Leaders recognized that if they didn't invest in a communication strategy that helped colleagues stay motivated, there was a risk of losing talent, causing more significant challenges for the business. The professional communicator's role was to explain how they brought value and what they'd receive in return, which we now call the employee value proposition (EVP).

As the decade progressed and we saw technology like laptops, mobile phones and the introduction of the internet, the opportunity to embrace different channels to hear from colleagues expanded. Two-way communication was critical for success, as it allowed leaders to provide feedback in the moment and listen to what was happening at the coal face of the business.

When we entered the millennium, social media platforms like Facebook, Twitter, Glassdoor and YouTube gave voices to many employees. These platforms allowed people to anonymously share their thoughts about working conditions and behaviours they'd witnessed in the workplace. There was an opportunity for people to communicate without access to official channels (ThoughtFarmer Intranet Blog, 2020).

No longer could leaders and line managers assume that conversations that took place internally wouldn't be shared externally. Leaders feared these platforms and tried to limit their use in their organizations by banning them from laptops and work PCs. In an organization Advita supported, regular weekly reports were sent to line managers, sharing who had been on social websites and for how long. Colleagues started to distrust leaders, which caused greater employee disengagement and poor performance. The majority of the workforce were becoming more digitally savvy than their employers, and with the introduction of smartphones, people no longer needed access to their work machines to browse the web or contribute to social media platforms.

However, over the past decade many organizations have started to use this technology as part of their key channel strategy and have embraced technological opportunities to build greater transparency. But now the challenge facing organizations is information overload, misinformation and disinformation, which can lead to mistrust, poor performance and disengagement. However, it's important not to undervalue how these channels have opened up possibilities that were not always available to many people, bringing greater inclusivity in how we communicate with our workforce. A robust communication strategy and plan, with inclusion at the heart, should address some of these concerns.

The purpose of internal communication
and skills needed to thrive

What's fascinating about the first ever employee-led magazine, the *Lowell Offering*, is that it was borne out of wanting to cultivate more inclusion between the 'factory girls' at different mills. The desire for them to understand some of the challenges they faced and bring a sense of belonging between the disparate communities saw the publication thrive. As the profession evolved, we saw the role of internal communication professionals shift. We became more involved in building better engagement with colleagues so they could share their ideas and contribute more to help the organization succeed.

However, as well as being able to write and communicate clearly, the skills needed to succeed as an internal communicator have also evolved over the years. In 2021, the IoIC published an updated Profession Map Framework which sets the benchmark for internal communication professionals and teams. The framework identifies six areas of activity and expertise needed for a modern-day communicator (see Figure 5.1). Alongside the six areas, there are also 10 behaviours internal communication professionals should adopt. We've used these 10 behaviours as a guide to expand on the attributes an **inclusive** internal communication professional should demonstrate:

- An active listener – this is a critical attribute for any inclusive internal communication professional. In fact, for all leaders who work and communicate with teams. We discuss the advantages of listening throughout this book, but to develop the art of active empathetic listening to build inclusive practices, you must:

  o Be interested in what the other person is saying. Pay attention to non-verbal cues such as body language and facial expressions. However, be mindful that some people who are neurodivergent may not portray certain neuro-typical behaviours. Don't make assumptions that someone isn't interested because they are not making eye contact or are distracted. It's also important that you give plenty of notice with clear instructions in what's required from the conversation. Try to keep instructions brief and use literal or exact language.

  o Be open to influence (don't enter the conversation with a pre-determined outcome).

  o The practice of productive disagreement (discussed in Chapter 4) is important but ensure you give people time to process information. Don't interrupt them or rush people to finish their sentences.

○ Ensure that you reiterate by paraphrasing what you've heard, this will help the other person know you've understood what they've told you.

○ Consider peer-to-peer sharing and support so you can understand where your learning opportunities are.

○ Create an environment of trust (see Chapter 2) and ensure you follow up with feedback, including clear communication of the next steps.

• Empathetic – put yourself in someone else's position and understand their point of view. Brené Brown once said that it's not about walking in people's shoes but how you listen to their story about what it's like to walk in their shoes – and believing them, even if your experiences don't match (Brown, 2021). Building inclusive cultures through effective communication can sometimes be frustrating when things are not moving quickly. We can build trust quickly and stronger connections when we take an empathetic approach. Empathy will allow us to tell stories and connect the dots effectively so we can build relationships. We need to understand the barriers and blockers others are facing. If we don't channel empathy, people will remain distant, and it'll be challenging to do our job well.

• Tenacious – as we shared at the start of this chapter, you will need an abundance of tenacity to build inclusion. This work isn't easy, and you will face a bucketload of resistance. To build more tenacity, remember to set clear goals for what you're trying to achieve (we explore goals further in Chapter 6). A robust communications strategy with clear goals can help give you focus and determination to achieve your objectives. Some of this work will require an element of bravery as you will face criticism and resistance. Embrace this fear. Build a community of supporters around you and talk to others in similar situations.

• Analytical – having strong analytical skills can help us gather data, solve complex problems and make rational decisions. It can also help us execute our projects better and summarize data effectively. These skills are essential to cultivate inclusion and to build understanding with leaders on why this work is important. Establishing where your knowledge gaps are and seeking appropriate training to help you build more confidence is necessary. Read books, find a mentor or coach and learn how things work. Be curious and ask questions if you don't understand something (remember the SPARK framework from Chapter 4).

• Creative – Some people believe that you're born with creativity, but this isn't true. You can practice different skills to build a more creative mindset.

- o Step out of your comfort zone. Having a growth mindset to try new things and gain new experiences can help. Take a creative writing course, ask to work shadow a senior leader or apply for coaching or cross-mentoring with someone who works in a different field or is from a different demographic. This will not only help you gain new perspectives, but it'll also build courage and confidence in your work.

- o If you're feeling frustrated because you can't find a fix, step away from the problem and return to it later. Go for a walk, speak to people in your community, and ask questions in your team. Also, think about reframing the problem. For example, if you're struggling to develop a creative campaign for an awareness day, think about how you want people to feel when they see the campaign, what they are saying about it and how it makes them feel. Write it down as a story and allow yourself to explore your creativity without judgment.

- o Change your routine. Sometimes to get a burst of creativity, we may need to change our routine and do something different. Change your workstation around and remove clutter. Try sitting in a different location or on another office floor.

- Empowering – similar to tenacity, empowering others will be your super skill. Feeling powerless can be frustrating, but it's essential to channel that frustration into something more positive. Developing a sense of self-awareness can help boost your confidence (and those around you) and help you take charge of your actions. It's also important to share successes and recognize people doing great work. It's easy to focus on the things that are not working well, but we don't often celebrate the things that are.

- Adaptable – we are surrounded by constant change and since the Covid-19 pandemic, things are more uncertain than ever. We need to be able to adapt quickly to changes and updates without losing focus on inclusion and belonging. Embracing change, rather than resisting it, will help you build better resilience and remain positive in the face of adversity. To be more adaptable, observe the behaviours of others who embrace change well. What is it about them keeps them calm and in control? Ask curious questions, and don't be afraid to make mistakes.

- Trustworthy – we speak about trust at length in Chapter 2. If people don't trust you or your leaders, your job will be tough. You'll be micro-managed and treated as a postbox, which can not only stifle progress in terms of inclusion but can also cause significant disengagement.

- Curious – curiosity is a core skill for an inclusive communications professional. We've dedicated a section to curiosity in Chapter 4, where we
shared our SPARK framework in detail.

- Challenging – this attribute can cause many people to feel fear. Challenging others can take confidence, boldness and courage. It's even more
complicated if you're an underrepresented person working in a dominant
culture. The first step is to educate yourself on the topics where you
believe you're lacking confidence. Knowledge is critical for you to challenge effectively. We shared in Chapter 4 that your gut feeling is not
something that you should rely on solely. You need evidence and data to
support your argument and to challenge it effectively. Do your research,
write down your points using the information you've gathered and determine the consequences of not challenging. Also, remember that disagreement doesn't mean disliking the person, you can disagree on a point
without getting personal. It's about looking at different possibilities and
various outcomes.

FIGURE 5.1   The Professional Internal Communications Skill Map (Institute of Internal
Communication, 2021)

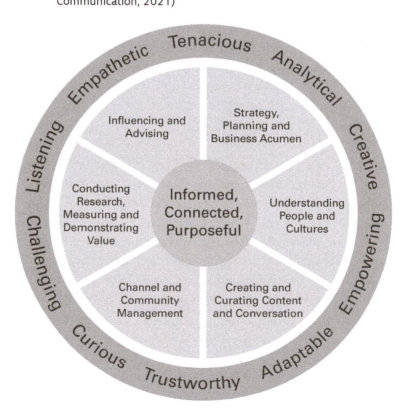

Defining inclusive internal communication

When we researched definitions, there was a myriad of different points of view and opinions on what role internal communication played in the organizations they supported. Each professional body, theorist, academic and influencer had their own take on the profession.

The IoIC say internal communication is 'to enable people at work to feel informed, connected and purposeful in order to drive organizational performance' (IoIC, 2018).

Dr Kevin Ruck, an internal communication academic, describes internal communication as 'Corporate information provided to employees that is also tailored to specific internal stakeholder groups (middle managers, line managers, functional and project teams, and peer groups) combined with the concurrent facilitation of employee voice that is treated seriously by all managers' (Ruck, 2020).

Jenni Field, a key internal communication influencer and author of *Influential Internal Communication*, describes internal communication as 'everything that gets said and shared inside an organization. As a function, its role is to curate, enable and advise on best practice for organizations to communicate effectively, efficiently and in an engaging way' (Field, 2021).

These definitions accurately represent the role internal communicators deliver in an organization. But if we reflect on the profession's history, we believe that communicators have lost their way in how they help people thrive in their roles. To be inclusive communicators, we must be responsible for challenging leaders who are not proactively considerate of inclusion and are not empathetic to the workforce's needs. As well as providing relevant information, building connections and ensuring that colleagues have an opportunity to have their voices heard. We also need to help build trust and understanding within an organization to create a foundation for healthy, productive and inclusive working practices.

To define **inclusive** internal communication, we believe:

inclusive internal communication enables powerful connections, demonstrates curiosity and cultivates belonging through two-way engagement. This results in trusted, clear and effective communication, allowing people to thrive in their work and impact organizational performance.

How internal communication can cultivate an inclusive culture

Internal communicators play a vital role in organizational culture. We are the ones who craft messages aligned with values, build connections between leaders and colleagues, instigate conversations about core initiatives and campaigns and bring people together to deliver on the mission, vision and purpose of the organization. A robust internal communication team can help build a cohesive, values-based culture that colleagues can buy into.

It's alleged that management expert Peter Drucker once said 'Culture eats strategy for breakfast' (Guley and Reznik, 2016), which implies that your company culture will determine your organization's success, regardless of how effective your strategy may be. If you don't nurture or support the people delivering your corporate strategy's objectives, it's doubtful organizational goals will be met. The culture of an organization exists whether or not leaders work on it. According to Edgar Schein, one of the world's top culture experts, culture is 'a pattern of basic assumptions – invented, discovered, or developed by a given group as it learns to cope with its problems of external adaptation and internal integration' (Schein and Schein, 2017).

Schein believes that an organization has three levels of culture: artefacts, shared values and basic underlying assumptions. The famous iceberg diagram shows how these three cultural elements may be identified in an organization (see Figure 5.2).

FIGURE 5.2 An iceberg model of culture

Artefacts: visible symbols, e.g. uniforms, posters, free fruit, games room, etc

Shared values: ethical statements and lasting beliefs which can influence the workforce in specific behaviours

Basic assumptions: unconscious drivers behind actions and decisions within an organization. Rarely discussed and difficult to find, often taken for granted

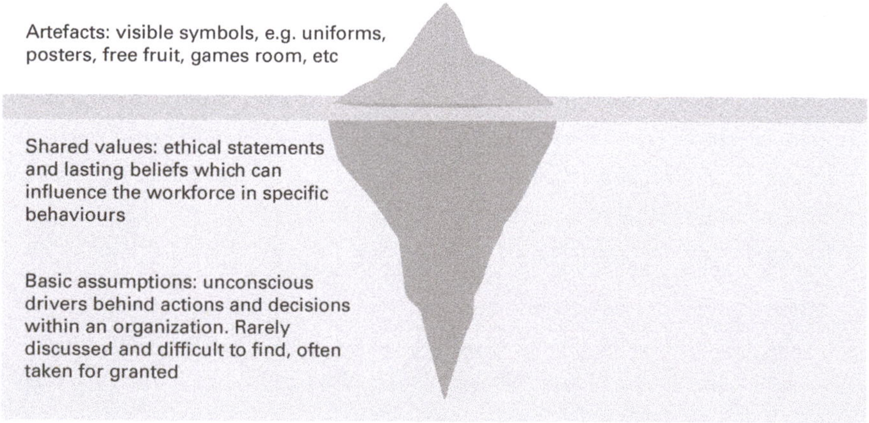

SOURCE Adapted from Schein's iceberg model of culture (Schein and Schein, 2017)

Artefacts

Artefacts are the visible symbols we see, such as the uniforms people wear, the posters on the walls, the ping pong table in the staff area and free fruit – things we can physically see that may influence the culture of the organization. The artefacts that last are often deeply tied to the underlying culture – such as which desk we sit at when we're in the office or how people dress at the organization. These symbols often influence how others perceive that culture. As internal communicators, we must observe these symbols and understand how colleagues engage with them. Artefacts can be easy to observe but also difficult to decipher, as each symbol will mean very different things to different given groups. If you're entering a new culture, you may not always understand why some people are tied to certain things, and you won't know unless you ask curious questions, a crucial part of our role as communicators. We mustn't allow our bias to make assumptions on artefacts alone. We need to observe, spend time with the groups and ask 'why do they do what they do?'. For example, you may walk into what feels like a great environment with free food, lounge chairs and sleeping pods which leads you to believe that the company cares deeply about their people. But when you start to ask questions and connect with others, you realize that people are expected to work 18-hour days and that the food and the pods are there because they don't want people to leave and be distracted from their work.

Shared values

Almost every organization has a set of shared values, more profound than the superficial artefacts we may see. Values are lasting beliefs which can often influence the workforce into specific behaviours. Shared values help colleagues understand what the organization expects of them and how they should behave when they represent the organization, internally and externally. Values guide how organizations make decisions; every colleague should align with them. However, one of the biggest challenges with shared values is that sometimes if the leader doesn't practice the behaviours behind the values, there will be a disconnect. Organizations spend time and investment developing core values, but often communication can be poor, and they end up stuck on walls or printed on lanyards. When they are not practised and lived daily, the culture will be misaligned, and disengagement will be rife. For internal communications, there are three easy steps we can follow to make sure that we help embed the organizational values in the organization.

1 **Reinforce shared values through written communication.** One of the most basic yet most effective ways to reinforce values is to mention them in written communication. This could be anything from talking about the company's commitment to customer service in an email to sharing stories about how colleagues can live out the values in your colleague briefings.

2 **Modelling values in leadership behaviours.** It's not enough to just write about values. Leaders need to ensure they are modelling them in their behaviours. As we shared in Chapter 2, colleagues are more likely to trust a leader if they are credible, reliable and empathetic. If they don't model the behaviours behind the values, they will lose credibility, and colleagues will not buy into whatever they are communicating. As internal communicators, we should encourage leaders to demonstrate the values in verbal and non-verbal communication.

3 **Use storytelling to bring values to life.** Real-life stories can be powerful. Showing examples of how values have played out in the workplace can significantly affect behaviours. When Advita worked at Manchester Airport Groups, she helped develop the Values in Practice (ViP) appreciation programme, which rewarded colleagues if they demonstrated one or more of the core values in their everyday work life. Each time a colleague went above and beyond in delivering that core value, they were awarded a values pin badge. They were given a gold colleague ambassador badge if they demonstrated positive action behind all five values. The stories shared were inspiring and explained how the values could enhance inclusivity across the organization.

Basic assumptions

Schein's third and final level of culture is basic underlying assumptions. These assumptions are often the unconscious drivers behind the actions and decisions within the organization. These assumptions are rarely discussed, nor are they found easily. As discussed in the bias chapter, assumptions are often unconscious beliefs, perceptions and feelings. These are the attributes that can create a toxic culture. We base our assumptions on previously learned things and don't often question why we made that decision. As part of our belief system, assumptions help us form judgments about others and draw conclusions, often based on our irrational beliefs. In an organizational context, assumptions play a vital part in daily work life. Since these assumptions are rarely discussed or dealt with openly, they can't be addressed or changed. There are patterns of behaviours we miss because the 'that's just the way we do things here' mindset often overrules any question around change. So colleagues either fall in line, face the microaggressions or exit the organization. The challenge with this basic assumption is that it's the single biggest destroyer of cultivating inclusive cultures.

However, it's essential for organizational leaders, with the support from communicators, to clearly understand their shared assumptions and how they can impact a high-performing inclusive culture from thriving. Here are some check-points to observe:

- What's happening around you? Are colleagues speaking up in meetings, or are they sharing ideas?
- Listen to what stories you're hearing, specifically gossip and speculation – are they about a particular person or groups of people? This will help you understand if there's any bias at play.
- How do people respond when they are speaking with senior leaders? Are they in agreement? Do they challenge them to speak up? Is there a pattern on who speaks up and who doesn't?
- What do people care about, and what are they paying attention to?
- How accessible are tools and resources? Are certain groups missing out because they don't have access?
- What behaviours do people ignore, and which are rewarded?
- How do people react in a crisis? Do they panic and start pointing fingers, or are they collaborative and focused on fixing the problem?

It can be difficult for leaders to get to the core root of people's basic assumptions if they don't know their team well. These assumptions are often deep-rooted and can be hard to unpack. As internal communicators and those responsible for communicating internally, we should be able to share our observations with the leader using the prompts above. We're often in a privileged position where we can see behaviours as we are generally independent of teams and departments. If these assumptions are not addressed appropriately, it will be challenging to cultivate inclusive behaviours (see Table 5.1).

TABLE 5.1 Top five inclusive behaviours

Ask powerful questions	Ask your leaders and colleagues regularly to help break down barriers. Asking powerful questions such as 'How can I help you succeed?' or 'What do you need from me to help you thrive in your role?' can transform relationships. Your communication will be authentic and purpose-led and will make a difference in how people perform.
Being curious and asking for regular feedback	These can help build better relationships with people across your organization. You don't need to wait for formal meetings or reviews. After a meeting or a project, you could ask 'What could I have done differently?' Use the SPARK framework shared in Chapter 4 to build more confidence in curiosity.
Challenging poor behaviours and practices	If you don't challenge poor behaviours or practices, your silence implies that you agree with the person acting poorly. Pay close attention to what people are saying and doing, and step in if you believe they are in the wrong. You can share your observations privately if you feel uncomfortable raising them at that moment, but make sure you have up-to-date examples and use coaching practices rather than accusatory behaviour.
Creating a safe space for colleagues to speak up	Creating safe spaces to allow people to share their thoughts can be very powerful. Don't let strong voices dominate the conversation; don't get defensive if you're challenged. Use our ALLMe 4A Framework in Chapter 6 to support you.
Being aware of biases and assumptions	Use the guidance provided in Chapter 4 to help you be aware of your biases and the assumptions you make. Ensure you have trusted voices different from you and can offer counsel and guidance when and when needed.

How internal communication can move from tactics to strategic deliverables

One of the questions communication professionals often ask is how they can move from being tactical to being involved in more strategic decisions. Decisions on culture and people usually sit with leadership and HR, but communications can also contribute significantly to the conversations. If cultivating an inclusive culture is a fundamental goal for your organization, they have to invite communicators to the discussion. We can offer appropriate guidance and advice on the best way to communicate information to the workforce and other stakeholders. We often have an umbrella view of the organization and understand what will work well and what will need some additional consideration. The Inner Strength i5 framework is one of the tools Priya uses when advising communication teams on being more strategic. Priya recognized that many communicators struggled to move beyond tactical deliverables and were treated like postboxes in their organization.

Five critical steps within the i5 framework will help you understand the knowledge gaps, where to focus and what other skills you will need to create an impact.

Implement

Implementation is the foundation of a communication professional's skills, but this shouldn't be mistaken for you simply taking orders. You have to be trusted advisors. Internal communication relies on writing, planning and delivering projects on time and within budget. This stage also allows us to think about what we need to do to ensure that our channels and messages are as inclusive as they can be. Sometimes the amount of strategic thinking required for the tactics can be undervalued. But if you're an expert internal communication professional, you will conduct a thorough debrief with your internal partners or clients to recommend how to deliver accurate information to the right stakeholder through the right channel and at the right time (Inner Strength, 2014).

Table 5.2 summarizes all the internal communication channels we may use today. This list isn't exhaustive but will guide you on what considerations you may need to make to ensure inclusive channels. Remember that even though some traditional channels have stood the test of time, tools and techniques are changing rapidly. This is why you must understand your workforce's demographics and the needs of your stakeholders so you can reach them successfully.

Interact

Interact is about relationships and research. The internal communication professional must have strong relationships that allow them to manage and advise leaders to drive cross-functional collaboration and manage to understand and communicate effectively with internal stakeholders. Interaction opportunities can build business acumen, help define culture and provide

TABLE 5.2 Popular internal communication channels

Channel	Description	Advantage/use when	Is it inclusive?
Email	Short for electronic mail, it allows you to send and receive messages to and from anyone with an email address.	To know that something was sent and received. New software now allows you to measure open rates, consumption and click-throughs. Using email databases, it is also possible to target and group messages. Don't teach them to ignore you by sending irrelevant messages.	When sending an email, sense-check that it's clear and concise. Have you avoided jargon and acronyms? Use gender-neutral terms such as 'Hi everyone' or 'Hi team' rather than 'Hey guys or girls'. Be mindful of some of the ableist language you may use, like 'crazy' or 'insane', and use 'outrageous' or 'intense' as alternatives. Also, consider if this information is available through another format for those who may find reading on the screen difficult.
Intranet	An internal website only accessible to those with permission.	Use the intranet to tell stories, highlight and archive announcements, connect to tools and serve as a document and information repository. Today's intranets also allow for targeting of tools, permissions and content.	Are your intranet pages accessible? If you don't know, ensure an accessibility review is undertaken and bring in experts if needed. Ensure that you use ALT text when using photos. Do your stories represent your organization, are your photos and images representative and can users quickly navigate their way through? Always conduct annual or bi-annual user-experience testing to see if any glitches need fixing. Also, avoid using 'click here' and share what they'll receive, e.g. 'view our latest end-of-year results'.
Direct mail/ postcard	Print pieces are delivered directly to home addresses.	Use when information applies to the entire family of the employee, or it is the best way to connect with a remote employee who does not have an email address. Some printed pieces can highlight programmes and direct stakeholders to information available electronically.	Ensure that the letters/postcards you're sending are accessible. If you're asking people to scan a QR code to access a website, be mindful that not everyone will have a smartphone or even the internet, so give alternatives if possible.

Newsletter	It can be print or electronic. It can consolidate information into one vehicle.	Newsletters can allow for storytelling and highlighting of relevant information. They are printed when employees do not have electronic access or they are meant to be printed.	Ensure that you avoid jargon and acronyms. If people are likely to print out the newsletters, then you need to make sure you are spelling out the URL links. Think about the colour contrast in your digital channels. Some colours can be hard to differentiate if you have visual impairments.
E-newsletter	This is an electronic newsletter distributed by email. Consolidates and highlights information in one vehicle.	An e-newsletter often highlights headlines and information so that employees can scan content and click through for more information. E-newsletters often lead to more detailed information on a website or intranet site. It's a great way of decreasing standalone emails. Tools now also exist to help you customize content delivered.	Don't ask people to 'click here' if you want them to visit a link. You must focus on what the user will receive rather than making assumptions about how they may interact with the e-newsletter. Be detailed and add descriptions for screen reader use. So 'view our latest CEO video' rather than 'click here to find out more'.
Poster	Creatively designed print documents are often put on a wall or bulletin board.	Many organizations use posters in high-traffic employee areas. They are used to raise awareness and drive action.	As with the above, ensure that the language is clear, concise and not ableist. Ensure that the colour contrasts are accessible for those with visual impairments and that images are representative.
Brochure/ flyer/leaflet	These printed documents provide overviews and snapshots of information.	Used when the intent is for employees to take information with them or take them home.	See above.

(continued)

TABLE 5.2 (Continued)

Channel	Description	Advantage/use when	Is it inclusive?
1:1 meeting	A conversation in person or over the telephone between two people.	When information needs to be shared, which is private. Often used by leaders and colleagues to discuss an issue one-to-one. We recommend one-to-one meetings for performance management and when a change programme may impact individuals.	If you're hosting the meeting, ensure everyone has an opportunity to contribute, observe those who may stay quiet or those who dominate the discussions and interject respectfully so others have the chance to share. Set the scene at the start and confirm the purpose of the meeting, the outcomes you're expecting to reach and how it's a safe space to challenge.
Huddle	These often refer to group or team meetings before a shift. They tend to be short: 5–15 minutes.	Use huddles with customer-facing or manufacturing/distribution colleagues – these work particularly well when you have multiple shifts.	See above.
Team meeting	When a team meets. Can happen in person or virtually.	Team meetings tend to happen regularly. Perhaps on a weekly or monthly basis. Larger groups like departments may establish a frequency of quarterly or bi-annually. Team meetings can provide updates, plan the following steps and recognize results.	See above.
Town Hall	Large meetings in an organization led by an executive or department leader.	The Town Hall is used for larger format company-wide updates on progress, information on strategy and recognition of success.	See above.

Annual kick-off/ conference	Once per year meeting to kick off the strategy.	Annual kick-offs tend to set the strategy for the year. They are designed to inform and inspire employees on what's ahead. They may include all employees, leaders only or a subset.	See above.
Video	Videos are filmed/visually recorded narratives.	Videos are used to provide updates or tell stories more entertainingly. Videos tend to get messages across faster. Videos can be expensive and professionally produced or created in-house. Employees tend to like authentic videos with light production for regular updates and enjoy seeing highly produced content for special programmes and focus areas.	Are the videos captioned? Have you transcribed them for those who prefer to read them? Can you listen to the audio only?
Podcast	A digital audio file that is recorded.	Organizations use podcasts when it's easier for employees to listen to content, such as employees who spend time on the road or travelling. They deliver a format that does not require screen time.	Have you transcribed the episode and produced a summary? Where will that summary be available?

(continued)

TABLE 5.2 (Continued)

Channel	Description	Advantage/use when	Is it inclusive?
Employee app	Employee apps allow employees to receive information and updates on their work or personal devices. A central team manages content.	These provide information delivered to employees' pockets and fingertips. During the pandemic and lockdown, employee app companies saw tremendous growth. Apps now also work with the employee database to target information and allow employees to choose the information they are interested in.	Do colleagues have access to free wi-fi in your organization? If not, will you compensate them if they have to use their data to download the app? Is the information on the app available elsewhere, e.g. the intranet, posters or team meetings? Not everyone will have access to a digital device, so be mindful of assumptions made.
Employee social network	Social networks used internally, e.g. Yammer, Workplace, etc.	Employee social networks democratize information, allowing every employee to post content within an internal social network. These social networks enable employees to share opinions, comments and updates and recognize one another.	Using infographics or diagrams, ensure you use accessible fonts and high-contrasting colours. Fonts such as Arial or Helvetica are accessible. All images should have alt-text descriptions. Limit the use of emojis, as they can slow down the experience for those who are using text-to-screen apps. Hashtags should always be in camel case #ThrowbackThursday
Group chat	Closed groups can text one another as a group.	Some organizations have tools that allow the ability to create internal chat groups. We often see that employees use public tools to create group chats.	WhatsApp and other chat tools are prolific in many organizations but are not often formal business channels. Sometimes people can feel excluded if they are not invited to a group, or can be seen as an invasion of privacy for others. Offer alternative solutions or, at the very least, provide guidelines that the team must follow.

Manager toolkit	Fact sheets and toolkits to assist managers/supervisors in sharing information with their teams.	Use toolkits when you want to create consistency in major organizational initiatives. They usually include background, timelines, key messages and questions & answers.	Provide alternative formats if needed, and follow the guidelines above in terms of clarity, avoiding jargon and acronyms.
Manager training	Communication training for managers.	When we want to help managers understand their communication role and how to use the information the organization provides to them.	Is the training accessible? Are you providing alternative formats?
Learning management system	An HR organizational development tool to train online at your own pace.	Some programmes may use business tools to help support communication efforts. Look at the organizational touchpoints and incorporate communications into those processes.	See above.
Training	Formal training programs in your organization.	Your organization may have formal training as it onboards and develops employees. Think about those touchpoints to integrate communication.	See above.
Digital workplace	Tools within the organization like HR, finance and operational systems.	Think about meeting employees where they already are. It may be wise to bring messages to employees within the tools they use for work.	See above.

TABLE 5.3 Top five research methods

Research method	Description	Advantage/use when
Meeting	Set up one-to-one or group meetings to ask questions and collaborate.	When you want to understand more about business initiatives and programmes. When you want to share strategies and updates. When you simply want to connect and build relationships. The real opportunity is to make these relationships outside your usual, siloed circle.
Engagement survey	Annual or regularly administered engagement surveys often managed by HR departments provide an engagement score and other insights.	The engagement survey is an important benchmark and asks vital questions on the state of engagement and disengagement in an organization. Since most engagement surveys include Gallup Q12 questions that measure retention, promotion and extra effort, they can be compared for changes year-over-year or against other companies.
Communication audit	Research to understand the state of internal communication in your organization.	Communication audits identify communication effectiveness, the usage of communication channels and communication preferences by employees. They are a great way to decide what is working, what can be improved and what is no longer necessary.
eNPS	Employee Net Promoter Score is a measure that asks employees one question: On a scale of 0–10, how likely are you to recommend our organization as a place to work?	Use eNPS for trends and changes and for benchmarking with other organizations. Promoters are 9–10, Passives are 7–8 and Detractors are 0–6. NPS is calculated by the per cent of Promoters minus the per cent of Detractors, giving you a score between −100 and 100.
Exit interview	HR often interviews employees leaving the organization to understand key issues.	Look at this information to identify recruitment, retention, engagement or reputation trends.

the communication professional with a unique point of view that can be shared with leaders and colleagues. A key opportunity for interaction is to understand leadership and employee perspectives through formal and informal conversations and feedback. To interact, the best practice is to start with research. Table 5.3 explores some of the best research methods.

Integrate

Integration is where the magic happens. As one of the few functions that stretch across organizations, internal communication has the opportunity to help the organization connect the dots. It's a role that cements the function's value since so many are focused on their own programmes and processes.

- **Connection** – Internal communication professionals need to identify both connects and disconnects. As we discussed in Chapter 2, a lack of trust or engagement usually revolves around what they see happening compared to what leaders have said. We can help fill the gap between ideas and action by assisting colleagues to be aware, understand, act and believe. We can also play a role in identifying the disconnects by matching what is being said to what is being done – the say/do gap.

- **Calendaring** – Internal communication and our communication channels can't exist in isolation. We need to create a communication calendar that lets us step back and look at the bigger picture. How are the awareness months connected to the overall business strategy? Are we at risk of bombarding colleagues with lots of disparate messages? Are we taking into consideration hybrid working? Is there a natural order in organizational programmes that reinforce one another? Can we integrate the messages or programmes to drive a more significant opportunity? Are we considering the demographics in our organization and how they access information?

- **Content strategy and key messages** – A crucial part of integration is how we map content strategies, key messages and a strategy for all supported programmes, including DEI initiatives. These messages must start with the organization's foundational messaging – its mission, vision, values, purpose and strategy. We need to be able to connect these to bigger concepts and serve to repeat and reinforce their importance.

- **Collaboration** – Internal communication professionals play an essential role in collaboration. We can ensure that there's representation around the table, as well as cognitive diversity. Because of the relationships built and understanding of who is who, we are often in the position to highlight who should be around the table and who has the expertise to solve real business problems.

- **Consistency** – We play a significant role in driving consistency, messaging and behaviour. Our role is to help enable, engage and empower others to thrive. Enable provides information clearly and succinctly that's easily understood, helps colleagues know what they need to do with the information or what is required and empowers them to make decisions when no one is watching. We also support the manager's conversations to ensure everyone is aligned and telling the same story. When information is missing, people will gossip and make up things that are not true.

- **Community** – this is an integral part of integration and an opportunity for communicators to build inclusive communities, especially if that community is not in the same space, has different roles and backgrounds, or is mobile and remote. Communication channels, information and access help drive culture by providing updates, celebrating milestones, addressing issues and challenges and recognizing success. Social tools also open opportunities for colleagues to connect through similar areas of interest and contribute to the organizational narrative. This builds teams and helps others in the organization not to feel alone.

Influence

Our greatest opportunity as communication professionals is not just to communicate on behalf of our organizations but, more importantly, to influence how our organization, its leaders and its people communicate.

Internal communication can help colleagues be aware, understand, act and believe. These are actionable and measurable terms and opportunities that have the potential to capture the heads, hearts and hands of those with whom we are communicating.

Although we tend to think of influence within the hierarchy, we have done much work recently to understand spheres of influence in organizational dynamics. In organizational mapping, key spheres of influence exist that many don't consider.

A senior internal communications professional, Mike Klein, focused on three kinds of influence that create followers that internal communication

TABLE 5.4 List of key influential people in organizations

Types of influential people in an organization	How they are selected	Behaviours demonstrated
Ambassadors	Formal representatives of the organization or initiative.	Managers, supervisors and colleagues who have received training on certain initiatives or programmes, e.g. change ambassadors are often seen as behavioural role models. The organization often selects them to lead, but there is no proof that they are influential.
Influencers	Selected by their peers and are often people that others listen to.	Influencers are often recognized by their peers for their experience and wisdom. There can be disconnect between who a manager believes is influential compared to those colleagues often seek out.
Advocates	Self-select to support critical initiatives.	This group is not often given much attention as a driver of organizational change or performance. But they can be critical in the success of initiatives if they are passionate and committed about the change or organization.

SOURCE Klein, 2018

professionals should consider. These influencers can help you identify where the gaps are, what's missing across the organization and what support is required for groups who may be marginalized or underrepresented (see Table 5.4).

Impact

Every request for communication support inside organizations should start with one fundamental question: What does success look like? Strategy is a buzzword today, yet many who use it don't understand what it means.

Strategy is planning that leads to successful results. It is not in the doing but the delivering successfully to the business results. What it's not is checking boxes to say something was done without understanding the reason or the impact the doing had on the organization.

When asking the question, if the internal partner or external client answers with tactics such as the success of sending a memo, creating a video or the leader being happy without being able to articulate a more extensive and specific outcome, it will reduce it as a priority.

Partners and clients must understand why it's essential to communicate the critical priorities of an initiative, as success must be measurable by using outputs, outtakes, outcomes and organizational impact.

Outputs are the tactics delivered, often cited by many internal communication professionals when asked for impact. It's the stuff implemented – the number of emails, newsletters, videos, and events created – yet in the absence of other measures to support impact, they may contribute to organizational noise versus value. We share more detail about measurement in later chapters, but the three categories of outtakes, outcomes and organizational impact are integral for communication professionals to understand (AMEC, 2022):

- Outtakes focus on consumption. Whether the colleagues received, paid attention to, comprehended or retained particular messaging.

- Outcomes are evidence of changes to or reinforcement of opinions, attitudes and behaviors.

- Organizational impact is whether internal communication has influenced organizational performance.

Measurement will allow us to define whether or not we've succeeded in implanting successful strategies, which can help people feel included and thrive in our organizations.

KEY TAKEAWAYS

- Internal communication and the impact it can have on inclusion isn't new and has existed in various forms for more than a century.

- Inclusive internal communication must include two-way engagement, the ability to challenge respectfully and active listening.

- We can't make assumptions about the cultures we support. We must ask relevant questions and observe before coming to conclusions.

- Basic assumptions are the unspoken rules and behaviors of an organization. Leaders need to be aware of this and address concerns directly, as this can create toxic cultures.
- Internal communication can play a significant role in cultivating inclusive cultures through effective channels, curious questions, advising and guiding, and observation skills.

REFLECTIVE QUESTIONS

- How often do you review your internal communication channels to ensure they are fit for purpose and inclusive?
- Have you recently reviewed your skill levels in the top 10 attributes needed to be a successful internal communication professional?
- Do you speak to different groups of people in your organization to help you identify where gaps might be?
- How much impact do you have as a communicator in your organization? Do you have strong relationships with leaders, and can you influence change?
- Reviewing the IoIC profession map, what skills do you need to build?

Bibliography

AFL-CIO (2019) Lowell Mill women create the first union of working women, aflcio.org/about/history/labor-history-events/lowell-mill-women-form-union (archived at https://perma.cc/LZP3-LLQX)

AMEC (2022) AMEC's Integrated Evaluation Framework, amecorg.com/amecframework/ (archived at https://perma.cc/JYE4-MVYV)

Brown, B, (2021) The Practice of Story Stewardship, brenebrown.com/articles/2021/12/05/the-practice-of-story-stewardship/ (archived at https://perma.cc/S7ZT-V2RL)

British Film Institute (2012) Just Billingham, player.bfi.org.uk/free/film/watch-just-billingham-no-3-1946-online (archived at https://perma.cc/QE56-MB75)

Field, J (2021) Influential Internal Communication. 1 ed. London, Kogan Page

Forgotten New England (2019) In his words – Dickens' visit to Lowell Massachusetts 1842, forgottennewengland.com/2011/11/09/in-his-words-dickens-visit-to-lowell-massachusetts-1842/ (archived at https://perma.cc/R5JM-QLL2)

Ghosh, J (2011) Fear of Foreigners: Recession and Racism in Europe, Race/ Ethnicity: Multidisciplinary Global Contexts

Guley, G and Reznik, T (2016) Culture eats strategy for breakfast and transformation for lunch, The Jabian Journal, journal.jabian.com/culture-eats-strategy-for-breakfast-and-transformation-for-lunch/#:~:text=You%20must%20 have%20heard%20the,executive%20of%20Ford%20Motor%20Company (archived at https://perma.cc/3664-JA87)

Heron, A R (1942) *Sharing Information with Employees.* 4 ed. California, Stanford University Press

Hill, M (2020, 14 March) Race row sent hundreds on strike in Preston, *Lancashire Post,* lep.co.uk/heritage-and-retro/retro/race-row-sent-hundreds-strike-preston-2450302

Inner Strength (2014, 16 September) Internal communication for business success from the inside-out, innerstrengthcommunication.com/blog/internal-communication-business-success-inside-out (archived at https://perma.cc/ SP9P-QHTA)

Institute of Internal Communication (2018) History, ioic.org.uk/about-us/history. html (archived at https://perma.cc/HWP4-S78A)

Institute of Internal Communication (2019) The birth of IoIC and early evolution of internal comms, voice.ioic.org.uk/item/721-ioic-70-part-one (archived at https://perma.cc/J266-7K7U)

Institute of Internal Communication (2021) The IoIC Profession Map: A framework for internal communication professionals, Milton Keynes, IoIC

IWM (2019) The workers that kept Britain going during the Second World War, iwm.org.uk/history/the-workers-that-kept-britain-going-during-the-second-world-war (archived at https://perma.cc/C3EE-BZ8V)

Klein, M (2018, 13 August) Four dimensions of internal influence: ambassadors, influencers, advocates and followers, changingtheterms.com/2018/08/13/ four-dimensions-of-internal-influence-ambassadors-influencers-advocates-and-followers/#comments (archived at https://perma.cc/AD64-MF2G)

Library Company (2012) Portraits of American Women Writers, librarycompany. org/women/portraits/farley.htm (archived at https://perma.cc/2YU4-N83U)

McGregor, D (1960) *The Human Side of Enterprise.* 1 ed. New York, McGraw-Hill Book Company, Inc.

Ruck, K (2020) *Exploring Internal Communication.* 4 ed. Oxon, Routledge

Schein, E H and Schein, P (2017) *Organizational Culture and Leadership.* 5 ed. New Jersey, Wiley

Smith, S (2011, 26 August) The workers rebellion of the 1960s, *Socialist Worker,* socialistworker.org/2011/08/26/workers-rebellion-of-the-1960s (archived at https://perma.cc/ER8M-XNQR)

The Gilder Lehrman Institute of American History (2018) Lowell Mill Girls and the factory system, 1840, gilderlehrman.org/history-resources/spotlight-primary-source/lowell-mill-girls-and-factory-system-1840 (archived at https://perma.cc/TP3E-N4P2)

ThoughtFarmer Intranet Blog (2020, 24 June) History of internal communication in the workplace, thoughtfarmer.com/blog/history-of-internal-communication-in-the-workplace/ (archived at https://perma.cc/H6AB-HZHL)

PART TWO

Frameworks and models

06 The 4A Framework to move DEI from performative to performing

07 Change and the Diversity Continuum

08 Focusing on the conversation versus the campaign

09 The intersectional approach for communicators

10 Why using inclusive language is essential in the workplace

11 How to build an inclusive engagement plan for DEI

12 Best practices to develop and communicate your DEI strategy

06

The 4A Framework to move DEI from performative to performing

While the first part of our book focused on important foundations of understanding in DEI, part two focuses on frameworks and models. Part One is intended to make you think. Part Two helps us evaluate and do the work. It's more practical and we hope that the various frameworks help you assess where your organization is in order to plan and deliver progress and results.

A Leader Like Me – The 4A Framework

This chapter explores the A Leader Like Me (ALLMe) 4A Framework for DEI. We review the cycle of acknowledgement, awareness, action and accountability needed to drive DEI on a macro level in organizations and at a micro level when dealing with personal relationships and crisis.

You will notice many frameworks and methodologies in this section are worth understanding. We love the use of these ways of thinking to help us understand our approach to both internal communication and DEI. Frameworks are not only practical, but they provide us with a way to measure and evaluate where we are and where we want to go. Frameworks are active versus static. They are directional versus stuck. They show us progress through steps that clearly establish what it takes to move to the next level. That tends to be how change works. It requires you to go through the steps and rarely can you miss one. In the DEI space, we simply can't go from ZERO to HERO in one fell swoop and that has quite frankly been part of the struggle. We need to emotionally and systematically work through each step over hours, months, years, lifetimes and sometimes generations. And it's not unusual to step backwards. We often say that DEI work feels like one step forward, two steps back. Our focus is on progress, not perfect.

The framework we want to start with is one that we created to talk about our recommended approach to DEI. It can help holistically in a big picture/ macro kind of way and it can be applied to incidents in an in-the-moment/ micro perspective.

The framework is the ALLMe 4A Framework we created several years ago when explaining our expectations of organizations and individuals who are committed to DEI. It includes:

- Acknowledgment
- Awareness
- Action
- Accountability

FIGURE 6.1 The ALLME 4A Framework

Acknowledgment

What does it mean to acknowledge? According to the Merriam-Webster dictionary, definitions include: 'to admit the truth or existence of' and 'to recognize as genuine or valid'. Acknowledgment is a critical first step in any DEI process or situation. We need to validate before we address issues and concerns. Without validation, we simply cannot begin.

To your audience, acknowledgment means: we see you, we believe you and we trust you. On the other hand, a lack of acknowledgment says loud and clear that you, and your perspectives, are invisible, are not important and simply don't matter. At the end of the day, acknowledgment in DEI is about empathy. It centres people or groups who are asking for help.

Acknowledgment, according to business coach Chris Westfall, involves a combination of empathy, trust and recognition. It means seeing from someone else's perspective; trusting that their perceptions are real and recognizing their efforts. In Westfall's book, Helice Bridges claims that 'Acknowledgment is missing from our workplaces. Our homes. Our schools. Managers point to what wasn't working. That approach reflects the punishment model we all grew up in. People don't say, "you did everything right". They say, "you missed that". And we'll always remember what we missed' (Westfall, 2022).

Acknowledge is the first step for a reason. Without it, everything that follows is superficial and unauthentic. It's probably why so many DEI programmes struggle. We jump to quick check-box actions to protect reputation without truly believing there is a real problem or real issues to solve. So what in the DEI space should we be acknowledging?

Acknowledge existence

Is the need for work and effort in diversity, equity and inclusion real? Are there inequities today? Do you believe it or are you simply trying to follow the crowd and do the bare minimum to look like you or your organization cares? Do you believe that there is an overreaction and that this DEI trend and focus will simply go away?

In order to make real progress in DEI, we need to acknowledge that there are challenges with diversity, equity and inclusion in your community, your organization, your country and the world. That there are injustices that simply exist. Remember that in acknowledging, you are not deciding who is to blame, but being very clear on the present state.

When dealing with an issue or someone pointing out an aggression, you need to acknowledge the perspective of the person pointing it out. The opposite is telling others that they are being too sensitive or overreacting.

Here is the reality: leadership teams are not reflective or representative of the communities, customers and the colleagues they serve. In colonized countries, there is preference given to white, non-disabled, cis-gendered, heterosexual males. This points clearly at a lack of diversity (check), equity (check) and inclusion (check) which presents a disconnect if we are an organization that wants to be seen as fair and just.

Organizations and individuals that acknowledge existence are not afraid to measure their present state, and talk about where they can improve.

Acknowledge importance

Acknowledging importance means you and your organization believe that addressing DEI is imperative for the organization in order to manage its reputation, risk, recruitment, retention and results. Let's not forget that DEI is the right thing to do to create a fair and just society where everyone is treated with respect and dignity and has the same opportunity to succeed. Importance means that the organization is willing to invest in DEI and look at changes that need to be made in order to progress.

We also need to acknowledge the importance of our commitment to DEI on the people who work for our organizations and with whom we interact.

When organizations and individuals acknowledge importance, they are willing to invest time and resources to driving change.

Acknowledge bias

As referenced in Chapter 4, we need to acknowledge that bias simply exists. It's not some made-up term and people who feel impacted negatively by bias are not overreacting. Professionally, we can acknowledge where bias may reveal itself in employee and customer experiences. Personally, we need to look at everyday interactions and acknowledge that what we have learned in our upbringings, regardless of our age, gender, race, ability or sexual orientation, has resulted in automated thoughts, decisions and actions that we need to unlearn in order to be fair.

Many organizations acknowledge bias by bringing in external experts to deliver anti-bias training. Realize that this is simply a first step since so many tend to focus on one-time or intermittent training that doesn't necessarily get embedded into behaviours when we recruit, retain and recognize our people. Remember that bias is a lifetime of learning. One training programme doesn't magically fix everything.

Organizations and individuals that acknowledge bias start with the discrepancies that exist when it comes to programmes, policies and procedures and ask how bias plays a role in creating inequities.

Acknowledge history

Imagine history simply being erased. Imagine the interpretation of your history is from a specific point of view, often that of the oppressor versus the oppressed? Imagine someone making light of your trauma?

We must acknowledge factual history not fictional stories that make those with privilege feel better about themselves. It is only through the clear understanding of what actually happened and why, can we begin to learn, heal and work towards a better future.

The world is full of examples:

The American Thanksgiving Story – For years, schools across the United States held pageants telling the story of what happened in Plymouth Rock when the pilgrims arrived on the shores of the new world. Local Native Americans welcomed the pilgrims and shared a feast with them. In truth, according to David Silverman, author of *This Land is Their Land: The Wampanaog Indians Plymouth Colony, and the Troubled History of Thanksgiving* (Silverman, 2019), much of that story is myth riddled with historic inaccuracies that are deeply harmful to the Wampanoag Indians whose lives and society were forever damaged after the English arrived in Plymouth. The true story is about death and disease brought by the pilgrims for colonial land expansion. Native Americans remember the pilgrims' entry as a day of mourning (Bugos, 2019).

Another example revolves around Holocaust denial. The United States Holocaust Memorial Museum says that "Holocaust denial is any attempt to negate the established facts of the Nazi genocide of European Jews (United States Holocaust Memorial Museum, 2022). Holocaust deniers claim that the Holocaust was invented to advance the Jewish interests. According to the United States Holocaust Memorial Museum, 'The denial or distortion of history is an assault on truth and understanding. Comprehension and memory of the past are crucial to how we understand ourselves, our society, and our goals for the future (United States Holocaust Memorial Museum, 2022).

Organizations and individuals that acknowledge history are transparent about the good, the bad and the ugly of their historical facts. Again, the key is about being curious versus judgemental. Many organizations and families have benefited from settlement, slavery, colonization and discrimination. It's important to be honest about history in order to chart the course to the future.

LETTER TO THE EDITOR FROM BOB BARNES, SEATTLE

The fact that the country now known as the U.S.A. was built on the backs of slave labor, and that a campaign of genocide was conducted against the people already living here, are irrefutable and historically proven. One can call these facts an insult to our history or, just maybe, acknowledge them in an attempt to heal and move forward.

Mistakes of the past are fated to be repeated unless we learn from them.

SOURCE Barnes, 2020

Acknowledge systems

We need to acknowledge that systems exist that create discrimination and barriers. They are not always conscious, explicit or visible; they can be pervasive under the surface. In fact, to many, they just seem the standard. They can be 'deeply embedded in systems, laws, written or unwritten policies, and entrenched practices and beliefs that produce, condone, and perpetuate widespread unfair treatment and oppression' (Braveman, 2022).

In an article about racial discrimination and health among Asian Americans (Gee et al, 2009), an iceberg is used as a metaphor. The top of the iceberg above the waterline is overt discrimination like hate crimes and poor treatment that are readily observable. However, the bottom of the iceberg that exists under water is the difficult-to-observe covert or symbolic discrimination. These include implicit attitudes, segregation, racial ideologies and institutional policies that have a negative impact. The researchers say: 'Systemic racism is so embedded in systems that it often is assumed to reflect the natural, inevitable order of things' (Braveman, 2022). And this applies to all marginalized groups.

That's the difficulty with systems and structures we are used to or comfortable with. They just feel common, comfortable, usual and ordinary… until you acknowledge that they exist to discriminate and maintain an unequal status quo.

Priya had an opportunity to work with a legal organization trying to increase representation. It was mind blowing to realize that decisions being made and policies being written that historically impacted higher numbers of Black and Indigenous individuals, and women, were written by mostly white men. In law firms, there is now the realization that a lack of diversity impacts law and legislation. As firms begin to try and drive change, they are looking closely at their systems and launching programmes in partnership with educational institutions to address representation.

Organizations and individuals that acknowledge systems take a look at what they can see at the top of the iceberg and spend time looking at the systems that have prevented diversity, equity and inclusion that exist under the surface to understand why.

Acknowledge pain

The conversations around DEI are often centred around pain and trauma. Around the world, the DEI stories that have impacted us the most focus on a traumatic incident, yet the reaction is so much bigger.

When George Floyd was murdered in 2020, there was the immediate trauma to him and his family, and it also unleashed the trauma of Black people who are regularly discriminated against and treated differently because of the colour of their skin.

The finding of mass graves in Canada at residential schools was more than the loss of lives – it was the generational trauma of Indigenous people whose land, culture and language was taken away due to colonialism.

When a shooter killed five and injured many more at a Colorado gay club in 2022, the LGBTQ+ community and their families feared for safety and security for themselves and their loved ones.

The 'MeToo' movement started with the Harvey Weinstein sexual abuse cases, yet unleashed traumatic memories for women around the world who had been sexually abused and often reminded of trauma that they had buried deep for years.

The appearance of swastikas painted in Jewish communities and synagogues resurrect memories of the Holocaust and its impact on families around the world.

The reaction to what feels to some like an isolated incident is often an accumulation of months, years or generations of trauma. We need to acknowledge the pain, where it comes from and not manipulate it for our own benefit. We need to also be careful of being desensitized to issues because they feel like everyday occurrences.

Organizations and individuals who acknowledge pain have empathy and are there for support. It's important when asking colleagues to share pain that they don't feel forced. Someone's pain can be used for education, with permission, but not for entertainment.

Acknowledge diversity

Often, a reaction to protect oneself from being seen as discriminatory is trying to claim that everyone is equal.

Phrases like 'I don't see colour' or 'all lives matter' tend to not be supported by facts. Here is the truth: not everyone is the same and not only is that okay, but it is wonderful. We need diversity of thought, experience and skill in order to thrive. The goal is not to be the same, the goal is to be treated equitably. That's why differences should not only be acknowledged but understood and celebrated.

When it comes to ability, age, gender, sexual orientation, race and experience, acknowledging diversity, and the need for it, in order to serve customers, can be an asset.

Organizations and individuals who acknowledge diversity recognize that opportunity exists when we bring different thinking, experiences and perspectives to the table.

Acknowledge effort

We thought it was important to add this category. Effort towards a more just world needs to be acknowledged on all sides. Let's acknowledge that, despite being constantly fed doomsday scenarios, most people want to do the right thing. Many of our biases are formed after birth through our circumstances and our communities through learning.

In order to learn new things, we must be part of the dialogue and discourse. Part of the work of DEI practitioners, internal communication, HR and leadership is to encourage the conversation versus shut it down.

We also need to speak up when we catch people doing something right and encourage effort and progress. Change is uncomfortable, and the only way the uncomfortable becomes comfortable is by getting used to it, as opposed to running away.

We also need to create safe spaces for people to make mistakes, acknowledge them, learn and move on. Yes, there are circumstances and lines that cannot be crossed when they present danger to security or safety or when what occurred was blatant sexism, racism, able-ism or homophobia. Our goal is to create awareness, correct and identify the preferred words, behaviours and actions.

We also want to be in a position where we can acknowledge progress. Communicating milestones and changes are worth the time and effort. We know that some will be sceptical and highlight that the small steps are not enough. However, here is our fear. If we continue to insult the efforts for progress in DEI, we can inadvertently stop the progress in its tracks or move it backwards. Sometimes it's easier just to keep things exactly where they are than be blamed for trying.

Organizations and individuals that acknowledge effort recognize value-based behaviours and highlight milestones and movements forward, even if they are small steps.

Awareness

The second A in our ALLMe 4A Framework is awareness. The definition of awareness is the quality of being aware; knowledge and understanding that something is happening or exists. It's about attention, consciousness, mindfulness, observance or observation.

For our framework, awareness is simply about the facts. In awareness, we do our research so that we can understand our starting point and think about what good looks like for our organization. Awareness centres on curiosity versus judgment. When we are aware of where we are today, we are in a position to start planning for tomorrow. So let's examine the role of awareness.

Where are we today

In Chapter 1, we made the case for DEI by taking a look at what diversity looks like in the world; in your customer base; in your community, or in the colleagues who work in your organization. Awareness begins by us asking: where are we right now?

When we start our organizational DEI programme, we now ask ourselves where we sit when it comes to these numbers. Let's be prepared to look under the covers and be either pleasantly surprised or horrified by the results.

Awareness is simply about what is. Where are we? What is our starting point? And the more thorough we are with the questions we ask, the more likely we are to create a platform that is an accurate jumping-off point for DEI efforts.

Diversity

- Is your organization diverse? How do you know?
- What are the factors of diversity that matter to your organization?
- What is the diversity of your community, customers, colleagues, leaders, board, suppliers?
- Does diversity change as you move hierarchically up your organization?
- What programmes has your organization put in place in the past to support diversity? Have they worked?

Inclusion

- Is your organization inclusive? How do you know?
- How would your colleagues rate inclusion?
- Is there a difference in opinion between overrepresented and underrepresented groups?
- What does inclusion mean to you?
- Are people expected to be someone different at work than they are at home?
- Do you see underrepresented groups code-switch (adjust language or behaviour) or assimilate in order to be included?

Equity

- Is your organization equitable?
- How does equity or lack of equity show itself in recruitment, retention and recognition programmes?
- What practices or protocols in your organization put some groups at a disadvantage?

When you look at those numbers and answers, can you say confidently that diversity is reflected in your organization, that it is inclusive and that it demonstrates equity?

So there is a clear red flag if your organization has acknowledged they need to work on and or invest in DEI, yet no baseline research has been conducted. The efforts will simply be random and superficial and the hope for progress of any kind will be nil.

Where do we want to be tomorrow?

Once we have established a baseline, we then have the opportunity to ask ourselves and our organizations what success in DEI looks like. These can be expressed in a set of goals that have been identified or a discussion about where we should be.

These can include diversity goals to correct any discrepancies that exist in demographic make-up. It can be practices that help people feel included and those that perhaps inadvertently put some at a disadvantage. We can get more concrete on measurable goals when we get into the next action planning steps.

Ask the questions, listen to the answers

In the awareness phase, we've seen many organizations conduct surveys and listening exercises with colleagues and other stakeholders. It gives colleagues a chance to contribute to action planning and feel like they have been part of a solution that is meaningful to them.

Self-identification

We've seen many organizations ramp up their efforts through self-identification questions and surveys to understand who works for them today. Just note that the biggest challenges revolve around trust. Colleagues need to understand clearly why the organization is asking and what it intends to do with the information. Where possible, it is important that the organization also provides a summary of its findings in order to build trust. Note that it is not unusual for colleagues who do not trust the organization or its leaders to choose not to answer these questions.

CAUT, the Canadian Association of University Teachers (CAUT, 2021), recommend the following:

- Have clear instructions on how to complete the survey.
- State the purpose of the survey and the reasons for which it is being conducted.
- Include a statement about legality.
- Include a statement about confidentiality.

They also encourage organizations to recognize intersectionality and allow participants to check all boxes that apply. After all, you don't want participants to feel like the survey itself is not inclusive. Most organizations do collect data on gender, sexual orientation, disabilities, indigeneity, and racialization.

Listening exercises

Many organizations have been actively conducting listening exercises through focus groups, think tanks and more informal coffee chats. What has been important in our work is that people are placed in groups where they feel comfortable to share their perspective without repercussions. It's probably the reason we, and other consultants, are brought in to provide third-party-administered and confidential exercises to help identify pain points and concerns.

There is an order to how vocal and safe people feel in expressing their true opinion, whether it is in support of DEI or against any effort:

- Anonymous surveys give us quantitative and qualitative feedback. The comments sections when people trust the anonymity can be quite raw and emotional.

- Anonymity on social media where colleagues can express their opinions via social media handles that make them hard to identify. Even when providing live Q&As, we've seen clients stop the ability for colleagues to ask questions live behind anonymity since some colleagues tend to be more emboldened to make discriminatory statements when they can't be identified.

- Focus groups, often managed by a third party. Colleagues tend to be more honest when they are around a table with peers with whom they can relate. They are less likely to pipe up about issues with a supervisor or leader in the room unless there is already an established culture of trust.

- From a diversity perspective, employee resource groups (ERGs) have often been used for feedback. You will hear very different opinions from various ERG representatives since their role is to try to be the voice for their group or cause. Just remember that it's difficult for the one member of a specific underrepresented group to speak for everyone.

As difficult as listening exercises tend to be in DEI, they are very important to conduct. It's also important to receive the negative comments, concerns and feedback in order to proactively prepare for messages and questions that address issues expressed. We would always rather be prepared than unprepared.

Open eyes, open minds, open hearts

It's important to approach the awareness step with an open mind and be prepared to be uncomfortable with what you learn. We'll remind you to observe your findings with curiosity not judgment.

CASE STUDY
Nike

Nike, Inc. claims to be working to build a more diverse, inclusive team that reflects the athletes and communities where they live, work and play.

On its website, it measures exactly where it is and clearly states its present numbers along with its plan. It started tracking measures like pay equity in 2017 and have continued to set goals and hold themselves accountable to results.

It reports its gender stats globally at the employee, director and VPLT levels and publishes US race and ethnicity at the three levels as well.

It also publishes pay equity stats as of 2020. Their data shows that for every $1 earned by men, women globally earned $1, and for every $1 earned by white colleagues in the US, racial and ethnic minority colleagues earned $1.

TABLE 6.1 Nike gender dashboard by level

FY21	All employees	Director+	VPLT
Female	49%	43%	41%
Male	51%	57%	59%

Nike has stated that its goal is to have 45 per cent of women in leadership positions by 2025.

It also plans to maintain the 30 per cent representation in racial and ethnic minority groups at the director level and above which is consistent with population demographics in the US.

SOURCE Nike Inc., 2022

Action

The third A is action. Action is a thing done; the accomplishment of a thing usually over a period of time, in stages, or with the possibility of repetition. It's about initiative and enterprise.

In our framework, action is about planning. It is about building hope and fostering involvement.

Action means being proactive versus reactive and actually having a measurable plan that forms the foundations needed to hold yourself and your organization accountable.

Once you have done your research and established a real baseline or starting point and have articulated what good looks like, it's time to ask, what are we going to do to get us from where we are today to the goals we have set for ourselves?

Action plan

Many simply start to do random things that are reactive, but an action plan sets out what you will do, who is responsible and when it will happen. As mentioned, organizations must build their DEI strategy and plan before a DEI communication plan can be created. The DEI communication plan should identify the changes that have been promised and identify how communication can create awareness, understanding, action and belief.

Elements of a DEI action and supporting communication plan may include:

- Timeline – Although many organizations will tend to create three- to five-year plans, we've seen organizations break down those plans into achievable and realistic one-year chunks that allow them to take steps in the right direction. With longer range initiatives, we've seen organizations provide realistic steps to build changes in the long term.

- Measurable goals – Goals identified must be SMART – specific, measurable, achievable, realistic and time-bound. It's okay to state long-term aspirations and provide shorter-term goals that demonstrate movement and progress toward change. Remember that attitudes and behaviours built over decades and centuries do not change overnight. What you are trying to demonstrate is commitment, vision and progress toward sustainable change.

- Roles and responsibilities – One of the big mistakes organizations make is expecting the DEI resource who has taken on the job to achieve change in a vacuum. DEI is culture change. It is change in everyday decisions and behaviours from individuals at every level of the organization and often requires collaboration with leaders and various departments. We'll provide a little bit more context when we talk about our areas of focus. At this point, many organizations can use RACI (responsible, accountable, consulted, informed) charts to identify who in the organization is responsible, accountable, consulted and informed. The DEI practitioner provides oversight.

- Priorities – One of the key opportunities in an action plan will help your organization prioritize the myriad of opportunities ahead. It's important to be able to explain why some initiatives were prioritized over others.

- Messaging – All key messages for the DEI plan should create clear linkages to the mission, values, vision, purpose and strategy of the organization. Remember that different messages may be needed to support colleagues through change.

Areas of focus

In Chapter 1 we talked about the elements on the DEI – why. These are the same areas that organizations can focus on in order to drive action:

- Rights – We focus on DEI because it is the right thing to do.
- Representation – We focus on DEI to represent our publics accurately and realistically.
- Retention – We focus on DEI to retain our best workers.
- Recruitment – We focus on DEI to both attract talent to our organization and grow talent within our organization.
- Reputation – We focus on DEI because our reputation matters.
- Results – We focus on DEI because it is linked to better business results.

As we review each of those areas, work with relevant operational leaders to identify how we can realistically get from where we are today to achieving future goals.

Questions to ask:

- Do we need to change policy?
- Do we need to look at process?
- Do we need to understand governance?
- Do we need training? Who needs the training?
- What is working today and what isn't?
- How can communication help drive action?
- Can we clearly articulate what employees need to do or do differently?

CASE STUDY
Financial Services Compensation Scheme

The Financial Services Compensation Scheme (FSCS) helps people get back on track by protecting them when authorized financial services firms fail. Since their launch in 2001 they have come to the aid of 6.5 million customers and paid out £26 billion in compensation.

At the FSCS today they recognize the importance of creating an equitable, diverse and inclusive workplace where everyone can succeed in achieving their personal and professional goals, balance their home and working lives and feel like they truly belong.

They believe strongly in championing inclusion at all levels of their organization and are incredibly proud to have been recognized in several national awards in this space: FT Financial Adviser Diversity in Finance Awards first ever Employer of the Year in 2019; being placed in the Inclusive Top 50 UK Employers for the last four years (the FSCS is the UK's 12th most inclusive employer) and in 2022 they were awarded the Working Families Top 30 Family Friendly Employers.

However, it hasn't always been like this. When David Blackburn, Chief People Officer, joined the organization in 2013, there was much to improve: little had been achieved in transforming workplace culture, increasing diversity or driving employee engagement. The data demonstrated how big a challenge they faced: only 43 per cent of employees thought the culture was positive; less than 10 per cent of the leadership team was non-white or female with no LGBTQ+ representation and overall employee engagement was 65 per cent.

The FSCS board had an ambitious vision: *FSCS into the 2020s – Protecting the Future*. To deliver this David **acknowledged** they needed an equitable, diverse and inclusive workplace. They were **aware** that it was important to have an environment where everyone was treated with dignity and respect, where productivity and customer experience improved because their workforce truly embraced the benefits that EDI can bring.

They took **action** by setting themselves several bold strategic diversity targets: to achieve 50 per cent female leadership by March 2022; to increase Black, Asian and minority ethnic leadership to 20 per cent and LGBTQ+ leadership to above 5 per cent across the scheme.

The FSCS knew that to deliver this increased diversity they needed **accountability** so they reviewed, refreshed and relaunched their approach, establishing new partnerships and platforms and to put internal and external communications at the centre of their approach to reach new audiences.

They celebrated differences internally via their weekly Monday bulletin, weekly message from their CEO, their Diversity, Inclusion & Wellbeing Hub, and featured employees' personal experiences wherever possible across both internal and external channels: Facebook, LinkedIn and Twitter.

They ensured that awareness sessions recognized the widest range of lived experience – from Neurodiversity Awareness Week sponsored by their Chief Counsel who is the parent of children who are neurodivergent to the 50th Anniversary of Pride and LGBT History Month led by David himself who is part of the LGBT community; to their new partnership with Carers UK which was launched in June 2022 by FSCS' Chief Executive; and their ongoing work on raising awareness and support for colleagues going through the menopause (they signed the Menopause Workplace Pledge in 2022), their senior leaders are active, visible champions.

Today they have higher levels of board, senior and executive diversity than ever before:

- In 12 months, they've increased the number of non-white managers from 17 per cent to 29 per cent and now report on backgrounds broken down by self-identified ethnicity.
- Over a third of FSCS employees come from non-white backgrounds.
- 75 per cent of the executive team and 67 per cent of the FSCS's board are female.
- They have LGBTQ+ representation at board, executive team, and senior leadership levels.
- 13 per cent of staff identify as LGBTQ+ (an annual increase of 7 per cent).
- They have also increased female representation in traditionally male dominated areas such as IT and data management from 8 per cent to 22 per cent.
- In 2022 they onboarded 40 new colleagues to the scheme across almost all teams and at all levels (50 per cent male / female, 35 per cent Black, Asian and minority ethnic and 7.5 per cent LGBTQ+).

Their intentional approach has not just transformed their business performance, it has made the FSCS a diverse and inclusive employer of choice and internal communications has been central to their success.

Most importantly they know their work directly impacts their colleagues' lived experience: 87 per cent of colleagues feel that they genuinely belong, 88 per cent feel that they can always be themselves at work and 91 per cent describe the FSCS as an inclusive and caring employer (May 2022 survey).

David attributes this progression to three simple actions to help organizations with their DEI journey:

1 **ENGAGE** – you need to proactively engage with your workforce through pulse surveys, people briefings, team meetings and virtual drop-ins; productivity, quality, innovation and great customer care are all achieved by engaging with others.

2 **LISTEN** – listen to their anxieties and concerns, answer them and build confidence.

3 **ACT** – Good words have their place: they signal behaviour. You can say all these things but unless you do them, your words will not build trust.

From performative to performance

Although Chapter 8 will focus on being performative versus driving real performance, we felt it was important to call it out in our action conversation. We encourage you to think long-term, sustainable change versus knee-jerk, check-box actions. We believe that these have the potential to hurt versus help when there is a disconnect between the promises made and the actions and behaviours of the organization.

Also keep in mind that the easier actions tend to be the performative ones. It's probably why we jump to using diverse stock imagery on our recruitment site without actually reflecting that diversity when people walk through your doors. It's the reason your ad campaign can talk about your commitments when your colleagues struggle to belong. It's easier to put up black boxes and rainbows than to change real policies to create equity.

Accountability

Our final A is accountability. Accountability is an obligation or willingness to accept responsibility or to account for one's actions. Ultimately, accountability is about measurement. We want to let people and organizations know that we are committed to driving change.

Measures

When we create communication plans and strategies for organizations, they have got to be measurable to identify success. The clearly articulated goals identified in the action phase need to be measured to show progress and correct challenges. We often provide a set of quick wins that can be achieved immediately to demonstrate action in the short term and break longer-term initiatives into shorter-term progress goals to showcase movement and let our colleagues know that we have not forgotten.

Our measures are inspired by the AMEC Integrated Evaluation Framework (AMEC, 2022) when it comes to measurements and goals to which we want to be held accountable.

Outputs

We define outputs by our tactics and actions. What did we do or do differently? What actions did we take? Were we on time and on budget?

Outputs could include:

- The policies or processes changed.
- Emails sent out.
- Communication and training created and delivered.
- Ads, brochures and websites delivered.
- Strategy completed.
- Celebrations, awareness and commemorative months and dates acknowledged.

Outtakes

Outtakes are about the consumption of our outputs:

- Clicks and views on our website.
- The number who attended training and meetings.
- The number who viewed our ads.
- The numbers that opened and read our materials.

Outcomes

Outcomes are the behaviours and actions changed as a result of our outputs and outtakes:

- Colleagues are reporting fewer microaggressions.
- Complaints from colleagues and customers are reduced.
- The sentiment has changed to more positive about the organization.

TABLE 6.2 Setting goals for accountability

Item	DEI goals	Communication goals
Organizational impact	Reputation – 50% fewer racial profiling incidents reported	Customer satisfaction increases by 10% and fewer incidents reported by the media.
Outcome	Colleagues use training to impact their behaviour	50% fewer complaints for racial profiling submitted
Outtake	Anti-bias training attended by 100% of colleagues	100% of colleagues sign up for training
Output	Anti-bias training introduced	Create a campaign to launch training – emails, manager tools, memos, posters

Organizational impact

Organizational impact is the impact on business results and measures:

- Better business results.
- More diverse recruitment.
- Higher retention and engagement stats.
- Better reputation.
- Improvement to employee and customer experience.

Progress not perfect

When it comes to accountability, it is important to provide updates on milestones achieved and progress on initiatives. One of the mistakes many make is that they want to have achieved a long-term goal fully before communicating and celebrating. By providing regular updates on what is working, where we are having challenges and how we are correcting ourselves in order to improve, we create an important conversation with colleagues that help them understand the value they are bringing to the organization, enabling them to stay the course and remain committed.

And the more you can connect the dots between changes being made and the impacts those changes are having on the organizations, the more colleagues begin to understand the relationship between DEI and business stability and success.

FIGURE 6.2 Gender Diversity Dashboard

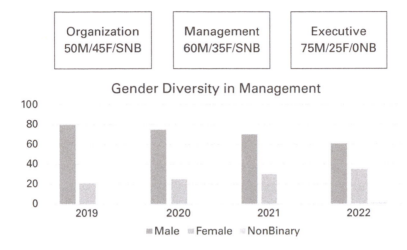

We've seen many organizations successfully create a DEI report card or dashboard that is shared quarterly or annually in order to clearly articulate goals and rate themselves as red, yellow and green against initiatives.

The art of the apology and the ALLMe 4A Framework (bonus)

We mentioned that the ALLMe 4A Framework can be used at a macro level for organizational DEI programmes and that it also provides a framework for micro incidents and situations.

When we are called out for a microaggression, it is natural for our first reaction to be defensive. We feel attacked and the human instinct is to protect oneself. The truth is that defensive, self-protective responses tend to make things worse and escalate the situation.

If you say 'You are overreacting', it is the exact opposite of acknowledgment. You are telling the person who feels wronged that you do not believe them or their perceptions and feelings are wrong.

If your instinct is to say 'I'm not racist, homophobic, sexist, ablest', you are essentially making someone else's pain about you. And if you are the individual with privilege in the situation, this is seen as a power play. It means that you and your feelings are more important than theirs.

Here are a couple of examples using the ALLMe 4A Framework.

Example 1: The wrong way

In 2019, Canadian sports personality Don Cherry used two words in a rant about buying poppies for Remembrance Day. He seemed to point out that immigrants did not buy them: '**You people**... you love our way of life, you love our milk and honey, at least you can pay a couple of bucks for a poppy or something like that.' His co-host Ron Maclean seemed to agree and the internet went wild.

Ron Maclean and Sportsnet, the broadcaster, apologized immediately. Don did not (Strong, 2019).

He told people they were overreacting and that it wasn't his intention to insult anyone. [Lack of acknowledgment]

At the same time he made his remarks, and completely unrelated, a newcomer group called Refugee613 was getting ready to launch a campaign asking new Canadians why they wear a poppy (CBC, 2019). [A general lack of awareness. His remarks seemed to be about assumptions versus facts]

He made it about himself versus who he hurt: 'I know what I said and I meant it. Still do. Everybody in Canada should wear a poppy in honour of our fallen soldiers. [Lack of action. I was right]

He refused to apologize or commit to reflection or doing better next time. [Lack of accountability]

As a result, Cherry was fired from Sportsnet after 38 years of hosting. In retrospect, he says he wished he used different words. He also blamed his co-host 'for burying him' when he publicly apologized, acknowledging the situation, showing awareness of how it came across, committing to action and being accountable.

Example 2: The right way

In 2022, singer LIZZO used an ableist slur in the lyrics of her song 'Grrrls'. Critics immediately spoke up and pointed out the issue on social media.

Her response (Peiser, 2022) was:

It's been brought to my attention that there is a harmful word in my new song, 'GRRRLs'. [Acknowledgement]

Let me make one thing clear: I never want to promote derogatory language. As a fat black woman in America, I've had many hurtful words used against me so I [understand] the power words can have (whether intentionally or in my case, unintentionally). [Awareness of learning]

I'm proud to say that there's a new version of GRRRLS with a lyric change. This is the result of me listening and taking action. [Action taken right away]

As an influential artist I'm dedicated to being part of the change I've been waiting to see in the world. Xoxo, Lizzo. [Accountability to do better]

As communication professionals, it is not unusual to be brought into crises and change efforts, like DEI, for our organizations. If we use the ALLMe 4A Framework of acknowledgement, awareness, action and accountability, we can help our organizations and leaders be more LIZZO than Cherry.

KEY TAKEAWAYS

- The ALLMe 4A Framework for DEI consists of acknowledgment, awareness, action and accountability.

- Acknowledgment is a critical first step in any DEI process or situation. We need to validate before we address issues and concerns.

- Awareness is about doing research and understanding the facts. It's important that you look at your baseline with curiosity not judgment.

- Action is important but we must have a plan to address issues. Actions need to be cross-functional and cross-organizational effort. Changes can't happen without influencing everyday and operational experiences.

- Accountability measures progress. It's important to set short-term and long-term goals and use milestone to create a transparent conversation on progress and challenges.

REFLECTIVE QUESTIONS

- Does the DEI work my organization is doing incorporate the ALLMe 4A Framework?

- Are there individuals or leaders in my organization that do not acknowledge DEI is important or an issue?

- Are we aware of our starting baseline when it comes to DEI? Have we been thorough in understanding where we are today?

- Do we have an action plan to address DEI or are we simply reacting?

- Have we got measurable goals and ways to hold ourselves accountable to progress?

- Do we communicate milestones in order to demonstrate movement to our colleagues?

Bibliography

AMEC (2022, 1 October) AMEC's Integrated Evaluation Framework, amecorg. com/amecframework/ (archived at https://perma.cc/XX6L-YDH7)

Barnes, B (2020, 25 September) Racial healing: Acknowledge history to move forward, *The Seattle Times*. Seattle, Washington

Braveman, P A (2022, February) Systemic and structural racism: Definitions, examples, health damages, and approaches to dismantling, HealthAffairs, healthaffairs.org/doi/10.1377/hlthaff.2021.01394 (archived at https://perma.cc/EYB9-ECG7)

Bugos, C (2019, 26 November) The myths of the Thanksgiving Story and the lasting damage they imbue, Smithsonian Magazine, smithsonianmag.com/history/thanksgiving-myth-and-what-we-should-be-teaching-kids-180973655/ (archived at https://perma.cc/CT78-LNDC)

CAUT (2021) Self-identification survey best practices, caut.ca/equity-toolkit/article/self-identification-survey-best-practices#:~:text=Guidance%20for%20Self%2DIdentification%20Questions,allow%20for%20more%20complex%20responses (archived at https://perma.cc/7G7X-XMHX)

CBC (2019, 12 November) Refugee group's poppy project lands amid Cherry bombshell, cbc.ca/news/canada/ottawa/poppy-newcomer-refugee-613-1.5356397 (archived at https://perma.cc/RD33-EZ8W)

Gee, G C, Ro, A, Shariff-Marco, S and Chae, D (2009) Racial discrimination and health among Asian Americans: Evidence, assessment, and directions for future research, *Epidemiologic Reviews*, 130–51

Nike, Inc. (2022, 1 October) Diversity, equity & inclusion, about.nike.com/en/impact/focus-areas/diversity-equity-inclusion (archived at https://perma.cc/8BCU-EKKP)

Peiser, J (2022, 14 June) Fans told Lizzo a word in her song was offensive. She changed the lyrics, *The Washington Post*, washingtonpost.com/nation/2022/06/14/lizzo-ableist-slur-lyric-apology/ (archived at https://perma.cc/PRS7-2CCT)

Silverman, D (2019) *This Land is Their Land*. New York, Bloomsbury

Strong, G (2019, 11 November) Don Cherry not apologizing for Coach's Corner poppy rant, CBC, cbc.ca/sports/hockey/nhl/don-cherry-fired-coaches-corner-1.5355764 (archived at https://perma.cc/58P3-ABSY)

United States Holocaust Memorial Museum (2022, 29 September) Explaining Holocaust denial, ushmm.org/antisemitism/holocaust-denial-and-distortion/explaining-holocaust-denial (archived at https://perma.cc/8Q3Q-HVQU)

Westfall, C (2022, 4 March) The importance of acknowledgement: How empathy drives leadership, Forbes, forbes.com/sites/chriswestfall/2022/03/04/the-importance-of-acknowledgment-how-empathy-drives-leadership/?sh=2bab14ca329b (archived at https://perma.cc/ER2D-AC82)

07

Change and the Diversity Continuum

This chapter explores the models and frameworks to help you with your DEI work. Models and frameworks, based on research, provide you with a way of assessing your present state and provide clarity around what positive steps look like in terms of setting expectations, benchmarking against best practices, progressive thinking and aspirational behaviour.

Models and frameworks, rooted in research and analysis make our jobs easier. They also make the work we do in internal communication, change management and DEI replicable. They help explain that there is a structure and process to the work we do that helps turn some of the anxiety into confidence, the newness into everyday realities, and help us understand that there is a process to the changes we're seeking.

In the last chapter we introduced you to the ALLMe 4A Model of acknowledgment, awareness, action and accountability. In this chapter, we will focus on various models that have inspired us and are applicable to the work we do in driving progress in DEI.

Remember that models and frameworks provide us with how-to approaches and help us set expectations realistically. They also lead us to ask questions in a discovery process to define who and where we are right now and help us map a way to get to where we want to be. Although the application of the models is the same, the answers to finding communication solutions to real business problems tend to be unique. That means that solutions are dependent on the organization, its culture, its leaders, resources, budget, technology and readiness for change.

The Change Cycle

One of the models central to change work is the Kübler-Ross Grief Cycle (Malik, 2022). It was created by Swiss-American psychiatrist Elisabeth

Kübler-Ross in her book *On Death and Dying* (Kübler-Ross, 1969) as she explained her research and findings on the five stages of grief and follows people's reaction to grief. According to Kübler-Ross, these five stages are:

- Shock and denial.
- Anger.
- Bargaining.
- Depression.
- Acceptance.

The Kübler-Ross Grief Cycle was adopted by change management as a model of how humans simply react to all change. We believe that the recent DEI work maps nicely to both change and grief as people adjust to a world that is changing too fast for some and too slow for others.

We've moved from distress during shock, denial and anger, to discomfort while we are bargaining and depressed and comfort, once we have accepted the new reality.

Inspired by the Kübler-Ross Grief Cycle, many organizations have developed their own adapted versions of how people manage change. For our

FIGURE 7.1 The Cycle for Change – Moving from shock to commitment

internal communication work, we created the following Cycle for Change that takes us full circle from shock to commitment. Many versions of the change curve or change cycle spend most of their time focused on negative reactions until there is an epiphany and people see the light. We believe the path to commitment takes longer and that work does not stop at acceptance but needs to continue to drive adoption and commitment from colleagues.

Let's take you through the cycle. Think about how we all react to change or loss that we don't control.

We always start with **shock**. Whether it's news of the death of a friend, your parents announcing their separation or divorce, learning that you have just lost a job or that your job is about to change, it is completely natural to be shocked or surprised. You often hear either your inner or outer voice say, 'This can't be real.' Shock is the OMG (oh my goodness) phase of change.

Shock quickly then turns to **denial**. This is when you question the news. You wonder if you heard or interpreted it correctly. Our voices say, 'I can't believe it', or 'They are just exaggerating.' You may believe that it won't really happen and think that they will change their minds tomorrow or will never go through with it. This may be the 'wait and see' or 'I'll believe it when it happens' phase.

Next, we move to **anger**. Once we understand that changes have happened that may impact us, it is natural to become angry or frustrated, especially when it feels scary or uncomfortable. Fear creates a fight or flight response and it's at this stage that we can feel defensive or disruptive. In our minds, when we're feeling powerless, we want to try everything we can to run away or defend ourselves. Our internal voices may be saying things like 'This has nothing to do with me', 'I feel attacked' or 'It's their fault, not mine.'

Anger often turns to **resistance**. This is when we realize that change is inevitable and happening and we have lost control. We may try really hard to hold on to what we feel we are losing. We put up our guards and try and protect what we have. We will also be looking for ways to stop change from happening. We may start feeling hopeless and helpless. The inner and outer voices are saying, 'We can stop this' or 'But we've always done things that way' or 'If it ain't broke, why fix it?'

During resistance, we may stop listening and stop working. We feel paralyzed and are afraid to do anything so it's best to simply stop and think. In DEI, it could also be the stage of self-reflection where we feel shame, guilt and remorse.

It's here that we see the first signs of **acceptance**. It could be a realization phase and is often the place where we have the potential to move from resistance to resilience. The voices here are saying, 'Am I part of the problem?', 'Do I need to change my thinking to move forward', 'Have I benefited from privilege?' Understanding that change is inevitable, we begin thinking of what changes in thinking and behaviour we need to personally make to adjust to our new normal. This may be a 'shrug the shoulder' and 'get on with it' phase. Our voices are saying, 'The train has left the station and I need to catch up', 'I have to either get on board or be left behind' or 'I'm willing to try something new'.

This is where we start focusing on **adoption**. At this stage, we're willing to learn new ways of thinking, doing and working. We need to understand and see what good looks like and our active role in change. Your voices are saying, 'What do I need to do or do differently' and 'How will I know that I'm getting it right?' When we are adopting, we need training, reinforcement and recognition. We also need to feel safe making mistakes as we learn.

Our final stage is **commitment**. After doing things differently, different eventually becomes acceptable. We learn to live with the change in our lives and we may learn it wasn't as scary as we thought it would be. We are comfortable in the new normal, we may believe in the new normal and we may actually be fans of the new normal. Our organizations are benefiting from the change and so are we. This is the 'What was I so afraid of?', 'I guess I was wrong', 'This isn't so bad after all' phase of change.

Reaction to change is HUMAN

The reason we talk about the Cycle for Change is twofold:

1 Reactions to change is human – The changes happening in DEI work are big changes. In some cases, we are changing processes, systems and biases that we all just accepted for years that we now are being ask to question. When practitioners put their change management hats on and expect these reactions and behaviors, they can be prepared to address them. If you are impacted positively or understand the reason behind change, you will tend to move faster through the Cycle for Change. If you feel you are impacted negatively by the change, you will resist more and it will simply take longer.

2 Internal communication plays an important role in driving conversations around change in order to help people move from one part of the cycle to the next. Without communication, employees and leaders may remain stuck earlier in the cycle and may never get to acceptance.

In the work we do with our clients, we've always talked about our role to help employees be **aware** of what is happening in an organization, **understand** why decisions were made, **do** the right thing and **believe** in the cause. We've also maintained that our communication role works hand in hand with the Cycle for Change. In fact, when done correctly, we use our knowledge of colleague sentiment to provide information that helps people along the journey from shock to commitment.

Although the following chart gives you an example of the channels and methods that can be used, they are intended to be suggestions to get you thinking about what will work for your organization.

Too often with change, leaders who have been planning change for months or years and have already gone through the cycle for change during their planning discussions forget that employees are hearing of plans often for the first time. Believing that one email sent at the beginning of a change announcement is enough to drive success is deeply flawed and often leads to the anger and resistance we continue to see in many organizations.

It's important to note that in our consulting work, we highly recommend that colleagues are involved and updated in the planning phase of any change project if possible. Although this is more difficult in projects that require confidentiality, we don't think this is the case for DEI strategies and plans. By involving colleagues in the creation of the plan, listening and addressing concerns, and providing updates on progress before changes are launched, you may get to acceptance, adoption and commitment sooner.

Questions for internal communication:

- When planning announcements of the DEI strategy or initiatives in the strategy do you think of where colleagues are in the change cycle?
- Do you involve colleagues in the planning and strategy and provide regular updates?
- Can you use the Cycle for Change to plan your communication activities?

The GDEIB model

The Global Diversity, Equity and Inclusion Benchmarks (GDEIB) is published by the Centre for Global Inclusion, which is a non-profit organization founded in 2017. Its mission is to 'serve as a resource for research and education for individuals and organizations in their quest to improve diversity, equity, and inclusion practices around the world' (Centre for Global Inclusion, 2022). The GDEIB is provided as a free resource for those who sign a user agreement.

TABLE 7.1 Communicating through the Cycle for Change

Change cycle	Communication direction	Channels and methods
Shock	Provide the facts • What is happening? • To whom and when?	• Launch announcement – prefer town hall/face-to-face followed up by an email announcement
Denial	Reinforce messaging • Provide background • Detailed timelines • Executive sponsor or c-suite led will make it more credible	• Provide managers/supervisors with facts sheets with Q&A to answer questions • Allow managers to share context on what this means for the department, team, colleagues
Anger	Explain why • Share the numbers and research • Share what change means professionally and personally • Share clear timelines to set expectation	• Share a case for change with further details • Research • Data • Information on competitive and social environment
Resistance	Be empathetic • Listen to concerns and address them • Provide examples and a path to success	• Listening exercises like focus groups and fireside chats • Change readiness assessments • Answer questions with facts
Acceptance	Provide direction • Tell them what to do • What has changed? • What is expected of them?	• Training • Presentations and regular updates on what's next • Use start/stop/continue – what does change, what stays the same, what do we stop doing?
Adoption	Recognize and reinforce • Recognize aligned behaviour • Reinforce direction • Show what good looks like	• Recognition programmes • Stories highlighting progress and people
Commitment	Share success • Updates on milestones achieved • Measure the results and share on a regular basis	• Measure results • Provide a report card or dashboard updated regularly • Showcase the impact of the change on the organization and its people

The first edition, named the GDIB, was published by the founders of the Centre, Julie O'Mara and Alan Richter, in 2006. They began with some research conducted by the Tennessee Valley Authority in the USA. O'Mara and Richter worked with 47 expert panellists (EPs) who represented different dimensions of diversity and were experts in many areas of diversity and inclusion around the globe. The intent was – and still is – to update the GDEIB every five years or as often as there are changes in the field now known primarily as DEI. The EPs served as more than just reviewers – they and the authors modelled inclusion as they worked together with the EPs to create the GDIB. The research involved several rounds of changes and refinement and they are proud to say that consensus was reached with this edition as well as with future editions.

The fourth and latest 2021 edition was the first one to adopt the new name GDEIB, as the field had evolved to include more focus on equity (the E is for equity) and social justice. The 2021 edition was also impacted by the changing way organizations are operating because of Covid-19, the global pandemic, the accelerated pace of change and increasing globalization. They also added a third author, Nene Molefi, a leading global HR and DEI consultant located in Johannesburg, South Africa. By this fourth edition there were 112 EPs to represent even more diversity, equity, and inclusion expertise around the world. In addition to the GDEIB itself, user tools (checklists, assessments, activities and handouts) and archived newsletters that include examples of how various organizations around the world have used the GDIB and the GDEIB to achieve the benchmarks are available. The GDEIB is available in English, Spanish, French and Portuguese. All the user tools are available in English, with several available in the other languages.

Although we will focus on highlights of the GDEIB model here, we strongly recommend that you pay a visit to its website (centreforglobalinclusion.org) to learn more about the Centre and the other things it does in addition to the GDEIB. As we go to press on this book, the Centre is planning several new GDEIB tools, products and services.

For our purposes, I want to point you to the model itself.

The following chart summarizes the key elements of the GDEIB DEI benchmarks.

There are four main groups and 15 categories that are important to create a world-class DEI initiative. You have the ability to rate your organization

TABLE 7.2 Summary of GDEIB DEI benchmarks

Area	Purpose	Elements	Description
Foundation	Drive the strategy	• Vision • Leadership • Structure	• A strong vision for DEI-aligned organizational goals • Leaders who are accountable for implementing the vision, setting goals, achieving results and being role models • Visible and dedicated support and structure with authority and budget
Internal	Attract and retain people	• Recruitment • Advancement • Compensation • Benefits and flexibility	• Recruitment done through a DEI lens • DEI integrated into professional development, performance management, advancement and retention • Job design evaluated for bias and compensation is equitable • Work-life integration, flexibility and equitable benefits
External	Listen to and serve society	• Social responsibility • Products and services • Marketing • Responsible sourcing	• Proactively work with community, partnerships and government • Embed DEI in product development to serve diverse customers • Integrate DEI into marketing and customer service • Source ethically and nurture underrepresented suppliers

(continued)

TABLE 7.2 (Continued)

Area	Purpose	Elements	Description
Bridging	Align and connect	• Assessment • Communications • Learning • Sustainability	• All assessments and research guide DEI decisions • Communication is clear, simple and a crucial force in achieving DEI goals • Educate to achieve DEI competence and confidence • Connect DEI and CSR efforts to increase effectiveness

FIGURE 7.2 The GDEIB Model establish the importance of foundations and bridging needed to impact internal and external activities (Centre for Global Inclusion, 2022).

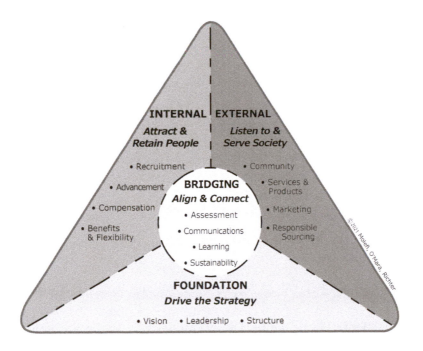

on each item in these 15 categories to assess the level of your organization by category. Levels are as follows:

- Level 1 is **Inactive**. This means no work has begun in DEI in this category.
- Level 2 is **Reactive**. This means you have a compliance-only mindset to meet legal or societal pressures.
- Level 3 is **Proactive**. This is when organizations start making plans and creating accountabilities.
- Level 4 is **Progressive**. Organizations are implementing DEI and seeing improved results and outcomes.
- Level 5 is **Best Practice**. These organizations demonstrate best practices and are leading the way.

Internal communication in GDEIB

You may wonder what GDEIB has to do with internal communication. We were pleased that communication is a key element included in bridging needed to align and connect. It sits appropriately in the centre of the model to connect foundation to internal, external and the other categories in the bridging group.

Even more interesting is that elements internal communication professionals need to be familiar with and have influence over are included in **every area and category** of the GDEIB when it comes to best practice.

Foundation

Foundation drives the strategy. It requires the organization and DEI to have a vision, for leaders to be visible and accountable and a structure that has authority and budget for success.

For the foundation group, organizations should think about:

What do we stand for? This includes the vision, mission, values, purpose and strategy.

Where are we going? This includes strategy and plans, short term and long term. What are the goals?

Who will lead? This is the leadership, responsibility and accountability of what will be measured and when. Importantly, it recommends that leaders are change agents and role models for DEI and, most importantly, are trusted.

How will we deliver DEI? Foundation, according to GDEIB, also states that the DEI structure and implementation be an important first step. How is DEI being resourced, where does DEI responsibility sit in the organization, what access does it have to leadership and what is the DEI plan?

The key to the foundation group is that we have to start with strategy and planning in order to set ourselves up for success and real progress.

Questions for internal communication:

- Have you articulated your organization's strategy, vision, mission, values or purpose? If yes, are there any natural linkages to the DEI mandate?
- Have you helped the DEI team clearly articulate the DEI vision?
- Are leaders at the c-suite actively involved and visible? What are they accountable for communicating in the plan?
- Who will lead and who will deliver communication? Do you have enough resources?

Internal

Internal focuses on processes to attract and retain people. It means recruitment is done through a DEI lens, DEI is integrated into the colleague life cycle including professional development, performance management and promotion, job design is evaluated for balance and there are equitable flexibility and benefits.

GDEIB states that the internal area is focused on attracting and retaining people. Internal communication professionals have an opportunity to ask questions and clearly articulate the following for colleagues:

Who do we recruit? Practices in how an organization attracts and hires colleagues and are these practices measurable, transparent and equitable?

How and who do we promote and retain? Practices in how an organization promotes and retains colleagues ensuring that there is equitable treatment of employees. For example, do diverse employees hold positions at all levels and functions and is turnover at an acceptable and even rate for everyone?

How do we design jobs to be equitable? Is DEI embedded in job design, classification and compensation? This category focuses on job design, classification and compensation. Is there pay equity and are jobs designed to be accessible to those who can deliver the work? They need to ensure performance, pay, bonuses and promotions are equitable and fair, and if they are not, state what the plan is for change.

What is it like to work here? The focus here is on work-life integration, flexibility and benefits. We can focus on practices in place that create a decent work environment, places value on colleagues' psychological safety, and show a respect for human rights.

Questions for internal communication:

- Is DEI embedded into policies and practices of recruitment, retention, promotion and culture?
- Are employees aware of these policies and practices, especially if they have recently changed or have been updated?
- Do you provide updates on progress?
- How do you embed these proof points into your storytelling?

Bridging

Bridging aligns and connects the foundation to internal and external areas. It includes assessments to guide DEI decisions, communication that is clear and simple, education to achieve DEI competence and a clear connection of DEI and sustainability efforts:

What do we measure and how often? We often say that what gets measured matters. GDEIB looks for assessments, measurement and research being conducted regularly on the overall organization and within departments. It also recommends that a reputation risk assessment on several DEI issues be conducted regularly.

Do we communicate clearly? The GDEIB sees internal and external communication as crucial to achieving DEI goals. The assessment asks that content is high quality, regular, easily located, accessible and translated.

Do we educate our people? Education is a key bridging point. In this section, GDEIB recommends that DEI learning is integrated and offered internally and externally and that education addresses racism, anti-racism, sexism, white supremacy, privilege, internalized oppression, classism/castism, homophobia, transphobia, religious bias, disabilities and mental health awareness. Education is not only for colleagues but also important for suppliers.

Do we connect DEI and sustainability? Here the GDEIB is looking for the organization to link DEI clearly to the organization's sustainability strategy based on ESG – environment, social and governance and the UN's Sustainable Development Goals. Specifically, DEI is seen as integral to the sustainability of the organization and the organization publicly reports on its performance and challenges.

Questions for internal communication:

- Do we measure and assess our organization on DEI and share updates?
- Do we have a communication plan that supports the DEI plan?
- Do we help employees understand why education is important and measure attendance and understanding?
- Do we create connections in our messages and stories that link DEI to business sustainability?

External

External is the final group in the GDEIB model that focuses on listening and serving society. It revolves around what the organization delivers to its customers, clients, communities and other stakeholders and has a direct relationship to business impact, reputation and results:

Are we proactive in the community? The organization lives its values and actively supports, invests in and advocates for DEI-related initiatives in the community, government and society at large. It takes bold, versus performative, stands on societal issues. The organization also addresses past behaviours and policies that have mistreated people. This is also an opportunity to encourage employee volunteerism in the community.

Does DEI impact how we deliver products and services? In this category, GDIEB is looking for innovation driven by diverse teams versus existing products simply retrofitted. Perhaps the organization uses technology or contributes to equity through its products and services?

Do we integrate DEI into marketing and customer service? GDEIB is looking for the contribution of diverse teams into marketing and customer service and ensuring that organizations are testing marketing strategies so that they are culturally relevant. There is an opportunity here to target markets and ensure that the organization understands the nuances and intersectionality of its base.

Do we responsibly and ethically source? At the high end, GDEIB standards are looking for sourcing from suppliers who have high standards for sustainability, ethical behaviour and fair trade. It also is looking for organizations to nurture underrepresented suppliers.

Questions for internal communication:

- Do we share community activities with employees and encourage them to get involved?

- Do we create connections between DEI and how we deliver products and services?
- Do we involve employees in innovation of projects and services?
- Do we ensure employees understand the why behind changes to marketing and choosing suppliers?

Final thoughts on the GDEIB model

There are two things we love about this model that are important to highlight:

1 While all 15 categories are important, communication is at the core. Communication, both internal and external, is an important part of bridging foundations to internal and external bottom-line standards. Without communication, it is hard to connect the dots and influence decision-making and behaviour. In fact, bridging connects the business and DEI foundation to recruitment, retention, recognition, reputation and results.

2 Each organization must determine how it prioritizes the importance of the benchmarks. You should start with the foundation group, and then most likely focus on either the internal group or external group or portions of both based on the organization culture and business priorities.

Let's think for a moment about the reality of how most organizations try and deliver DEI. Many begin with performative gestures like black boxes and rainbows on social media. They may then start expanding their list of cultural and commemorative days being celebrated to showcase inclusion.

When they are caught in a crisis or see others caught, they may add training – often as a reactive move. Some may see it as a check-box exercise, so once they've delivered unconscious-bias or anti-racism training, they believe they are done and no more action is required.

They may have suddenly become conscious of the fact that their advertising does not reflect their customers and communities, so you begin seeing racialized faces and various ability and genders showcased on their stock photos, promotions and ads. This can present a challenge when there are discrepancies between the images and who is actually running the organization which can lead to distrust.

Finally, the organization begins hiring to meet recruitment goals but fails to create an environment where new hires can thrive since there an unconscious expectation for diverse hires to fit into an established culture that does not value or understand the need for diversity.

Organizations approach DEI in many different ways. One of the reasons we like the GDEIB is that it approaches DEI from a systemic and change management approach. Benchmark is another term for standards that are written as desired outcomes or result statements, not as activities. One of the big challenges to effective DEI work is to focus on desired outcomes/ results rather than random activities that may not work as a system. The GDEIB organizes the benchmarks – a total of 275 of them – in a way to help organizations in various sectors, sizes and types around the world, to rate themselves on where they are today and what outcomes must be met to rate higher base on global best practices and the advice of 112 EPs.

We learned from the authors that the most constant feedback they receive is that the GDEIB is comprehensive and is a model that works.

Diversity, equity and cultural continuums

If you search for 'diversity continuum', you will be presented with multiple frameworks, many that have been inspired by the work of the Centre for Global Inclusion. We found some interesting ones worth exploring in this section on models and frameworks. As we discuss them, you may find the model that is perfect for you or find pieces that you can fit together to work for your organization and purpose.

We first heard of the Diversity Continuum from colleague Jefferson Darrell, founder and CEO of Breakfast Culture based in Toronto. Jefferson delivers DEI audits, strategies, training and presentations to help move the needle on DEI in organizations. He often shares the Equity Continuum© by Trevor Wilson first introduced in the book *Diversity at Work: The Business Case for Equity* (Wilson, 1996).

The Equity Continuum

Trevor Wilson's Equity Continuum has six stages and is numbered zero to five (Wilson, 1996).

DENIAL

In the denial stage, we don't think there is anything broken or believe there is a case for change. We would like to continue exactly how we are. A good example occurs in housing, when someone applies for rental who is perceived to be different from the dominant culture in the area. Unfortunately, it has been the case that Black people have been denied acceptance even if they

TABLE 7.3 Trevor Wilson's Equity Continuum

Level	Stage	Description
0	Denial	Organizations see no need for change.
1	Compliance	Legislated equity means you have to make changes in accordance to the law.
2	Moving beyond compliance	Organizations want to do better and start looking at corporate social responsibility (CSR) and see DEI as a way to be better corporate citizens (ESG).
3	The business case	Organizations see that diversity could be a business advantage.
4	Integrated	Organizations start to bring DEI practices into strategies and business operations. This is where inclusion happens, an active decision to include people, products, practices for competitive advantage.
5	Integrated and equitable organizations	Organizations believe in human equity. Their DEI practices are simply the way they do things.

SOURCE Wilson, 1996

have the references and good credit. They are denied because there is a bias from a safety and security perspective and people are comfortable keeping things exactly how they are.

COMPLIANCE

Compliance involves making changes once a law has changed. Going back to the rental housing example, if it is illegal, a landlord can no longer deny entry and if they do, can potentially be sued and mired in legal battles because of their decision. Because of this fear for their reputations, they create new direction and rules. It is forced compliance, not because it is the right thing to do, but because legal and public pressures force them to change.

THE BUSINESS CASE

The business case is when organizations realize that there is money to be made by diversifying. Leaders start looking at market expansion and targeting opportunities. They simply focus on the business case. When it comes to our rental example, landlords may start to realize that neighbourhoods are changing and that the up-and-comers who are young professionals are more diverse today. Having a reputation as a non-inclusive neighbourhood is now impacting rental pricing. They can choose to allow more diverse clientele in to positively impact the bottom line.

INTEGRATED

Once integrated, organizations may then realize that they need to look beyond their customers and change themselves to gain different perspectives. They can start by adding staff or hiring leaders. They also need to look at their own practices and any unconscious or conscious biases that exist in recruitment, retention and recognition. They may listen to the research that tells them clearly that a more diverse team leads to different and better outcomes. In our rental example, now we often see real estate agents, landlords and staff who are more representative of the renters they want to attract. They may promote their multiculturalism and accessibility as an advantage and seek to advertise in publications that target new markets.

INTEGRATED AND EQUITABLE

In the integrated and equitable stage, inclusive practices are simply 'the way we do things around here'. Organizations look at recruitment and hiring and encourage representation that reflects their communities and customers, they embrace differences and everyone feels that they belong. Neighbourhoods become vibrant and diverse and thrive because of it.

Let's take a look at Lululemon to illustrate the Equity Continuum.

CASE STUDY
Lululemon

In 2005, Lululemon's former CEO Chip Wilson told the *Calgary Herald* that his organization would lose money if he made garments larger than a size 12 and then made headlines in 2013 when he suggested that women's bodies were to blame when customers complained about tights that were see through and tearing (Fillippo, 2020). He was clearly not only in denial but truly believed that the company's reputation relied on it focusing on a specific body image. It put Lululemon's reputation at great risk and as a result, Wilson was forced to step down in December 2015 since 'some of his comments have started to take away from the brand' (CBC News, 2015).

It wasn't until the end of 2020, after a few quarters of negative and limited growth, that the company took what it calls its first step into inclusion with sizes expanding in a limited number of styles up to size 20. This opened up a market that Lululemon didn't know existed. It also started expanding its advertising and promotion of diverse customers and they are now reaping the benefits. Their annual revenue for 2022 grew year-over-year (YOY) by 42 per cent and is tracking at close to 28 per cent YOY as at the quarter ending 31 October 2022 (Macrotrends, 2022).

Lululemon is probably sitting between levels 3 and 4 – they have made the business case and are starting to integrate into business practices. Their employee Net Promoter Score (also known as eNPS) is strong on male and female employees but are quite neutral when it comes to diverse employees. They rate in the top 5 per cent for women and in the top 15 per cent for diversity, though they still have work to do (Comparably, 2022). The company ranks number one versus its competitors but still has an overall diversity score of 75/100 while its gender score sits at 85/100.

TABLE 7.4 The Cultural Competence Continuum

Cultural competence	Description
Cultural destructiveness	• Forced assimilation to dominant group only • Everyone should simply be the same • We stomp out differences
Cultural incapacity	• Racism, stereotypes, unfair practices • Differences are wrong • Some of us are superior to others
Cultural blindness	• Differences ignored • Treat everyone the same but meet only the needs of the dominant group • See the difference, act as if you don't • We ignore that the differences have an impact
Cultural pre-competence or sensitivity	• Explore culture issues • Ready to assess the needs of the organization and individuals • See differences, but respond inadequately • We want to be sensitive but don't know how
Cultural competence	• Recognize individual and cultural differences • Ready to seek advice from diverse groups and hire culturally unbiased staff • We see the difference, understand the difference • We interact with other cultural groups in ways that recognize and value their differences
Cultural proficiency	• Implement changes to improve services based on cultural needs • We see the differences and respond • We honour differences and view diversity as a benefit • We interact knowledgeably and respectfully among a variety of culture groups

SOURCE The Center for Culturally Proficient Educational Practice, 2022

The Cultural Competence Continuum

We love the work from Dr Andrew B Campbell on Culture Competence (Campbell, 2020). He uses the work of the Center for Culturally Proficient Education Practice which was built for the use of school districts (The Center for Culturally Proficient Educational Practice, 2022).

This continuum truly resonated with us when we saw it and we had share it with you. As women of colour who grew up in Canada and the UK – Priya, as an immigrant coming to a new country in the 1970s, and Advita, born in Manchester in the early 1980s – we could relate to the stages in this continuum. In fact, it was the conversations about our experiences that led to our A Leader Like Me business.

CULTURAL DESTRUCTIVENESS

We keep different people out of our countries, our neighbourhoods, our schools, our friend groups, our families, our teams and our businesses. We simply close the doors. We never question why, and how our interactions, behaviours and decisions may lead to the uniform outcome, it simply is the way it is, even when our countries, communities and customers are diverse.

CULTURAL INCAPACITY

In this stage, people are let in, but we simply act out our biases consciously. We're not afraid to treat people differently because we believe in our own superiority. We believe our characteristics of gender, colour, religion, ability, sexuality, body image, education and socio-economic status give us the right to treat other people unfairly. We make crude jokes and tell 'the others' that they are too sensitive. We feel we have the right to use derogatory terms. In this case, we open doors and actively mistreat. Both of us remember being called the P word in two different countries, in different decades, so that others could demean us and make us feel small.

CULTURAL BLINDNESS

In this stage, we simply ignore differences. We tell anyone different to aspire to think and behave like the dominant group. We say that the differences don't matter but the impacts are clear. We let you in the door and will accept you if you are like us. You dress like us, you think like us, you have the same education as us (or more in many cases), you talk like us – language, accent, terminology – and you disassociate yourself from anyone different. Both of us remember wanting so much to assimilate that we lost important elements of our culture, language and relationships in order to change to be included.

The one thing we didn't lose was our food but that was kept quietly to our homes since we were often insulted bringing anything stinky in our school lunches. We both remember friends telling us 'I don't see colour', and telling us that we fit right in. In fact, we worked hard to do so, disassociating ourselves from our culture. It's in this stage that you will also see code-switching. The 'underrepresented' person assimilates in professional/public spaces whilst showing up culturally in personal/private spaces, and often feels like a fraud in one or both.

CULTURAL SENSITIVITY

In this stage, there is a transformation that can lead to equity. We are willing to learn about races, religions, perspectives, experiences, challenges and cultures the are different than our own. We want to explore these differences but are afraid of getting it wrong. We'll ask more questions (sometimes seeming insensitive in the process), we'll read books, we'll take training, learn a new language, travel to different parts of the world and try new foods. We have made the conscious decision to expand our horizons and experiences, even though they may be new and uncomfortable at times. We try to be empathetic to the viewpoints and experiences of others. Priya's husband is Canadian, with British roots. When they first met, he was open to trying new foods and stepping out of his comfort zone. It wasn't always a pleasant experience, especially when he was used to meat and potatoes with limited flavour, but he kept at it, willing to at least try. We can also relate as we try to understand different perspectives of sexuality, gender, disability and race. The conversations may have been out of our comfort zone at first but as we began to understand and build relationships, we became more open and conscious about our own biases.

CULTURAL COMPETENCE

In this stage, we actually see differences and value them as opportunities for growth. We ask questions, build relationships, expand our circles, hire for diversity and seek to make our offerings more accessible. We're conscious of biases and the systems that create them. We include a variety of perspectives in our research. Our research highlights that PR and internal communication suffer from a lack of diversity, yet colleagues are diverse. The lower levels of our organizations, in communities where our clients are based are diverse, and their customers are diverse. Imagine that a uniform group of leaders and communication professionals are providing advice and counsel from a uniform point of view and experience. When we are culturally competent, we may decide to cover our shoulders and wear longer dresses that cover our knees when entering a Catholic church in Italy. We ensure there are vegetarian and vegan options for friends who are visiting our homes and ask about allergies. We add ramps to our office spaces to ensure accessibility and captions to our programming. We add alt text to our images. There is something powerful about walking into a space and seeing leaders like us on stage and in a room.

CULTURAL PROFICIENCY
In this stage, we see the differences and respond to them, honouring the differences, viewing diversity as a benefit, and interacting knowledgeably and respectively among a variety of groups. We simply plan for differences and see it as a competitive advantage. Keep in mind that as we become culturally proficient in more spaces, as the world expands and becomes more connected, new perspectives will also enter our spaces. At this stage we are probably also becoming aware of the accumulative effects of intersectionality. That's why we may never be completely culturally proficient but may hover between competence and proficiency as our understanding evolves.

The Organizational Diversity Climate Continuum

In 2004, Cheryle Hyde and Karen Hopkins conducted research on diversity climates of human services agencies based on diversity audits conducted with 161 non-profit and public human services agencies (Hyde and Hopkins, 2008). We wanted to highlight it to you because you may clearly see connections to your organization and the work you do.

The Organizational Diversity Climate Continuum speaks directly to discrepancies in representation both inside and outside organizations. They identified the following diversity climates.

TOKENISM
Tokenism happens when only a few staff or management members are from underrepresented groups. At this point, organizations' diversity related effort consists of trying to meet legal requirements or reflect mandated policies. They may also start making cosmetic changes to publicity efforts to add diverse images to marketing, recruitment and promotional materials.

SEGREGATED CULTURE GROUPS
This occurs when staff and clients are from different culture groups. In this case, the research stated that organizations would tend to take a nuts and bolts approach to diversity to close cultural gaps. This may include check-box

TABLE 7.5 The Organizational Diversity Climate Continuum

Diversity climate	Staff composition	Diversity related effort
Tokenism	Few staff or management from underrepresented groups	Cosmetic • Legal compliance and mandated policies • Publicity changes – make brochures and images look diverse
Segregated culture groups	Staff and clients from different culture groups	Nuts and bolts • Goals are diversity oriented • Programmes and services are culturally sensitive • Personnel procedures impacted
Staff pluralism	Diverse staff but uniform management (define – same characteristic)	Engagement/investment • Community outreach • Funding for training • Staff development or mentoring
Management pluralism	Management is diverse	Embedded • Mission/vision reflect commitment to diversity • Accountability mechanisms • Long-range planning and problem solving

SOURCE Hyde and Hopkins, 2008

hiring goals centred around diversity. There was also a focus on ensuring programmes and services were culturally sensitive and staff were trained on personnel procedures.

STAFF PLURALISM

In this example, organizations saw diverse staff that reflected clients and community but management was not as diverse. Organizations in this situation make diversity related investments to drive more diversity at the top including community outreach to find future management recruits that were more diverse. They also tended to fund more development, training and mentoring opportunities for staff to help move them up internally.

MANAGEMENT PLURALISM AND INTEGRATION

In this climate, management is diverse and there is representation and participation of all cultural groups throughout the organization. In these stages, diversity related effort is embedded. This means the mission and vision reflect a commitment to diversity, there are accountability mechanisms and long-term planning and problem-solving that drive sustainability.

This continuum focuses specifically on the discrepancies between clients, staff and management when it comes to diversity. In many cases it tells us what we already know – that we are way behind on truly embedded DEI in organizations.

We see constant examples where the staff and management make-up of organizations are at odds with the communities and customers being served. One thing to note is that that the research highlights a similar diversity-related effort when management is diverse and when there is integration and representation throughout the organization at all levels.

In fact, in a recent Forbes article on the benefits of a more diverse leadership team, Daniel Hooman from Agile Partners shared that 'democratizing companies and enriching mental models starts with leaders first, as the bottleneck is always at the top of the bottle'(Forbes, 2021). It actually is at odds with the bottom-to-top method that most organizations are trying to use. The truth is that it will take 10–20 years for changes to occur while we wait for more junior, front-end staff to make it to the upper ranks, and that depends on their retention as well.

We see this quite often in the PR agencies and communication teams we work with. They are quickly trying to encourage the hiring of junior resources to drive diversity in their teams versus hiring at leadership levels.

How to use models and continuums

- Find the continuum(s) that resonate(s) with you and your organization.
- Understand where you and your organization sit in the continuum(s).
- You may want to hire a third-party agency or consultant to conduct the research for an unbiased opinion.
- The language in the continuum(s) may help you articulate where your organization is today and where it needs to focus next. It also may help you make the case for additional and dedicated resources.
- Giving leaders a clear view of where they and the organization realistically sit and what great looks like may inspire them to change. Having research, data, numbers and facts also help you build a case for change.

KEY TAKEAWAYS

- Frameworks and models help us understand our present state and what next steps look like.

- DEI is a transformational change project. Use the change curve to understand human behaviour and the Grief Cycle.

- GDEIB resources are available for free to anyone wanting to progress in DEI. The website published by the Global Inclusion Council is steeped in solid research and provides tools and templates you can use to drive progress.

- A variety of continuums can inspire us to progress through change. We've shared a number of those that have resonated with us, but encourage you to do your research as well.

- Work is not a quick fix. It can take years to create your plan and then implement change. You must focus on progress and moving forward as a sign of success versus completion.

REFLECTIVE QUESTIONS

- Where do I sit personally on the change curve or continuums presented?

- Where is my leader or my organization right now on the change curve or continuums presented?

- Can I use one or more of these frameworks or models to articulate where we are today and the work that we need to do to be successful?

- Am I looking for a quick fix or am I willing to do the work?

- Are you the one who is resisting or in denial?

- Will we need to bring in external resources to help with the assessment of implementation of change?

Bibliography

Campbell, D A (2020, 11 June) Growing in cultural competence: A requirement for championing equity, diversity & inclusion, YouTube, youtube.com/watch?v=D5XhOwqb6sU (archived at https://perma.cc/LD7Z-BL75)

CBC News (2015, 2 February) Lululemon founder Chip Wilson steps down from board of directors, cbc.ca/news/canada/british-columbia/lululemon-founder-chip-wilson-steps-down-from-board-of-directors-1.2940109 (archived at https://perma.cc/C24L-YRHV)

Comparably (2022) Diversity at Lululemon, comparably.com/companies/lululemon-athletica/diversity (archived at https://perma.cc/7WCP-E2QR)

Dixon-Fyle, S, Dolan, K, Hunt, V and Prince, S (2020, 19 May) Diversity wins: How inclusion matters, Mckinsey, mckinsey.com/featured-insights/diversity-and-inclusion/diversity-wins-how-inclusion-matters (archived at https://perma.cc/V7S4-32WK)

Fillippo, E D (2020, 16 September) Lululemon's move towards 'size inclusion' draws mixed reviews online, Yahoo! Style, ca.style.yahoo.com/lululemon-size-expansion-draws-mixed-reviews-161921890.html (archived at https://perma.cc/K34S-6A3K)

Forbes (2021, 24 June) 14 important benefits of a more diverse leadership team, forbes.com/sites/forbescoachescouncil/2021/06/24/14-important-benefits-of-a-more-diverse-leadership-team (archived at https://perma.cc/TSV9-DGLF)

Hyde, C A and Hopkins, A (2008, 11 October) Diversity climates in human service agencies, *Journal of Ethnic & Cultural Diversity in Social Work*, 25–43

Kübler-Ross, E (1969) *On Death and Dying.* New York, Macmillan

Macrotrends (2022, 19 December) Lululemon Athletica Inc Revenue 2010–2022 | LULU, macrotrends.net/stocks/charts/LULU/lululemon-athletica-inc/revenue#:~:text=Lululemon%20Athletica%20Inc%20revenue%20for%20the%20twelve%20months%20ending%20October,a%2042.14%25%20increase%20from%202021 (archived at https://perma.cc/N39C-HQM5)

Malik, P (2022, 24 February) The Kübler-Ross Change Curve in the workplace (2022), Whatfix, whatfix.com/blog/kubler-ross-change-curve/ (archived at https://perma.cc/3RHQ-67TF)

The Center for Culturally Proficient Educational Practice (2022) The Continuum, ccpep.org/home/what-is-cultural-proficiency/the-continuum/ (archived at https://perma.cc/ZU3B-HCGR)

The Centre for Global Inclusion (2022) centreforglobalinclusion.org/ (archived at https://perma.cc/Y29C-FTK2)

Wilson, T (1996) *Diversity at Work: The business case for equity.* Toronto, John Wiley & Sons

08

Focusing on the conversation versus the campaign

From some of the case studies we share in this chapter, it's clear that performative action can severely affect the reputation of the organization and the leaders who work there. When leaders don't take the time to understand a subject or an issue beyond a few words in a statement, it demonstrates a lack of interest or intention to see change happen. We must hold ourselves and others accountable for their actions, and consequences must be in place to demonstrate that we care about DEI work in our workplace. If we don't care and we are only promoting issues at a superficial level, the leadership behaviours will impact performance which will affect the bottom line, causing many businesses to lose good talent and their reputation.

In this chapter, we will focus on:

- How to avoid performative and tokenistic actions within the organizations we support.
- The action we need to take as internal communication professionals.
- How to manage awareness days to avoid overwhelming colleagues.
- The steps we must take to be more DEI focused.

Throughout this book, we've spent some time explaining the importance of inclusion and how we can positively influence change. However, one of the many challenges facing businesses is understanding how to take meaningful and intentional action and make a difference to people in their workforce. Alongside this, we also need to consider how we're supporting our leaders to build a responsible business that can positively influence the environment around us. Over the years, we've witnessed organizations and businesses falling into the pitfall of performative work. If we don't take the time to understand the impact performative behaviour can have on individuals and seriously consider what changes we need to make to address the systemic inequalities facing groups and underrepresented communities, we're in danger of causing more harm than good.

Performative and tokenistic behaviour

Before we continue, we must understand what the terms performative and tokenistic mean in communications. On a personal level, performative allyship, sometimes referred to as performative activism or optical allyship, is when you demonstrate support for a cause or for a group who are marginalized or discriminated against, but your actions are not helpful or, worse, your behaviour actively harms the very people you're supporting. Tokenistic behaviour is when there are no meaningful actions behind the platitudes and no desire to break away from oppressive systems. It's driven by a tendency to show solidarity with the cause, often due to the 'bandwagon' effect, but this behaviour can frequently cause distress to those communities we're supposedly supporting. This behaviour can dim the light on the actual issue; instead, the spotlight is shone on the apparent activist rather than the communities they help. At an organizational level, performative measures can seriously impact mental wellbeing for many colleagues, as often they are lured into a false sense of security, but in reality the campaign is to avoid being called out.

Writing an article or filming a video of a leader sharing their thoughts on a specific cause is a crucial step, but it isn't meaningful if it doesn't follow suitable actions. Real hard work occurs when leaders step into uncomfortable situations, take action and fight against injustice by helping to change ineffective systems and policies that can disadvantage minority groups. Sometimes they will have to make difficult decisions to step away from opportunities if they go against what they've shared across their organization. For example, if gender equality is a focus area in your organization, but your leader agrees to speak at an event that doesn't have any women represented, do you think colleagues will believe any communications you send out about gender equality? If people can't see change, the words leaders share won't mean anything.

Even though performative action has existed for many decades, it has gained more traction after the posting of black squares, with the hashtag #BlackLivesMatter, in protest of racism and police brutality following the murders of George Floyd, Ahmaud Arbery and Breonna Taylor in the USA in 2020. However, the initial purpose and mission of the black squares were to show solidarity with Black artists and hold the music industry accountable for benefiting from Black people's work without giving them any credit or compensation. Two Black women, Jamila Thomas and Brianna Agyemang, spearheaded the mission, asking Instagram users to use the hashtag #TheShowMustBePaused on the first Tuesday in June 2020.

On 2 June, the black square was misused. Without any context or information on the origins of the black square, social media users began to post, believing that the movement was designed to show support during the Black Lives Matter protests. Though this act may have been well-intentioned, many activists spoke against the black squares. The squares were silencing the voices of people, and stories that could have made a difference were not seen, such as protests against police violence and supplies that folks needed to support the cause. Activists asked people to remove the squares and instead take meaningful action, such as helping to amplify voices and donating money and goods to organizations supporting the protests (Wellman, 2022).

Many brands also jumped on the bandwagon. They used the opportunity to talk about their plans to address equity, diversity and inclusion. They shared powerful statements, apologized for getting it wrong and explained how they would take action. But when some in-depth analysis took place, it was clear that some of these organizations didn't have meaningful plans to address the challenges facing Black people and people of colour (Fashion Round Table, 2020).

We know from the work we supported during the June 2020 protests that business leaders felt pressured to speak up and show solidarity but critically share what they were planning to do to help Black colleagues. Most of the statements were generic, leading to many leaders being questioned on how much they genuinely cared. It was clear by many of the statements that not much thought had gone into understanding what needed to be done to make a real difference. The lack of action and tokenistic gestures led to many colleagues speaking up about the injustice they frequently received as Black colleagues in their workplaces (Venn, 2020). In 2020, Reformation, a sustainable clothing brand based in the US, posted on their Instagram page about how they support Black Lives Matter and the work they planned to do to help recognize Black people for their contribution. However, an employee at Reformation, a brand that roots itself in social justice through sustainability, spoke out about how the company's CEO treated her as a Black employee. Elle Santiago, a former assistant manager at Reformation's flagship store in Los Angeles, posted on Instagram about her experiences, which led to the CEO of Reformation immediately stepping down from her post (Moore, 2020).

These performative actions don't just apply to racial inequalities. The term 'rainbow-washing' is often used to describe brands' marketing tactics for performative activism for a commercial gain for LGBTQ+ matters. Organizations and businesses have been held accountable for supporting Pride Awareness Month when it's clear they don't care about the injustice facing the LGBTQ+ community. An investigation by USA Today found that seven Fortune 10 companies earning the Human Rights Campaign Foundation's 'Best Places to Work' donated to politicians in 2020 who voted against LGBTQ+ interests (USA Today, 2022). In March 2022, on International Women's Day, a Twitter bot shared the gender pay gap of companies that posted statements on how much they care about gender equality. This led to many organizations retracting their statements and either republishing a carefully worded new press release or staying silent (i News, 2021).

These examples demonstrate that a public display of performative action is no longer accepted. Corporations that expect their colleagues to stay quiet on causes that impact them or their peers directly will struggle to manage the narrative internally. With social media, many colleagues now have a ready-made platform where others are willing to listen to what they have to say. Business leaders don't hold a monopoly on what is shared with their customers or the media anymore. Even if they don't want to expose themselves, colleagues can create covert profiles and share what's happening internally by leaking information to back up their claim. On Twitter, several 'hidden' profiles from colleagues inside organizations share stories of poor behaviour and performative action. These profiles attract thousands of followers, and many of their messages go viral.

One example is a tweeter called 'Minoritised NHS Manager™', who started their Twitter profile in May 2021 and has now attracted more than 5,500 followers. The stories they share are based on experiences of racism that they or their peers have experienced in various NHS trusts across the UK. As communication professionals, we may hold power over some of the channels. However, if we don't offer opportunities for two-way feedback for people to share their frustrations, we will lose control of the narrative and, worse, trust in what we do, leading to colleagues creating their external platforms.

What makes a good ally in communications?

An ally aligns with, promotes and supports groups and individuals different from them. Allies are intentional with their actions to help those from marginalized and underrepresented communities. Being an active ally means being prepared to stand up and support people who are unheard or ignored in rooms where they are often the minority. For example, do you speak up when the only woman in the room is asked to fetch the drinks or take notes in a meeting? If one of your friends shares a racist joke, do you explain that not only is it inappropriate but why it's inappropriate? As an active ally, it's not enough to say you're not sexist, racist, ableist, homophobic, etc. You have to be actively 'anti' and educate people why it's sexist, racist, ableist or homophobic. As an ally, you take time to learn and unlearn behaviours about the challenges and adversities facing underrepresented minorities without expecting any accolades for yourself. To do this effectively, we must be aware of the inequalities facing colleagues in our organizations.

Questions to consider:

- What makes your organization committed to the cause? How are they demonstrating passion and intention in making a difference?
- How is the cause aligned with the values and ethics of the organization?
- How are you supporting the underrepresented voices, and what platform are you giving them so that colleagues can use their voices effectively?
- Are behaviours reflecting the messages you're communicating? For example, are leaders always available for conversation? Do you provide opportunities for two-way feedback accessible to all?
- What meaningful changes have occurred since the last awareness month or day?

As Chapter 6 explains, our role is to encourage two-way communication, connect leaders with the workforce and ensure colleagues understand how they contribute to the organization's success. However, as well as understanding the areas you need to improve and challenges you need to address, you must recognize the good work also taking place. This will help raise morale, demonstrate progress and inspire people to continue to take action.

Taking action

Even though a part of speaking up and showing solidarity may be driven by morally wanting to do the right thing, there's also an economic benefit in cultivating an inclusive culture. Consumers who saw brands taking performative action have lobbied customers to stop shopping there. Investors are now requesting organizations to have a robust DEI strategy that addresses the adversity some underrepresented colleagues face in their organizations. Research and studies have also shown that people won't apply for opportunities if they don't believe the organization invests in diversity, equity and inclusion initiatives. With performative actions on display more publicly than ever, organizations must be more mindful of how they position themselves as an inclusive employer.

In 2022 Adidas came under fire for not addressing the antisemitic hate spoken by Ye, an American musician formerly known as Kanye West. Many organizations associated with Ye withdrew their contracts and immediately spoke up about Ye's behaviour. Adidas stayed notoriously quiet even though the hashtag #BoycottAdidas was trending on social media (Bloomberg UK, 2022). It wasn't until one of their employees, Sarah Camhi, their director of trade marketing, spoke up via LinkedIn (Camhi, 2022) to say she would no longer align with the brand that they took a stand. Camhi shared that even after global inclusion week, Adidas didn't communicate internally with their Jewish employees about the hate shared by Ye. This post received more than 22,000 likes and almost 1,000 shares. Adidas also saw their share price fall significantly during this time. A few hours later, Adidas announced they would withdraw their multi-million-pound brand partnership contract with Ye. Whether or not this action was in direct response to a colleague speaking up or the plan was already in place, this demonstrates that brands and organizations can't afford to stay quiet on essential matters.

We appreciate that no rash decisions can be made when millions of pounds are involved. However, when powerful brands like Adidas speak up frequently and with authority about inclusion and diversity but stay quiet for too long about issues impacting their bottom line, consumers and colleagues will lose trust in everything they do. In organizations, we often face situations where values are under the spotlight. It shouldn't matter how uncomfortable the topic is; every colleague must have the opportunity to talk openly about their feelings, and their concerns must be addressed. Not acknowledging the problem and not allowing employees to have a safe space to share their concerns will encourage them to speak up on platforms where they will be hard to ignore.

The role of internal communication to help prevent performative actions

Some organizational leaders often expect internal communicators to communicate messages about inclusive practices and take the lead on DEI communications. But many communicators we've spoken to are often overwhelmed with knowing where to start and how they can articulate the purpose without being performative.

There are several reasons for this:

- Leaders are often not clear on what the corporate DEI objectives are.
- There's no commitment to change or to take meaningful action from senior directors.
- Values and powerful statements don't match the behaviour, and there are no consequences for limited action.
- Inclusion isn't baked into the culture and is often sprinkled on top.
- There's no buy-in from decision-makers.
- There's a fear culture of getting things wrong, so people don't ask questions.
- The words don't match the behaviours, so there's inconsistency in the messages.
- It's left to one person to fix, typically a DEI director.

We know that many of you reading this book will be responsible for writing content on behalf of your CEO and senior directors. You will often have to make your leader sound knowledgeable and demonstrate that the organization genuinely cares about some of the causes impacting underrepresented people. However, when organizations communicate messages without alignment with the broader corporate objectives, it's evident that the purpose is more about 'looking good' rather than 'doing good'. At this point, the question to consider is whether your workplace has a DEI strategy or a communications strategy for DEI. If it's the latter, it's essential to consider whether or not the work you're doing will help make a difference to those fighting against oppressive systems or whether it's more about accolades and status symbols.

Approaching these challenges isn't the role of the communications professional alone, but we do need to ensure that we do our part to support colleagues. A crucial part of our role will be to ensure that leaders who want to express solidarity with fundamental causes do so with authenticity and intention. When allyship is authentic, there is an obvious attempt to transfer the benefits of privilege and give opportunities to others. Performative ally-ship can stifle progress and suppress genuine efforts to cultivate inclusive workplaces. Surface-level activism in the workplace and across various channels can disguise poor culture. Underrepresented colleagues can feel isolated and are often gaslit into believing their feelings are invalid because people will have fallen for the minimal effort towards various movements such as poster campaigns, 'heart-felt' videos from leaders and several train-ing sessions. But these activities are totally meaningless if behaviours, processes and systems don't change, and some colleagues continue to receive unfair treatment.

Before you start to plan your messages and campaigns about an aware-ness day or month, you need to consider five key questions:

1 How does this campaign align with the DEI strategy and corporate objectives?

2 What are the key goals of the campaign and messages (think SMART – specific, measurable, achievable, realistic and time-bound)? For example, to increase DEI training attendees by 20 per cent by the end of quarter four.

3 What do you want people to think, feel and do with the campaign you're communicating?

4 Do you have leadership buy-in from all leaders, and do they know what you need from them?

5 What personal accountability is expected from colleagues and leaders to implement change?

How to manage awareness days

Over recent years, we've seen an explosion of awareness days. According to the United Nations awareness month calendar, almost 200 days recognize various causes from across the globe. Knowing where to start and what to acknowledge, particularly a global business, can be overwhelming. Some businesses try to cover almost every awareness day or month, leaving the organization with information overload and insufficient time for colleagues to learn and observe. Other companies stay silent as they don't want to offend anyone or they don't deem it necessary. In wanting to ensure no one is excluded, we can often ignore feedback and expect our colleagues to consume information at a record pace which can cause disconnection and disengagement – and sometimes resentment.

Being aware of what work needs to take place to help cultivate an inclusive environment is critical. It's impossible to take meaningful action if you are not intentional with what you expect people to do with the messages you're sharing and what you hope to see change. A part of the work we do in organizations is to ensure that we communicate effectively with intention, purpose and expectations. Otherwise, we will just be seen as 'post boxes', and ultimately, we will not have the authority or the influence to question decisions.

If you don't have a DEI strategy that aligns with the corporate strategy, it will be challenging to identify key organizational priorities. You will end up sending out information that isn't accurate, highly likely to be meaningless and probably serves no purpose to colleagues. Changing mindsets and helping people understand why inclusivity is essential takes time, energy and focus. You can't create campaigns or messages without understanding the problem you're trying to solve, and you can't solve every problem simultaneously. A DEI strategy should help identify the gaps and what to do to ensure effective change. Using the DEI strategy, we should be able to create an inclusive communications strategy and a plan that considers the most effective way to ensure colleagues in the organization are included and belong. Awareness days and months must be more than just a poster or an email. Our role is to encourage people to make the required changes through impactful communication channels and processes.

CASE STUDY
Moving from performative to performance

In an organization that Advita supported, the communications director struggled to engage people with the various DEI campaigns they were running. When Advita reviewed the recent campaigns, a pattern emerged. Every campaign was almost a replica of the previous year. There were just words on a poster and no explanation for what call to action colleagues were expected to deliver. In focus groups, almost 80 per cent of colleagues felt that the campaigns the head office sent out were a carbon copy of all the other awareness days. Colleagues complained that they thought they were being told off or were not told what to do with the information. Underrepresented colleagues said that they felt unheard. They explained that the gestures felt tokenistic as nothing had changed for them, and everything felt fake.

When reviewing the materials for the campaigns, Advita asked the communications team to show data on the impact the campaigns were having across the organization. The team were unable to provide this information. Not understanding the key priorities led to many colleagues receiving, on average, four different awareness campaigns over a week. One colleague was so overwhelmed that they added a rule to their emails that directed any email that contained the word 'diversity', 'inclusion' and 'equity' into a separate folder in their inbox. The organization was in turmoil, and colleagues were highly disengaged with DEI initiatives, causing team friction. It was clear from the observations that the organization needed to focus their energy on understanding the purpose of what they were trying to achieve.

Working with the team, Advita created an inclusive communication plan which focused on three critical areas based on the data gathered from employee engagement surveys and HR data: recruitment, retention and sickness. The organization worked on producing some SMART objectives. They started with their 'big' why and shared outcomes with their colleagues. They were also clear on what colleagues could expect to see from leadership in terms of behaviours. They practised what they preached and reviewed their quarterly objectives, working with agility and intention. They could get ahead of the curve and pre-empt any challenges by listening, tracking and asking curious questions.

After reviewing their inclusion gaps, the organization focused on four key awareness days/months a year: International Women's Day, Pride Awareness Month, Black History Month and International Day of People with Disabilities. Advita used the ADKAR (awareness, desire, knowledge, ability and reinforcement) change framework developed by Jeff Hiatt, the founder of Prosci (Prosci, 2021), to help them create a plan that would motivate change and understanding. They clarified that colleagues can still share their stories about important days and months with them through the colleague's social network. People were encouraged to share their personal stories and why that specific cause or community mattered to them. Every religious holiday was recognized via the colleague calendar, and these dates went into every senior leader's calendar so they could celebrate these momentous occasions with their team.

The five-step process to understand DEI focus

The previous case study didn't happen overnight. It was a six-month process involving plenty of uncomfortable conversations and addressing poor behaviours that had been ignored for many years. When we work with organizations, the lack of time is something that leaders raise frequently. It's often driven by some target they must achieve or a negative story in the media that they need to manage. When we encourage leaders to slow down and think about the impact they'd like to have, it can sometimes cause distress and panic. But even though it may feel painful in the short term, thinking things through with patience and intention can pay off in abundance in the long term. We use a five-step framework to help leaders and communicators identify their gaps and to help them avoid performative actions.

Step one: What is the data telling you?

Understanding data is a non-negotiable first step. What is the organizational data and information telling you? And we don't only mean things like Net Promoter Scores (NPS) or engagement surveys, but also exit interviews, retention numbers, sick days, mental health days, promotional opportunities, what articles people are reading, the themes on social networks, etc. Do fewer women receive promotions? Do you accept applications from a broad range of candidates? Is there a pattern on sick days and the type of sickness people are off with? In one organization we supported, people from different religious backgrounds took more sick days during their religious days because the organization didn't communicate their flexible holiday guidelines effectively. The flexible working policy was a global initiative, but people assumed all colleagues would read the staff handbook. The communications team worked closely with HR to create a plan to ensure that colleagues understood their holiday entitlement. The following year they saw a decrease in sickness and a performance improvement.

Step two: Identify your knowledge gaps

You can't be an ally if you don't know your knowledge gaps and what things you need to unlearn and learn before addressing the inequalities facing certain groups. You need to be honest about the contributions you may have made to some of the performative decisions in your organization – did you avoid captioning a video because you were short of time? Did you make excuses for not challenging a leader on an inappropriate blog because you didn't want to 'ruffle feathers'? Understand what the key DEI goals are for the organization and what will be needed from the communications team to help cultivate an inclusive culture. To do this, you may need to understand the experiences of certain groups in your organization. Delve deeper into the employee experience process and what is missing for specific groups. You may not be directly responsible for changing these policies, but you can certainly influence change through education and knowledge building; if we want to make a difference in the world of work, we must sometimes come to terms with some uncomfortable truths. Once you're open to understanding and learning, your confidence in this area of work will allow you to develop impactful communication plans to help you make a difference.

Step three: Build a case for change

If the organization is serious about making a real impact, they need to invest in appropriate resources and give you adequate budgets to manage DEI communications effectively. Using the information you've gathered from step one and the work you've done to educate yourself on the inequalities facing certain groups, you can confidently build a robust case study for additional support. This could include conducting an inclusive communications audit to identify your channels gap, bringing in creative experts who understand the inclusive cultural practice on board or recruiting a dedicated DEI communicator.

Step four: Build relationships with key internal influencers

We discussed in Chapter 3 the lack of diversity in PR and communications. This means it's unlikely your communications team will be diverse regarding age, gender, disability, race, religion and sexuality. To address this imbalance, we highly recommend that you build a team of influencers and supporters who you can use as a sense check. We wrote about the impact of influencers in Chapter 5 and the benefits they can bring to the team. They will also be able to tell you what is happening across the organization and keep you informed of any updates.

Step five: Stay consistent

As we mentioned in an earlier chapter, programmes and initiatives fail because we don't stay consistent. Not being consistent and letting people down will deplete trust. If you've promised a weekly news update with the latest DEI news, ensure that you deliver this. If the data shows that it's not working, then be open about why you're changing the channel and ask your workforce how they would prefer to receive the information. If behaviours are not changing, remember the ALLMe 4A framework: acknowledgement, awareness, action and accountability, which we shared in Chapter 6.

Do diversity targets work?

Arthur Chan, VP of Diversity, Equity and Inclusion at Planned Parenthood in San Francisco, once said, 'Diversity is fact and inclusion is act', a statement that we stand by (Chan, 2021). There have been continuous debates on whether having diversity targets is performative. The UK and USA Equality Acts prohibit the use of quotas, but targets remain legal as long as they are not used to justify recruitment or progression of less suitable/qualified candidates because of their protected characteristics.

We firmly believe that measuring progress is complex if targets don't exist. If targets are arbitrary, then colleagues will disengage, and organizations will struggle to retain talent because no one wants to be seen as a 'diversity hire'. But we encourage the leaders we work with to proceed with caution as targets can be a check-box or tokenistic exercise if not executed appropriately. Targets can also be linked to terms like positive discrimination. Some people will confuse the term positive discrimination, which is unlawful (unless strict occupational requirement applies, like a women's refuge requiring female-only staff members or supporting a candidate who has a disability), with the term **positive or affirmative action**. Positive discrimination is when the organization appoints someone who is underrepresented because they want to achieve their target, but that candidate doesn't possess the skills needed to do the role.

Positive or affirmative action is when you actively encourage the increase of more qualified and skilled applicants from diverse backgrounds to apply for opportunities. To support applicants, organizations will take steps to remove barriers or obstacles that may stop people from underrepresented groups from applying for opportunities (we discuss inclusive language in Chapter 10). Organizations are permitted to take steps to help candidates in circumstances where they are disadvantaged because of their protected characteristics or have specific needs connected to a protected characteristic. For example, suppose your workplace lacks women in senior leadership roles. In that case, you may use a broad range of media for advertising for the position and ensuring that the language used in the job advert is inclusive and doesn't use terminology that might deter women from applying. You could also actively promote policies such as flexible working to attract more candidates from diverse backgrounds.

However, it's important to note that when some organizations hire underrepresented people, they rarely think about the support needed for that individual who is often the only minority voice in the room. People often blame the inadequacies of their colleagues rather than considering the lack of support from their leader or team. In situations like this, communication is often poor, and people end up excluding that individual from conversations, meetings and projects as it's likely that the leader probably doesn't have the appropriate skills to manage the discussions. When this happens, other peers unfairly tag them as the 'diversity hire', which can knock confidence and cause friction in the organization. If leaders cannot communicate effectively and provide safe spaces for people to speak up, then it's highly likely that those who often feel excluded will not be able to succeed. As communication professionals, we should be able to support our leaders by developing feedback channels, for example, frequent pulse checks and focus group conversations. If we have these standard mechanisms in place, we should be able to capture feedback early so we can address issues quickly. It's also possible that these colleagues will often face micro or macro aggressions from others. Reviewing the information from the focus groups and pulse checks will allow you to step back from the situation and provide accurate recommendations against the information you've gathered which will help remove bias and assumptions.

Why active listening is powerful against performative action

Internal communicators work closely with various teams and leaders. In Chapter 5, we shared that listening was one of the core behaviours internal communication professionals must possess. When you start moving towards being an inclusive internal communication professional, you will sometimes hear things that may shock you. You'll listen to stories and examples from others which you may struggle to comprehend, which can lead to challenging conversations with leaders. They may say things like:

'I don't believe that could have happened.'

'They are being a bit sensitive.'

'I think they are making that up.'

'Of course, they'll say that they are underperforming.'

'No one has ever said that before.'

Active listening plays a significant role in cultivating inclusion in an organization's culture. Listening will also help address performative and tokenistic gestures as you'll be able to hear directly from your colleagues on what's working and what needs more work. A report by Howard Krais, Mike Pounsford and Dr Kevin Ruck in Spring 2021 (Krais et al, 2021) found that organizations that listen to their colleagues can feel fairer and help leaders connect with their teams better. Listening can also help bypass mistakes and poor judgments of errors, allowing leaders to stay ahead of the curve. However, various systems need to be in place to help colleagues be heard, from surveys and one-to-one conversations to focus groups and listening hubs. In the listening report, Krais et al share 14 different listening methods in order of preference:

1 Big engineered survey
2 General pulse
3 Specific pulse
4 Leaders listen online
5 Internal digital platforms
6 Leaders listen face-to-face
7 Face-to-face manager listening sessions
8 Monitor digital discussions
9 Face-to-face focus groups
10 Interviews with employees
11 Employee resource groups
12 Online manager listening sessions
13 Staff suggestions scheme
14 Online focus groups

Surveys took the number one spot, but leadership followed closely regarding how colleagues are often heard in organizations. The report also established that 'face-to-face' interaction (virtual or physical) is critically important to colleagues. If these face-to-face opportunities are not available, building trust and connection with teams will be challenging. We also mentioned briefly in Chapter 5 about acknowledging and being aware of colleagues who are neurodivergent. It's incredibly important to be mindful of the different channels you are using to gather information and feedback. Some of the options listed above won't be appropriate for some groups and it's important you ask people their preferred method. Some people will feel uncomfortable speaking in large groups and may prefer a one-to-one conversation or a survey. Others may prefer a survey and a focus group. Not giving people choices can stifle inclusion and you will be in danger of listening to people who may not be as representative as you believe. Remember, giving people choice on how they want to share feedback will not only help people who are neurodivergent but also other groups, such as people who may not speak the native language.

Listening also ensures that we track and measure impact, which is vital in these listening sessions. To do this effectively, we recommend asking standardized questions about engagement, inclusion and belonging. These questions must be broken down by demographic so that you can identify where the genuine gaps are. If you don't break it down by demographic, results may be inaccurate, and it'll be tough to address what actions are needed to support various underrepresented groups. Keep questions brief and be aware of how many questions you ask.

Below are examples of questions you might ask in all listening activities. These questions are not exhaustive, and some may not work for your organization or the time you have available. Still, it's advised that two or three of these questions are asked consistently to establish rapport and understanding:

- Do you feel appreciated for the work you do?
- Do you feel heard if you have an idea or a thought?
- Do you feel you can progress in this organization?
- Are there any projects you'd like to work on?
- Are there any parts of the culture you'd like to change?
- What do you need from your manager to help you thrive?
- If you were leading the organization, what would you change?
- Do you have the opportunity to learn?
- Do you have everything you need regarding resources to help you in your role?
- Do you have any blockers? If so, what can we do to help you?

Once you have logged the answers to these questions, you will see where the gaps are and what the organization needs to do to address key issues. To ensure your leaders are aware, it's recommended that you share responses (anonymized) in a dedicated report that you can provide senior leaders quarterly. This report should be used as a milestone checker to track progress throughout the year.

Some of your leaders may get defensive when feedback about their team or behaviour is scrutinized. Therefore it's important to encourage leaders to actively listen to what colleagues are sharing and not to refute but to learn, digest and understand what practical actions need to happen. To get leaders to trust what you're saying, you must listen actively to what they are sharing with you. When you hear stories of injustice, it's difficult to remain composed but remember to present the facts and share the consequences of what may happen if nothing changes.

We understand that you are not responsible for every decision your organization makes about DEI activities or how certain months or days are recognized. However, we are accountable for being trusted advisors to our leaders and ensuring we're guiding them the best we can, especially if we want to avoid crises and manage reputations. As we shared in Chapter 4, this work takes time, energy and tenacity. We need to challenge with confidence and share consequences. It's not easy, and mistakes will be made – that's okay as long as you continue to progress.

KEY TAKEAWAYS

- Performative and tokenistic gestures can be harmful and can cause disengagement in organizations.

- Internal communications have the privilege of supporting leaders to ensure they are being authentic in their messaging and are making an actual difference in the workplace.

- As communication professionals, you need to identify where your knowledge gaps are before you can become an active ally for the communities that you serve.

- To avoid making mistakes or poor judgments when it comes to publicizing awareness days and months, you need to listen actively to your colleagues.

- The role of an internal communicator is to ensure you are aligning your organizational messages to the values and ethics of the organization. If not, you should call out poor behaviours and address misalignment against DEI objectives.

REFLECTIVE QUESTIONS

- How do your awareness days and months impact workplace culture – have you seen a significant improvement since the previous year?
- Do you give colleagues options on how they would like to feed back?
- Have you ever conducted an in-depth analysis of your communication channels to see the inclusion gaps in your messaging?

Bibliography

Bloomberg UK (2022, 25 October) Adidas cuts ties with Ye, absorbing €250 million profit hit, bloomberg.com/news/articles/2022-10-25/adidas-is-said-to-end-kanye-west-partnership-after-controversies?leadSource=uverify%20wall (archived at https://perma.cc/Y6WU-QVCJ)

Camhi, S (2022) LinkedIn, linkedin.com/feed/update/urn:li:activity: 6990451298189918209/ (archived at https://perma.cc/VT7S-C3QM)

Chan, A (2021) LinkedIn, linkedin.com/posts/arthurpchan_diversity-is-a-fact-equity-is-a-choice-activity-6709122719918755840-WU76/ (archived at https://perma.cc/CNA3-E23A)

Fashion Round Table (2020, 22 December) How brands lie to us through performative activism, fashionroundtable.co.uk/news/2020/12/22/how-brands-lie-to-us-fashion-brands-and-performative-activism (archived at https://perma.cc/F4NM-DTQ2)

i News (2021) Gender pay gap bot Twitter account highlights salary divide of firms that post about International Women's Day, inews.co.uk/news/gender-pay-gap-bot-twitter-account-international-womens-day-2022-companies-1504409 (archived at https://perma.cc/2G9P-KCG4)

Krais, H, Ruck, K D and Pounsford, M (2021) *Who's Listening Report Three.* London, PR Academy

Moore, B (2020, 12 June) Reformation CEO Yael Aflalo steps down after allegations of racism, Women's Wear Daily, wwd.com/business-news/business-features/reformation-ceo-yael-aflalo-resigns-amidst-racism-charges-1203653021/ (archived at https://perma.cc/3QUQ-BEUY)

Prosci (2021) The Prosci ADKAR Model, prosci.com/methodology/adkar#:~:text=The%20Prosci%20ADKAR%C2%AE%20Model%20is%20one%20of%20the%20two,%2C%20Knowledge%2C%20Ability%20and%20Reinforcement (archived at https://perma.cc/LEZ2-RUEY)

USA Today (2022) Hiding behind rainbow flags: These companies' political donations don't match their support of LGBTQ issues, eu.usatoday.com/story/money/2022/06/07/brands-rainbow-donations-politicians/9643841002/ (archived at https://perma.cc/V9VV-TH3R)

Venn, L (2020) These brands are getting called out for their messages about Black Lives Matter, The Tab, thetab.com/uk/2020/06/04/these-brands-are-getting-called-out-for-their-messages-about-black-lives-matter-159681 (archived at https://perma.cc/4YQK-RE2M)

Wellman, L M (2022) Black squares for Black lives? Performative allyship as credibility maintenance for social media influencers on Instagram, *Sage Journals*, 8(1)

09

The intersectional approach
for communicators

Many organizations fail to incorporate inclusion and belonging because they don't acknowledge how someone's age, class, disability, ethnicity, gender, sexuality and other characteristics interconnect to form a unique lived experience. For inclusion to be taken more seriously and embedded into the organization's culture, leaders must consider that many of their colleagues have multiple layers to their identity. Many communicators don't consider these multiple layers when communicating with groups of people and often put single labels on different characteristics based on the assumptions and stereotypes that they have formed through their own lived experiences.

In this chapter, we will:

- Discuss the importance of intersectionality.
- Discover why employee resource groups are not as effective as we think.
- Consider how communicators can influence change through effective communication.
- Explain why personalization is important to cultivate inclusion.

Before we delve into how we can influence change in our organizations by considering intersectionality, it's essential that you understand the term and the history of why it's in existence today.

Defining intersectionality

Intersectionality was first coined in 1989 by Professor Kimberlé Williams Crenshaw, a US critical race legal scholar and civil rights activist who founded the African American Policy Forum at Columbia University. Crenshaw created the term in her research paper to critique antidiscrimination theory and raise awareness of how it fails Black women by denying that they've faced discrimination due to their overlapping identities. The term reflects the macro-level forms of oppression and privilege associated with characteristics such as racism, sexism, and ableism. Crenshaw describes how ethnicity, gender, class, background and other characteristics 'intersect' and overlap. She says: 'Intersectionality is a metaphor for understanding the ways that multiple forms of inequality or disadvantage sometimes compound themselves and create obstacles that often are not understood among conventional ways of thinking' (Crenshaw, 1989).

The paper rejects the notion that human beings belong to only one identity category and that one social type doesn't define a person. She discusses that Black women are often excluded from race or sex discrimination cases because the focus is usually on the most privileged in those groups, e.g. men of colour or white women. This exclusion means that people with multiple identities, such as women of colour, are often left without social, organizational and legal protection. They may struggle to receive the support they need to recognize that they are struggling with racism and sexism because, more often than not, we view discrimination through a singular lens. Crenshaw was encouraged to develop intersectional theory due to the legal case of DeGaffernreid v General Motors. Five Black women sued General Motors for discrimination following a collective redundancy. They lost the case because General Motors could prove they hired both Black people and women. But what the law didn't recognize was discrimination against people who were both Black and women – a law designed and established to protect communities and subordinate groups like theirs. Even in organizations today, many dominant cultures benefit from intersectional discrimination. Their focus is often on 'single axis' models of discrimination, so the lived experiences of those with multiple identities are not considered. This is partly because political liberation has focused on single identities, such as feminism and anti-racist movements, allowing the adoption of homogeneous categories that exclude minority intersectional experiences (Smith, 2016).

Professor Crenshaw's work was amplified further in 2015 when the *Oxford Dictionary* included the term intersectionality. From that point, it started to transform the field of social sciences and feminist studies, which previously only focused predominantly on gender. Her research and studies on this topic have helped define and shape how we understand discrimination, privilege and bias in multiple characteristics, specifically for women of colour. However, it's important to note that Crenshaw wasn't the first to question the inadequate treatment of women with multiple characteristics. In 1977, the Combahee River Collective, a Black lesbian feminist organization, wrote a statement about the discrimination they faced due to racial, sexual and class oppression. The powerful message shared their experiences on the systemic oppression they faced, not only as women but also as Black gay women (Combahee River Collective, 1977).

We often celebrate and raise awareness of feminist movements, but gender equality is known to focus predominately on the experiences of middle-class white women and the discrepancies they faced against white middle-class men. During the first wave of the feminist movement in the 19th century, British feminists Millicent Fawcett and Mary Carpenter embraced the idea that Indian women should be enslaved and need to be taught how to be civilized. The American suffragettes often formed an alliance with white supremacists to advance their cause for women's rights. Susan B Anthony, a suffragette, often celebrated for her part in women's rights, once stated: 'I will cut off this right arm of mine before I will ever work or demand the ballot for the Negro and not the woman' (Wesleyan University, 1996)

Even recently, there has been an outcry on how the media report missing women, calling it 'Missing White Woman Syndrome'. The term was coined by journalist Gwen Ifill, who said this amplifies stories of missing white women while often ignoring marginalized women of colour (Eversley, 2021). According to the Black and Missing in America organization, nearly 40 per cent of missing people in the USA are people of colour, even though African Americans make up only 13 per cent of the population (Black and Missing, 2022). According to a research report by the American Society of News Editors, newsroom editors tend to be white and male, so bias and discrimination can play a big part in how we share these stories (American Society of News Editors, 2018).

You may wonder how this is relevant to your work as a communicator. We're often the storytellers in the organizations we support. We communicate key messages, raise awareness, connect leaders with the workforce and develop campaigns to help demonstrate how much the organization cares about inclusion and belonging. But as demonstrated by the American Society of News Editors research and the data we shared in Chapter 1, we rarely work in diverse teams. This limited diversity means we are unlikely to consider the different intersectional challenges facing the workforce regarding the communication we share. For example, we may curate stories for International Women's Day, but are we considering a wide range of women from different diverse backgrounds, not only in terms of race but sexuality, disability, age, class and religion? If you look back at your last International Women's Day video, blog or stories, was it a fair reflection of the colleague population and the customers/clients you serve? Did the awareness day change anything in the organization for underrepresented women? As discussed in our chapter about performative measures, it's important to reflect on the purpose behind these campaigns and why they are being promoted.

The challenge with employee resource groups

As communication professionals, we are encouraged to lean on our employee resource groups (ERGs) to help craft inclusive messages that engage various communities. We also have the responsibility to help promote the work the group does to our colleague population through our communication channels. In some cases, you may even receive an invite to be part of some ERGs to help them engage better with stakeholders.

Almost 90 per cent of Fortune 500 companies have employee resource groups (Diversity Inc, 2022). Many of these organizations believe their ERGs will help solve some of their diversity, equity and inclusion challenges, but this isn't always true. ERGs have been part of corporate life since the mid-1970s. They are sometimes referred to as affinity groups or staff networks, and they help people come together around a shared identity. These networks allow colleagues to connect, collaborate and converse with each other in a safe environment. The ERGs can be instrumental in helping to shine a light on specific issues that can impact minority colleagues. The people who belong to these groups want to create a positive workplace culture and feel like they are contributing to the DEI efforts within the organization.

Even though, in our experience, most of these groups are reasonably well managed, they are run on the goodwill of underrepresented minorities who want to help cultivate change in their organization. Leaders often make the mistake of thinking that because they've created these groups, all their DEI issues will be fixed. However, because volunteers often lead these groups, often from the mid-management level, they rarely have the authority, the budget or the resources to create the impact they need. In some instances, these groups don't have the buy-in from senior leadership and can lack direction. For many volunteers, this is in addition to their day job, and consideration of time reimbursement is rarely given. The biggest concern we often witness is the lack of support given to the leaders of these groups. Many are struggling with burnout, guilt and confidence issues. They are battling not only for themselves but the members of their group. Many are mentors and coaches taking away the responsibility from line managers, who are often not equipped to manage the complexities that intersectionality can bring to organizations. However, because of the pressures on some ERG leaders to 'fix' the issues, they can sometimes become protective of their members and put incredible pressure on themselves leading to mental health and wellbeing issues. When this happens, the ERGs can cause silos and divisions, and they can sometimes end up hindering cultural progression. Some of these groups also rarely consider intersectionality and ultimately label people with a specific characteristic rather than consider the multi-level identities each person brings. This behaviour can lead to poor practice and sometimes cause 'Oppression Olympics', where various groups compete against each other to battle for who has the most oppression and who deserves more support over another group.

In our case, we are both women and women of colour. When we worked within organizations, we didn't wholly fit into the ERG descriptors, so we struggled to belong anywhere specifically. We were often torn on which part of our identity we should show up as and which part of our identity we should favour over the other. We both wanted to contribute to the conversation in the women's network and support the work in the Black, Asian and Ethnic Minority network. However, in each group, the discussions were usually centred around the most dominant voice in the room, which can happen when there's no set purpose, sponsor or objectives.

CASE STUDY
Are ERGs helpful?

Advita supported one organization a couple of years ago with their inclusive communication strategy. A part of this work involved speaking with the ERG leads. There were several ERGs in this organization, but each worked independently and in a silo. In one of the group-wide inclusion meetings, Advita attended with the DEI director, each group leader would shout over each other, highlighting frequent poor behaviour. As Advita observed the conversations, she noticed that there was no common purpose for the groups. There was a small budget that everyone fought over, and no set agenda in any of the meetings. The ERG leaders fiercely protected their group and often refused to allow entry if they didn't fit the criteria they had self-imposed. Because of this exclusion, other colleagues set up their groups, which led to several ERGs being set up without any process or permission. The leadership team were fearful of saying no in case they were accused of not being supportive. The communications team struggled to prioritize work and was often accused of discrimination because some groups felt others were getting more attention. This led to chaos and uncertainty, which was the reason for the behaviour that Advita witnessed. To solve the issues, Advita advised the leadership team to have clear outcomes for the DEI strategy, allocate fair budgets and resources, provide a process so that people can set up groups fairly and provide appropriate support to leaders in facilitating meetings. Advita also worked with the communications team to work on their communications plan, which they could present to the ERG leads so that they could forward plan events, awareness campaigns and the support this would require. Everyone knew what to expect.

The most successful ERGs are those where volunteers understand their role and are rewarded fairly for their time. It's where ERG leads are recognized as leaders and are part of the talent pipeline. They are often invited to have conversations with CEOs and senior directors. The groups are often open to anyone who wants to support, including allies; they have an executive sponsor and resources allocated to run the groups effectively. They are all working towards the same goal and are helping to drive change for the better.

Different dimensions of diversity

Now you're aware of intersectionality origins and the impact it can have in the workplace, it's essential to understand how the primary dimensions of diversity can interact with personal, social/cultural and organizational environments. In 1990, Marilyn Loden and Judy Rosener developed a framework on the different aspects of diversity within individuals and institutions; they named it the diversity wheel (Loden and Rosener, 1991). The Canadian Research Institute for the Advancement of Women expanded on the wheel in 2009 and called it the Everyone Belongs CRIAW-ICREF's Intersectionality Wheel (Simpson, 2009). The CRIAW-ICREF's wheel was developed as part

FIGURE 9.1 The Privilege Pyramid

SOURCE Diagram adapted from the Everyone Belongs CRAIW-ICREF Intersectionality Wheel; Simpson, 2009

of a toolkit to help leaders in organizations understand the different aspects of intersectionality they may not have considered outside of the 'standard' protected characteristics.

We've adapted the wheel to make it more relevant to the challenges facing people in current times (see Figure 9.1).

In Figure 9.1 the top of the pyramid represents our distinctive circumstances, power, privilege and identity. The more power and privilege we have often determines the influence we have in the society we live in. Being privileged doesn't mean that you haven't suffered or faced adversity, or those without that privilege are always right. Having privilege means that we may not understand what it's like to be treated differently whether that's because we belong to the dominant culture, or that we have a good education. We're noting this here because we've seen how defensive people can be when the word privilege is mentioned. When you review the Privilege Pyramid, do take some time to understand your privileges as we all have privilege in some areas in our lives over others. The descriptions in the second tier represent aspects of our identity from our work history to citizenship. Again if we have a steady job, permanent residency and have had a great education, we will have more privilege and power than others. The third tier represents the different types of discrimination that can impact our identity directly and the bottom tier represents the larger forces that can reinforce the exclusion we may feel.

This pyramid will give you a starting point on the different types of intersectionality and how you must consider people's experiences without putting people in singular boxes. However, the descriptors in these tiers are not exhaustive, and many more words belong in the pyramid, particularly from Indigenous groups. Depending on where you live and the different laws you have around equality and fairness, we highly encourage you (or in collaboration with your DEI team) to create your belonging pyramid based on the demographics of your workforce and customers.

If we want to create a fair, equitable working environment, then reviewing the intersectionality of our workforce will help us identify where the gaps are and how we can help people in our workplace thrive. We must consider the full range of identities and change how we think about privilege, power and processes. When considering how you communicate to your workforce, would you say your communication is inclusive and accessible? We don't mean only in terms of the channels you have available (which is essential), but also the language you're using, the physical spaces you have available and the services you're providing. In an organization Advita was asked to support, she spoke with the communications team tasked with creating a campaign to help colleagues understand how they could access the Employee Assistance Programme (EAP). The team developed a communications plan on how they would do this and set objectives and milestones so they could track progress. When they launched the campaign, engagement was much slower than they anticipated. When Advita conducted an inclusive communications audit, she discovered that their campaign wasn't considering the intersectionality of the workforce. The team had made assumptions based on people's job roles and the privileges afforded to them as a communications team, such as frequent access to their desktop, higher salaries and regular office hours. Their campaign hadn't considered life on the frontline in terms of irregular hours, no access to technology and limited line manager support. They didn't consider colleagues for whom English was their second language or who didn't have the skills to learn how to use the EAP app. They made assumptions that everyone must have a smartphone, and everyone would want to download an app that would save them money. They failed to understand that due to systemic barriers and inadequate accessibility, most colleagues felt excluded rather than included. The team could not acknowledge some of the challenges and blamed the technology rather than their communication tactics. When Advita conducted focus groups, some older colleagues felt silly asking questions about how to use the system because they could hear the frustration in the voices of their peers, so they stopped asking.

We know that time, resources and budget can influence how we engage and communicate with our colleagues. But accessibility and inclusion are a big part of our work, and we must consider how we implement fairness into our communication practices.

Applying an intersectional approach to inclusion

As communication professionals, we must understand differences in privileges and the oppressive systems some groups face. You don't need to know absolutely everything about a group or a community, but you do need to be aware that most people with various characteristics will see a difference in how they are treated and the access available to them with things like funding, power, jobs, safety and support. It's also worth remembering that it's a combination of different parts of their characteristic that will impact the behaviours people see around them, such as age, race, sexuality, geographic location, language barriers, religion, gender, education, etc. If we want to engage fairly with communities, we need to consider how we can curate an intersectional approach to our work. Below are some steps you can integrate to help evolve your knowledge and learning.

Step one

Recognize that multiple forms of systemic discrimination can stop people from accessing opportunities in the workplace and beyond. Be mindful of these and what's within our remit or influence to change. For example, we only send training opportunities available through email, excluding people who may not regularly access email. Are we only sharing staff offers through the colleague app without considering that some people may not know how to use the app or even have enough data to access the app?

Step two

Understand how forms of systemic discrimination can intersect and present unique challenges for people. Intersectionality goes beyond recognizing multiple forms of discrimination. It's equally important to acknowledge how different forms of discrimination intersect, which can create a unique experience for that particular community. For example, the obstacles facing an Asian immigrant woman, for whom English isn't her first language, will be different from those facing a Black man who was born in the UK and studied at an Ivy League college. As an ally committed to intersectionality, we may review the barriers facing women accessing opportunities in our workplace. However, we would also look at how we may raise awareness of the challenges facing immigrant women of colour who may struggle with language barriers, nuances and cultural behaviours.

Step three

Go to the communities directly and listen to what they are telling you about some challenges they may face. Respect their voices and centre the people who are directly impacted. As an intersectionality ally, this may mean that you will support the storytelling of those affected by policies and practices and ensure their suggestions are heard in rooms they may not have the privilege to access. For example, suppose you are hosting a breakfast event introducing a new chief executive. In that case, it's essential to think about the challenges facing parents or guardians who have caring responsibilities or those who may not be able to travel in peak time. You may not be able to change the event, but you can certainly ensure that you provide alternative dates or a different form of access to the new CEO.

Step four

As difficult as it is for a communicator to express multiple voices and consider a range of thoughts/ideas, we need to accept that there's no singular way to experience an issue. Consider all perspectives before making significant changes to processes and policies. We can sometimes allow our bias to confirm our thinking without considering the consequences of what we are doing. For example, if you decide to remove the printed staff magazine and replace it with a colleague app, not only should you consider the impact on non-desk based colleagues but also those who may be neurodivergent and need clear instructions on the change, or people who are struggling to afford their mobile phone bills.

Step five

Using data to form a viewpoint is extremely important, but often the available data focuses on the singular aspects of individual identities, e.g. how many people are white British, how many people are women, how many are aged over 45, how many people have disabilities, etc. Highlighting disaggregated data ensures that we include the experiences of communities with intersectional identities. For example, data may show that overall, people from South Asian communities are generally well educated, but when you investigate further, there are significant differences among South Asian communities who are from a Bangladeshi or Pakistani heritage, and they often face more substantial discrimination due to Islamophobia.

From our experience working with other communication professionals, we know that time and resources are often cited as why we are not creating a more personalized experience for our colleagues. But when we spend the time to consider the benefits of taking an intersectional approach, we can make a significant difference in the experience of our colleagues. However, if we resist creating a framework to consider intersectionality in our workplaces, we will only ever communicate DEI topics at a peripheral level, and behaviour change is unlikely to happen.

The argument against intersectionality

We must also share our thoughts on the argument against intersectionality, as it's a frequent debate that can cause critics to misrepresent the original definition. As we shared earlier in the chapter, the discussion around intersectionality was driven by Black feminists who were excluded from mainstream feminist and anti-racism movements. In the 1990s, academics incorporated intersectionality theory into social sciences and moved away from studying groups in homogenous blocks. Critics, like conservative commentator Ben Shapiro, believe that embracing intersectionality is a form of identity politics, where your opinion is only valued depending on the number of different groups you belong to (Shapiro, 2020). He uses the phrase 'Oppression Olympics', which can occur in some cases, as demonstrated by the case study 'Are ERGs helpful?' earlier in this chapter. But this is more likely to happen in organizations with limited support or resources, with a short window of interest before leaders stop paying attention to some of the work that needs to occur. So, individuals who want to belong, thrive and have equal opportunities are left defending their rights and fighting for their communities. For so many years, minority groups have and continue to contend with oppression and poor behaviours. They fight for their needs, the generations before them and those who will come after them. When they finally have the opportunity to make a difference, they will do everything in their power to ensure they can leave a legacy of change behind because they never want anyone to experience what they have experienced. Leaders and allies need to recognize the symptoms that lead to some of these behaviours and provide adequate support. They must disarm and dismantle interlocking systems that exploit people and cause internal organizational battles.

One of the biggest challenges with intersectionality is that critics and supporters see the approach as linear. Often supporters misrepresent the term and use it to separate the oppressed from the oppressors, but this isn't about one person; it's about the systems in which those individual lives and work. Are those systems designed to benefit one type of person over another? Do the environment and the structure allow everyone to thrive equitably? Are we considering fairness for all groups? Are we giving equal coverage and support to the different groups struggling to be heard? We should be able to allocate appropriate resources to ensure we are supporting the groups that need the most help, and we should be able to explain the why behind our purpose to the broader workforce.

Intersectionality isn't about taking away from one group and giving it to another. It's about ensuring that we don't look at an individual in one dimension without considering the various intersects they may have. It ensures we don't make assumptions about someone's lived experience based on one characteristic or without considering other traits.

In an interview with *Vox*, an online magazine, Crenshaw shared that she never intended for her term to be used in current social science work and be the topic of debate (Coaston, 2019). For her, it was about recognizing that social equality can't exist if we don't consider age, class, disability, ethnicity, gender, sexuality simultaneously. If we don't think about how these characteristics exist alongside other categories, such as citizenship, social mobility, and language barriers, we are in danger of not allowing people to live as their authentic selves.

How internal communication can support intersectionality directly

As discussed in Chapter 2 about trust, curiosity is our superpower as communication professionals. With our curious skills, we can identify and examine systems of oppression within our organizations and influence change through effective communication and support. Using intersectionality as a methodological tool to understand inequalities facing our stakeholders can help us to develop messaging and communication that's powerful and effective. It removes the oversimplification of the way we tell our stories and helps us curate meaningful content that will help all people thrive, not only the most dominant culture.

A part of this work will be to ensure that our channels consider various intersects of our colleagues. As mentioned earlier in this chapter, looking at demographic data is essential to ensure you communicate as effectively as possible with your colleague population. But you need to dig deeper and see if there's any correlation with sickness, retention, performance, location, education, citizenship, etc.

Understanding the differences and similarities will give you a better indication of the colleague population, allowing you to address any inequalities within your communication channels. For example, your data may tell you that a certain number of your colleagues who travel on public transport tend to be off sick more than those who have the privilege of travelling by car. Looking further into the data, you might discover that women over the age of 55 tend to be off sick more frequently. Looking deeper, it may tell you that these women are off sick because they are struggling with anxiety caused by menopause. Rather than creating a generic wellbeing campaign to address sickness overall, you can create bespoke content for that population on a channel they can access while travelling on public transport. You may encourage your leadership team to bring in experts to speak on that specific topic or share stories of women so you can raise awareness across your organization. You could influence the policy change, allowing more flexibility in allowing people to choose where they work so they do not have to sacrifice their progression in the organization. This basic example demonstrates how considering intersectionality in our communication work can make an impact and help everyone thrive in their work.

We understand that you may face a challenge in accessing data and insights that will give you this level of clarity. If you struggle to find information or data, we suggest you collaborate with other departments, such as HR, IT and finance. Alternatively, we recommend you do more research, e.g. focus groups, audits, pulse checks, interviews, etc, to understand your data set. We also know this level of personalization requires budgets and resources that are not often available. If this is the case for you and your team, we encourage you to consider the return on investment. For example, how much does it cost the business in sick days per month, and how much could you save them by creating meaningful bespoke campaigns? We know it isn't easy, and it will take time. Adjusting your mindset from being a communications professional to a business leader with communication expertise is critically important if you want to influence and create impact.

The personal approach

Sending mass emails or newsletters can be counter-productive in cultivating a more inclusive culture. Throughout this chapter, we've written that people are not the same, even if they have similar backgrounds and lived experiences. We've shared examples of why intersectionality is important and how we can't make assumptions based on our irrational beliefs and experiences. However, when delivering communications, we use a 'one-size' fits all approach. This standardized approach to a communications strategy is outdated and doesn't consider the individual requirements people need to do their job well. To address some intersectionality challenges, we must consider what personalization looks like in the organizations we support. As well as it being the right thing to do, research shows that when colleagues feel connected to the company, performance, innovation and profitability is high (Gallup, 2020).

In the external world, we receive information and messages that are customized to our preferences and interests. Why do we struggle to create a bespoke experience for our workforce? From our experience, many internal communication teams don't treat their colleagues like customers, and that's a mistake. The customer user journey is a significant part of how the marketing team decides which campaigns to run and who receives what information. They spend time and energy truly understanding their customer base, likes, dislikes, behaviours, patterns, personas, etc. This process helps them invest in the right markets with the right messages. So why do we struggle to follow the same process for our workforce? When we delved deeper into personalization challenges, three common themes frequently emerged: lack of time, lack of budget and lack of metrics. We wrote about the lack of metrics in the previous section so let's look at the lack of budget and time.

Lack of time

We know that time is one of the biggest challenges facing internal communication teams across most businesses. We are expected to do more with less and are often not as well-resourced as other departments. However, sometimes we can be our worst enemies because we struggle to push back on requests as we don't know how to say no effectively. The teams that don't say no often don't have a robust communication strategy or plan that identifies their top priorities for the year ahead. For the inclusive communication strategy to be impactful, it must align with the overall business strategy, and the executive leadership team must sign it off. When you don't have a strategy that's been signed off and approved, it's challenging to push back on requests. This means you will focus your energy on delivering tactical initiatives, leaving you with limited time to invest in programmes that will create a greater impact.

Lack of budget

Not having enough money to do what we want is a debate that's been part of the internal communication industry for many decades. When requesting more resources or a budget, we need to prove the value we bring to the organization and how we deliver against the business objectives. No business leader will invest in a function if they can't see the benefit. You need to show that if you receive the additional budget, you will ensure it will give a good return on investment. As we shared earlier in this chapter, we need to shift our mindset to becoming more business leaders with communication expertise. If you're not confident with numbers, invest in programmes and courses like finance for non-finance managers or consider a skills exchange with your finance business partner.

The power of technology to help create a more personalized experience

Investing in the right technology can transform communication and bring a much more tailored experience to the workforce. The most effective communication strategies that consider personalization are the ones that integrate with different technologies from intranets, emails, mobile apps, digital signage, town halls, social networks, etc. Allowing colleagues to choose how they want to receive information, pick their preferred method of communication and have a tailored dashboard just for them can be powerful. An organization Advita supported gave colleagues an option on what they wanted to see on their intranet dashboard. Those who were deskless could choose what news they wanted to receive via the app (everyone opted-in for the urgent organizational news updates). Over six months, the organization saw that more people were connecting over critical stories on the internal social media site and their bi-monthly pulse check survey responses increased by 19 per cent and engagement increased overall by 14 percentage points.

Steps to take to start your personalization journey

Step one

Review the current communication channels you have in place. To do this, we recommend you conduct an inclusive communications audit, which will allow you to understand who gets what and how often. We share more about this in Chapter 11.

Step two

What budget and resources do you have available? It's essential to be realistic at this stage as this will determine how much investment you can make and what further investment you need.

Step three

What's your data telling you? You will need to dig deeper than the basic data, for example regarding gender split, how many are women of colour and how many are men? From that data, can you identify different age groups? Can you get hold of educational information? Can you find information that tells you the average salary of the organization? This information will help you understand where the gaps are in your messaging.

Step four

Start small. You will need to prove that personalization is effective before you receive further investment, so consider making small changes and track milestones. For example, can you segment your colleague population through email lists? Can you host special town halls for those workers who are deskless and may require a slightly shorter event? Can you provide a five-minute audio update for colleagues on the road? Tracking the impact on things like retention and sickness will be critical when you develop the business case for more funding. Create a dashboard of improvements and ensure you're sharing this with key business decision-makers.

Step five

Keep your colleague population informed. Ask them what they'd like to see and speak with them frequently, as they may have some interesting creative ideas. Even though we're looking at personalization with a communications lens, you will also be able to feedback information to other teams, such as training and development or facilities.

Using a range of communication channels to create a personalized experience can revolutionize belonging in the organization. We can only do this if we're prepared to invest some time, resources and budget into creating a remarkable colleague experience. Remember, it's progress, not perfect.

KEY TAKEAWAYS

- When you approach DEI without considering intersectionality, you risk excluding many demographics in your organization, which can lead to performative and tokenistic actions.

- If you don't consider intersectionality, then you are unable to influence the oppressive systems to change.

- Cut the data by different demographics so you have more of an understanding of who you are communicating with and what help they need.

- Empowering those with some privilege to be active bystanders and allies for those who may be disadvantaged is essential if we want to create equitable systems and processes.

- An intersectional approach can only thrive if you have the support of your leadership team and sponsors. This work needs investment, time and resources. Without that support, it won't be possible to address the inequalities facing minority groups.

REFLECTIVE QUESTIONS

- Do you know the intersectionality of your team and the leaders you support?

- Do you understand the demographics of your organization?

- Can you access internal data easily? If not, who do you need to work with to gain access?

- Have you considered the impact intersectionality may have on some of the messages you send out?

- Have you introduced a more personalized approach? If not, what support do you need to make changes?

Bibliography

American Society of News Editors (2018) How diverse are US newsrooms?, googletrends.github.io/asne/?filter=gender (archived at https://perma.cc/ F3EE-CZ4C)

Black and Missing (2022) blackandmissinginc.com/statistics/ (archived at https:// perma.cc/PS6D-YHL7)

Coaston, J (2019, 28 May) The intersectionality wars, Vox, vox.com/ the-highlight/2019/5/20/18542843/intersectionality-conservatism-law-race-gender-discrimination (archived at https://perma.cc/JY79-QSCQ)

Combahee River Collective (1977) *The Combahee River Collective Statement*, American Studies Yale, americanstudies.yale.edu/sites/default/files/files/ Keyword%20Coalition_Readings.pdf (archived at https://perma.cc/WUY5-V3UF)

Crenshaw, K W (1989) Demarginalizing the intersection of race and sex: A Black feminist critique of antidiscrimination doctrine, feminist theory and antiracist politics, *University of Chicago Legal Forum*, 1989(1), 139–67

Diversity Inc (2022, 11 July) Examining the history of ERGs and how to get the most out of them, diversityinc.com/examining-the-history-of-ergs-and-how-to-get-the-most-out-of-them/ (archived at https://perma.cc/QQ7K-BCPP)

Eversley, M (2021, 4 October) When women of color disappear, who says their names?, *The Guardian*, theguardian.com/us-news/2021/oct/04/when-women-of-color-disappear-who-says-their-names (archived at https://perma.cc/NYG9-8GER)

Gallup (2020) *The Relationship Between Engagement at Work and Organizational Outcomes*. New York, Gallup

Khokha, S (2017, 7 November) New film introduces world to Berkeley's disability rights pioneer Hale Zukas, Berkleyside, berkeleyside.org/2017/11/07/meet-berkeley-man-helped-lead-disability-rights-movement (archived at https://perma. cc/U3E8-NWNG)

Loden, M and Rosener, J (1991) *Workforce America, Managing Employee Diversity as a Vital Resource*. 1 ed. New York, McGraw-Hill

Shapiro, B (2020) What is Intersectionality?, assets.ctfassets.net/qnesrjodfi80/6BhQ kKs1jiG2eYSAqOGgMo/e9da47995fd795f62c525a93dbd6010c/shapiro-what_ is_intersectionality-transcript.pdf (archived at https://perma.cc/S6ZR-WDDS)

Simpson, J (2009) *Everyone Belongs – A Toolkit for Applying Intersectionality*. Canada, CRAIW- ICREF

Smith, B (2016) Intersectional discrimination and substantive equality: A comparative and theoretical perspective, *The Equal Rights Review*, 16, 73–102

Wesleyan University (1996) Black women & the Suffrage Movement: 1848–1923, wesleyan.edu/mlk/posters/suffrage.html (archived at https://perma.cc/EF44-K8PE)

10

Why using inclusive language is essential in the workplace

Words are powerful. They can inspire, motivate and persuade or cause harm, annoyance, rage and upset. Words can influence how we interact, from the people we communicate with within our community to those we vote for in power. How we communicate can also influence culture and behaviours in our organizations. Think about your organization or an organization you've worked at previously. Did you ever feel you had to adjust the way you spoke or wrote your emails? Did you at any point feel uncomfortable at some of the words people used? When we're embedded in an organization's culture it's difficult to spot issues with how people communicate. Which is why it's important to take a step back and reflect on whether or not the language we use is contributing to the oppressive systems that often surround underrepresented groups of people.

Inclusion and accessibility expert Ettie Bailey-King argues that we need to go a step further in our quest to build an inclusive culture. She believes that our focus shouldn't only be on inclusion but on anti-oppression (Bailey-King, 2022). We believe Bailey-King has a valid point. We don't live in a world that's equitable. However, changing the environment around us so we build equitable ways of working shouldn't be dependent on a handful of people. We all must take responsibility and ensure that we take a stand on how we deconstruct the oppressive systems that surround us. We know it's not easy to develop new habits in writing or speaking. It takes months of unlearning, intentional effort, mistakes and overcoming fear, but when consideration is given to how we communicate inclusively, the organization, the people we work with and the systems that surround us will see tangible benefits.

In this chapter we will:

- Explain the benefits of inclusive language.
- Explore how you can integrate inclusive language into your everyday communications.
- Include a sample of common terms that will help your inclusive language journey.
- Share how to manage inclusive language online.

What we've shared in this chapter is intended as a guide to help start the conversation in your organization. We can't cover every nuance or phrase. There will be terms stated which will ignite debate and discussion. There will also be words we've suggested you use that will evoke anger and annoyance. It's okay for you to feel that way. It takes time for people to understand the rationale, and time is sometimes something we don't give ourselves. However, whether you take our guidance or not, knowing how some words could cause direct or indirect hurt and exclusion is essential.

An important point to note. It's not our role, as communication professionals, to be the 'language police' and tell every person we meet what they should and shouldn't say. But it's our job to lead by example, influence and educate where we can through the stories we share and the campaigns we promote. We must ask questions and be curious on why certain words and language are used to describe situations or people. Ask curious questions and encourage a discussion – it's the only way to break down boundaries, cultivate change and help people feel included in our workplace.

Throughout this book, we have shared our thoughts and research on why cultivating inclusion is essential and how we can address some key challenges in organizations as communication professionals. We've explored how an inclusive culture can help organizations increase their profitability, performance and overall engagement in the workplace. However, a crucial part of cultivating inclusion depends on how people in our organization feel included in the conversations and the communications we share across the workplace.

Inclusive language is the words and phrases that avoid biases, slang and expressions that discriminate against people based on their identities. Cultivating an inclusive culture is impossible if we don't understand why inclusive language is critical to help people belong and feel included. It can take conscious effort and continued learning to communicate without bias and discrimination. As well as avoiding offence, it ensures that we treat everyone with dignity and as equal members of our community. You might be reading this and believing that sometimes we take inclusive language too far and that it's impossible to say anything without someone correcting you. But here's the thing. Language constantly changes: how we describe things, reference people and introduce new words to our vocabulary. Our everyday speech is full of new words, helping us express ideas that didn't exist 20 years ago, like Google, blog, paywall, etc. If you believe things are changing too quickly or people take more offence now than before, we suggest you take some time to understand your biases and beliefs. You can't build inclusion or use inclusive words if your barriers and beliefs hold you back. It's okay to disagree with some of our explanations, terms and references in this chapter, but it's not okay to completely disregard how language can help improve belonging.

The history of inclusive language

From the work we've undertaken over the years and from external research, belonging can be challenging if you don't see yourself represented in any form of communication (Deloitte, 2021). The conversation around inclusive language, specifically around gender, has been bubbling away for a few hundred years, but some believe it was a movement that started in the early 2000s. In fact, discussions on gender-neutral terminology have been an ongoing debate since as far back as 1375 when the singular 'they' appeared in the medieval romance *William and the Werewolf*, to describe an unnamed person. However, grammar purists argued that using the singular 'they' was an error because a plural pronoun can't be used as singular (Learn English, 2019). However, 'you' was a plural pronoun that had become singular, replaced with thou, thee and thy, and was used as singular for centuries (City of West Hollywood, 2018). So you could argue whether the debate was really about grammar or more that some grammar traditionalists (the majority of them male) feared losing dominant masculine language demonstrating power and hierarchy.

In the 1970s, Casey Miller and Kate Swift, both American feminists, created a manual called *The Handbook of Nonsexist Writing* (Miller and Swift, 2000). The book stated that the existing sexist language in literature excluded women, and gender-neutral terms should be used in writing. Simultaneously, conversations about gender ideologies in academia were being discussed, and in 1975 the National Council of Teachers of English published a set of guidelines on the use of non-sexist language. This publication led to backlash from purists who believed that the guidelines were 'mischievous and unnecessary' (Alter and Millicent, 1976). However, this backlash wasn't only pertinent to the 1970s. In 2019 the European Commission's inclusive language guidelines sparked controversy (Boffey, 2021). The handbook set out gender-neutral forms of address and other phrases to ensure that all Europeans felt included in communications. However, the critics of the manual stated that the guidelines were trying to erase Christian beliefs (it was suggested that the word Christmas should be avoided). Critics believed that the handbook was in danger of dividing communities. The inclusive handbook was withdrawn with the promise of an updated version to be published. There's no doubt some mistakes were made with the handbook, but ultimately this demonstrates that some people are uncomfortable with change. To be told what to say and not to say can cause conflict and resistance. For some, things are moving quickly, and for others, not quickly enough, which often leads to conflict.

To address some of the conflicts you may face when supporting organizations with inclusive language support, you may need to explain the why behind the change. In this book, we've tried to explain the importance of understanding the 'why' behind diversity, equity and inclusion. Why is it important to you? Why is it important to your leaders? Why is it important to your colleagues? And why is it important to your organization? And if it isn't essential, then understanding the reason why that is the case is equally important:

- Is it because they don't care?
- Is it too hard?
- Are they scared about making a mistake?
- Do they think it's all woke nonsense?

If you don't have open and honest conversations about the blockers and barriers, then like the European Union inclusive language guide, there's the risk that people will resent it rather than see it as a tool to support them.

Before you can start to create a document, like inclusive language guides, you have to understand the purpose. You must understand your workforce, what matters to them and what they need from the guide. This research will allow you to create something meaningful for your organization or clients. Difficult conversations shouldn't stop work from progressing. We're in danger of losing the art of communication thanks to fear that often surrounds us because we're afraid to make mistakes or learn how to have productive disagreements. You need to enter those discussions with an understanding that everyone will have a different point of view (we're not a monolith) and listen to what some people are telling you.

As we said earlier, the way we speak and write constantly changes based on new technologies, products, experiences, migration, trade, the environment and social change. The explosion of new technology has created a whole other world of language, where people now use symbols, gifs, emojis and abbreviated words like 'lol' (laughing out loud) and 'IMO' (in my opinion) to communicate with each other. As we travel and experience new cultures, we adopt words from many different places, such as sushi, shampoo and a la carte. We create new words by combining words such as brunch (breakfast and lunch). The reason for sharing these examples is to demonstrate that even though some believe that changing how we communicate is too 'politically correct' or 'woke', we've continuously evolved our language and are capable of adapting. It doesn't matter what dialect we speak. We need to continue to be curious, ask questions and avoid assumptions.

How we communicate can help build relationships and forge connections. For many, language has been embedded in our vocabulary through learned behaviours, repetition and culture. But when we don't have exposure to communities different from ours, we will struggle to understand how for some, the words we use can be steeped in negativity. This can often create barriers in systems and processes around us, which can discriminate against people based on their age, disability, ethnicity, gender, race and sexual orientation. To create a fairer and more equitable society, we must be aware of how we contribute to these oppressive systems that directly or indirectly impact underrepresented people.

The inclusive language mindset

Changing our mindset around common terminologies that are not considered inclusive can be complicated and sensitive. How we communicate with others is beyond the workplace, and often our friends and family can significantly influence our language and words. Many of us don't realize that some of what we write or say may be offensive to others or that certain words may imply bias or discrimination against someone's characteristics. It's important to note that when you start observing your language and some of the terms you may use, it can bring discomfort. We may get defensive or feel ashamed that we've been using phrases and words that some people may have been hurt by or found uncomfortable. But this is all part of learning, and rather than feeling defensive, it's critical to keep in mind the ALLMe 4A framework we shared in Chapter 6: acknowledgment, awareness, action and accountability. To create an inclusive culture in our organizations, we must go outside our comfort zones and be prepared to adopt an inclusive mindset.

It can be challenging to do this when each person has different preferences and a unique background. But to foster a culture of inclusivity and to ensure you're using terms that are free of bias, discrimination or prejudice, follow the five steps below:

1 **Don't be afraid to be called out.** It doesn't matter how culturally aware you are. You will make mistakes with language. Spend some time asking for feedback from your team and peers. Ask them to call you out if you're trying to change certain behaviours and words. For example, Advita continuously used the word 'guys' when referencing groups of people, so she asked her team and friends to call her out if she used the term in their company. Being called out is difficult; many of us don't mean malicious intent, so when someone accuses us of being 'racist', sexist', 'ableist', etc, we naturally enter defence mode. It's human instinct. We want to protect our community and ourselves from harm, and we feel the same physical reaction as our ancestors would have if they were facing a sabre-tooth tiger millions of years ago. Our brain's job is to keep us safe, and it hasn't evolved as quickly as the world around us. So, even though the risk of a sabre-tooth tiger attacking us is now impossible, our brains still have the same flight, freeze or fight behaviours if we believe we're facing some sort of attack, physical or verbal. When you feel defensive, reflect on why you think that way. What is causing that reaction, and what steps do you need to move forward? They may be right or wrong, but gather your thoughts and respond appropriately. Often, we see people's behaviour but not the intent behind that behaviour.

2 **Expand your community.** What we don't know, we don't know. If you're spending your time with people who look like you, talk like you and have similar lived experiences, then try to expand your networks so you can learn from observing and connecting with others. As we've said, language is complex, and many nuances exist. So spend some time connecting with people in your organization and understand some of the challenges they may face. However, be aware that it's not the responsibility of other people to educate you or to give you free advice.

3 **Look inside your organization.** Are all your senior leaders of one demographic with similar lived experiences? If so, is their language influencing the way you communicate with others? Are you asking for feedback from your colleagues, including those who may be quieter or underrepresented? If we work in an organization with a dominant culture, then we need to ensure that we're not biased towards one type of tone or language. Be mindful of not only using quantitative data to make judgments on culture. Speak to people directly, host focus groups and ask them questions about communications and language used. If you're a global organization and have multiple dialects in your workplace, seek expert advice and ensure that the translations are accurate and represent the words you're sharing fairly.

4 **Understand that change can take time.** Sometimes action bias can take over when we are in a place of discomfort and shame. We want to address the issue without considering the consequences or impact. But we have to take the time to listen to what people are sharing with us and learn how we can make a substantial impact rather than performative measures, as shared in Chapter 8.

5 **Explain why.** So often, we jump into change without sharing the why, which can take people by surprise. In Chapter 7 we wrote about the Cycle for Change, and the steps people go through when they are experiencing change. It's important to be aware of this and understand that some people will need detailed explanations on 'the why' more than others. It's important that we are consistent in our messaging and continue to explain how inclusive language can cultivate inclusion and help improve workplace culture.

Principles of inclusive language

Inclusive language principles must apply to all forms of communication, including conversations, meeting papers, documents, letters, emails, newsletters, reports, press articles, webpages and 'corporate' publications. To help your workforce understand what inclusive language means, we advise creating an inclusive language guide, so people have some guidance. However, an inclusive language guide won't answer all the questions. It has to be a starting point, with the understanding that it's a working document. It's virtually impossible to cover every nuance, detail or the latest thinking. The guide is likely to cause some disagreement, but you have to look at the broader purpose of the document and ensure it addresses key concerns from the research you have undertaken.

The guide should give the following:

1 An overview of the behaviours expected and how people can support to cultivate inclusive cultures.

2 The principles to consider when you're writing communications, whether that's internal or external.

3 Recommendations for what language you should and shouldn't use when discussing topics such as age, disability, gender, marriage and civil partnership, pregnancy and maternity, race, religion and sexuality.

The guide must be clear, accessible and as straightforward as possible. It's not a rulebook; it's a guide which will continue to evolve, change and adapt over time. To give you a starting point, we've written examples to help support you with some common inclusive language barriers. You need to understand that this is a guide aimed at English-speaking organizations based on the equality acts from Canada, the UK and the USA. There will be terms and references in the examples we've shared below that you won't agree with, and there will be references to standards that may not be appropriate for all countries. We highly encourage you to do your due diligence and research before implementing any policy or guide within your organization.

The inclusive language guide

The guiding principles

1 **Active voice.** Writing in an active voice helps make your communications more accessible. It's also beneficial when English is the second language for people (e.g. 'the town hall will take place at noon') rather than the passive voice (e.g. 'at noon today the town hall will be taking place'). However, where the object of a sentence is the most important, the passive voice may be appropriate, e.g. 'The employee was inducted into the organization'. Not only does this bring some clarity, but it also reduces bias towards systems of power.

2 **Self-identification.** While this inclusive language guide helps clarify preferred standard terms, every individual's lived experience is different. Use words that reflect how an individual or a community chooses to talk about themselves. For example, some people who belong to the Deaf

community prefer identity-first language (where you put the condition or the disability before the person) rather than person-first (where you emphasize the person before their condition or disability). You must ask people if you're unsure.

3 **Be curious.** Writing to ensure you are being as inclusive can be complex and will require an element of sensitivity. If you're in doubt about how to refer to a community or a person, be curious and educate yourself. Expand your network, connect with others who are different from you and start learning about topics that require further clarity. If you can't ask people or are unsure, use the inclusive language guide as a starting point and do the best you can.

There will be some fear when you try to write inclusive communication: some people will be worried about making mistakes or may even disagree with the information in the guide. That's okay. Remember that there's no definitive answer to what inclusive language is. It'll depend on context, country and individual. As we've said, be curious, ask questions and be respectful. However, be mindful that repeated mistakes may cause a lack of respect and can be distressing for others. If it continues or it's on purpose, it could signify bullying or discrimination, which is unlawful and must be managed through the appropriate process.

CASE STUDY
FleishmanHillard Inclusive Language Workshop and Global Vocabulary Guide

Words matter. They shape our thoughts, perceptions and our reality. They have an impact on how people feel. Communicators striving to advance diversity, equity, and inclusion (DEI) and issues of justice might find themselves stuck in what global PR agency FleishmanHillard defines as the 'DE&I Dilemma'. The DE&I Dilemma is the passion to move forward and make meaningful change while simultaneously feeling stuck in the present reality. It is the intense fatigue we often feel with trying to move forward when some days, looking around, it feels like nothing has changed.

As a company striving to become the most inclusive agency in the world, FleishmanHillard launched the Inclusive Language Workshop to give people the opportunity to address the power of language. The Inclusive Language Workshop and Global Vocabulary Guide are tools they use to guide their teams and clients on how to do better, *now*. They are not future-facing strategies or tactics – they are instruments to drive and inspire real change *today*.

FleishmanHillard knew change must begin with language. They believe that concepts like racism are often learned, largely determined by the vernacular we pick up throughout our life; they are not intrinsic to who we are, which is why rethinking word choices and investigating language can be a conduit of social change.

In the training they offer their clients, they explore some of the commonly used phrases that some people may come across every day; for example 'boys will be boys' or 'white space'. They recognize that each of these phrases are rooted in historical oppression and discrimination. But perhaps when used people either didn't know what they meant or did not intend to use them in a derogatory manner.

Boys will be boys emphasizes that people should accept that boys or men have noisy, aggressive or loud mannerisms, and that's just a part of the male character. White space is a manifestation of colour-based biases, which enforces that white is good over black or dark. Think of beauty products that claim to make skin colour lighter.

FleishmanHillard also believe that beyond language choices, it's equally important to frame and phrase what we are trying to communicate in a way that's inclusive, how we choose to use our words, and by adopting a *person-first* approach in communications. They teach individuals to think about and centre people as that will allow them to become better communicators, and eventually help eradicate decades-old references rooted in discriminatory words and phrases. Take the example of a person with a disability. They might be perfectly comfortable with being referred to as a 'disabled person', or they might prefer 'person with a disability' or no reference to the word 'disability' altogether. Everyone has a unique experience, therefore when directly referencing an individual, it's always advisable to first check with a person about how they identify.

Maria Khan, Account Director and Global Language Lead at FleishmanHillard, says:

'A guiding principle of inclusive language work is to keep evolving because language is ever evolving. Learning, exploring, and understanding the context of the words must be a life-long commitment if we are to help remove systemic barriers and support liberation. Each of us has different life experiences, and no two people will interpret language the same, but the beauty of inclusive and mindful communications is that it transcends our unique experiences'.

'We must get comfortable with being uncomfortable, and give people grace to make mistakes. Being comfortable with the uncomfortable, however, isn't enough in itself; it's a starting point and it must be followed with relentless pursuit of knowledge and *real action* because that is what will ultimately drive change in our communications, and in the world'.

Inclusive terms

This guide is a reference tool to help you think about some of the terms and phrases you might use. Remember, the information we share is from our research and experiences. The phrases and words we've shared below will likely change depending on geographies, location, culture, etc so please undertake extensive research before implementing the guidelines in your organization.

What is discriminatory language?

Language discrimination occurs when people are treated differently because of their characteristics and identities.

Discriminatory language includes words and phrases that:

- Reinforce stereotypes, e.g. all doctors are men, and all nurses are women.
- Exclude certain groups of people through assumptions, e.g. people from China can't speak English well.
- Reinforce derogatory labels, e.g. all people who are homeless have an alcohol problem.
- Patronize or trivialize certain people or groups or their experiences, e.g. autistic people can't work.
- Cause discomfort or offense, e.g. women should stay at home and look after the children, not go to work.

Ageism

A report in 2021 by the United Nations claims that 50 per cent of people hold ageist attitudes, which can lead to poor health and reduced quality of life for older persons (WHO, 2021). The review also shared that age is also a determining factor in who receives medical treatment and procedures.

To tackle age discrimination, you must understand that it can apply to anyone, both older and younger adults. Ageism for younger adults is often seen through areas such as employment, housing and politics. In 2022, the UK Government passed the Elections Act 2022 policy when voting to eliminate voter fraud. The list of identification which will be accepted includes concessionary travel passes for older people, but travel passes can't be used by young people or students (Toynbee, 2022). Critics of this new act have argued that this move will deliberately exclude young people and minorities from voting, as the UK doesn't provide a free mandatory national identity card which may help to mitigate some of these challenges (WHO, 2021).

Alongside being aware of potential discrimination externally, you have to be mindful of unacceptable comments such as 'They won't understand how to do that as they are past it.' You should only refer to age if it's relevant in your communication, for example, where funding is only available for a specific age group. Avoid using age to describe an individual or a group where it's not relevant, for example 'old workforce' or 'young and energetic team'. Instead, you could say 'experienced workforce' or 'effective and vibrant team'.

Reflection points

- Age discrimination can be a barrier to many opportunities for older and younger people. Be aware of how the language around age may inadvertently discriminate and cause stereotypes.

- Ageism can seriously affect people's health and wellbeing, and cost our societies billions of pounds. It's important to use evidence-based strategies, improve how data is collected and undertake robust research to build a movement that can change how people think, feel and act towards age and ageing.

- To understand ageism, you must check in on your bias, beliefs and attitudes on stereotypes that suggest certain ages are either good or bad at things. For example, try not to assume because someone is young that, they'll be good at technology, or if they are older, they won't understand technology.

TABLE 10.1 Inclusive language to use when communicating about age

Inclusive language	Not inclusive language
Older person / people	Old man / lady, OAPs, pensioners
Younger person / people	Young man / girl, kiddo
Energetic, driven	Young at heart
Youth, learners, teenagers, students	Immature, kids
Adolescent	Juvenile
People over... / people under...	Senior citizens, youngsters

Disability

Approximately one billion people have disabilities worldwide (Humanity & Inclusion, 2022). This means that more than one in eight people alive are living with either visible (i.e. paralysis) or invisible (i.e. depression, diabetes, HIV) physical, mental or neurological conditions.

Ableism assumes that there's an 'ideal' body and mind and that if bodies deviate from this ideal, they don't have value. The **social model of disability**, developed by people with disabilities, says barriers in society are disabling people rather than their impairment or difference (Scope, 2020). In November 2022, US Airlines reported mishandling more than 800 wheelchairs in October 2022 (Wichter, 2021). Media reports have shared stories from people who have been stranded and left alone for hours because airlines have forgotten them or there have not been enough resources to support them. In September 2022, a video went viral on social media of disability campaigner Jennie Berry who had to drag herself across the floor of the airplane because no aisle chair was available. It's claimed that a staff member told Ms Berry that she should wear a 'nappy' when travelling. The story sparked fury across social platforms leading to a petition for aisle chairs to be made mandatory on all flights (ITV News, 2022).

As communication professionals, we need to consider the reputational impact on organizations caused by poor behaviours of colleagues due to inexperience or lack of education. We may not be responsible for training and development, but we can certainly influence our leaders through feedback from our colleagues and external media. It's also critically important that we avoid tokenistic gestures and defining individuals against their disability/condition if it's irrelevant to the communication we are writing.

Reflection points

- Focus on the person, not their disability (while being aware that in some instances, such as the Deaf community, being deaf is often seen as part of the person's identity).
- Avoid medical labels, they don't say anything about the individuals and they reinforce stereotypes.
- Be mindful of how you describe a person's disability, and don't imply weakness or abnormality. Avoid using terms such as 'suffers from', 'afflicted by', 'victim of', etc. These phrases imply hopelessness and passivity.

TABLE 10.2 Inclusive language to use when communicating about disability

Inclusive language	Not inclusive language
Non-visible disability, physical disability, cognitive disability, learning disability	High functioning, low functioning
... uses a wheelchair	Wheelchair-bound, confined to a wheelchair, in a wheelchair
Deaf (with a capital D), hard of hearing, partial hearing loss, partially deaf	'The deaf', 'fallen on deaf ears', closed ears, tone deaf, hearing-impaired
Blind, blind people, limited vision, low vision, partially sighted	'The blind', vision-impaired, visually impaired, blindsided
Person living with dementia	Victim of dementia, battling with dementia
Accessible car park	Disabled car park

Gender, sex and sexual orientation – understanding common terms

Discrimination against someone's sex, sexual orientation, gender or intersex status is unlawful in some countries (there are still 69 countries that have laws that criminalize homosexuality). Depending on which country you live and work in, understanding some standard terms in the context of gender, sex and sexual orientation is essential.

Cisgender is when someone's identity is the same as the gender they were assigned to at birth.

Gender expression is how someone may choose to express their gender identity. It could be through how they dress, speak or act. How someone looks or dresses doesn't always reflect their gender identity.

Gender identity is each person's individual experience of gender. Gender identity can correlate with a person's assigned sex at birth or differ from it.

Non-binary, gender fluid or gender queer don't identify as either male or female. Some people have a gender that blends the two elements, and others don't identify with either. Other terms include bigender and agender.

Sex refers to biological attributes based on your organs, hormones and chromosomes. People can be male, female and intersex.

Sexual orientation describes your physical or emotional attraction to others (e.g. straight, lesbian, gay, bisexual).

Transgender is a term for people whose gender identity differs from their sex at birth. Some transgender people may transition at any point in their lives. During transitioning, a person may change their clothing, appearance, name, pronouns or identity documents. They may also undergo hormone therapy or other medical procedures or surgeries. But some transgender people may not pursue any medical intervention which doesn't delegitimize their transgender identity.

A Stonewall report in 2018 shared that 40 per cent of LGB+ workers and 55 per cent of transgender workers have experienced workplace conflict, compared with 29 per cent of heterosexual, cisgender colleagues. More than a third of LGB+ colleagues say that they hide their sexual orientation or gender identity at work because of negative behaviour from their colleagues (Stonewall, 2018). It's vital to consider how we communicate information to our colleagues when referencing different identities and terms. As we've shared throughout this chapter, language evolves, but it's our responsibility to keep ourselves updated with what's happening. For example, in the UK, the term 'transsexual' is still referenced in the Equality Act 2010, but it's now generally considered outdated and misleading (CIPD, 2019).

Reflection points

- Use gender-neutral terms instead of making a sex distinction, e.g. you or they/their/them, not he/she or him/her.
- Don't make assumptions about people's gender or sexuality. Make every effort to replace 'husbands and wives' with 'spouses and partners'.
- Avoid gender-based expressions that highlight gender stereotypes, e.g. 'man up', 'you throw like a girl', 'that's a woman's job' or 'even my mother could do that!'.

TABLE 10.3 Inclusive language to use when communicating about gender, sex and sexual orientation

Inclusive language	Not inclusive language
Transgender person	A transgender, transgendered, transsexual
Crossdresser (if self-identified)	Transvestite (unless self-identified)
Gender affirmation, sex reassignment surgery, gender confirmation surgery	Sex change, the sex change operation

(continued)

TABLE 10.3 (Continued)

Inclusive language	Not inclusive language
Gay / lesbian	Homosexuals, lifestyle choice
Sexual orientation	Sexual preference
Chair	Chairman
All, people, folks	Ladies and gentlemen, guys, girls and boys
Agreement	Gentleman's agreement
Humankind, people	Mankind
Doctor, nurse	Female doctor, male nurse

Mental health

Approximately 20 per cent of adults in the UK experience a mental health condition. With so many people experiencing common mental health problems, being respectful and thoughtful around the words you use about mental health can positively impact everyone.

Using person-centred language to avoid negative labelling and to prevent people from being defined by a condition is essential. However, using mental health language for everyday emotions is not the best way to describe what you mean. Using words like 'crazy' to describe a busy day or 'OCD' to describe someone clean and tidy can be problematic. These words often minimize the debilitating issues experienced by people with a clinical diagnosis.

Reflection points

- Try to focus on the person's experiences instead of labelling them in medical or prescriptive terms.
- Avoid using terminology to refer to a situation metaphorically, e.g. 'I've had a crazy day!' or 'I've had an insane time'.
- Breaking down the stigma around mental health is crucial for helping people talk about their mental health so they can access life-saving therapeutic interventions.

Neurodiversity

Around 10 per cent of the population is neurodivergent. Neurodiversity relates to the fact that no two brains are the same. This means that our

TABLE 10.4 Inclusive language to use when communicating about mental health

Inclusive language	Not inclusive language
Mental health condition	Mentally ill
Living with bipolar	They're bipolar
Person who has... (bipolar, depression, etc)	Crazy, mad, insane
They have depression	They're struggling with depression
Discharged	Released (from hospital)
A person experiencing a mental health condition	'The mentally ill', 'suffering from depression', 'victim of OCD'

biological make-up results in natural differences in how we communicate, problem-solve and use creativity. Autism, dyslexia, dyspraxia and ADHD (Attention Deficit Hyperactivity Disorder) are all in the range of neurodivergence.

Reflection points

- People with neurodivergent identities experience a broad range of emotions, thoughts, behaviours and sensory experiences that are different from neurotypical people.

- People don't have 'neurodiversity'; they are neurodivergent. Neurodiversity isn't a trait that an individual can possess, it's a biological characteristic.

- Identity-first language is often preferred by some people in neurodivergent communities, for example, the autistic community (Autistic Advocacy, 2019). If you're unsure, ask, because not everyone is the same.

TABLE 10.5 Inclusive language to use when communicating about neurodiversity

Inclusive language	Not inclusive language
Neurotypical person	Normal
Person with dyslexia	Dyslexic
Affected / impacted with autism	Suffers with autism
Condition	Disorder, impairment
Person with a brain injury	Brain damaged

Race, religion and ethnicity

Dismantling racism requires addressing systemic bias, from structural to linguistic. Conversations on race, religion and ethnicity can only progress if we are willing to make mistakes so we can correct them. There is no one-size-fits-all language for discussing race, religion and ethnicity, but we should review the words we use from the community's perspective, not the dominant group's power structure. We must use the most specific terms to describe a person or a group.

Race is a social construct to categorize groups of people, usually based on their physical traits regarded as typical amongst people of shared ancestry. Ethnicity is a term used to describe a social group with a shared cultural identity, including religion, cultural traditions, language and customs. To ensure we communicate as inclusively as we can about race, religion and ethnicity, it's vital to be as clear and specific as possible. For example, before using a broad term such as Black, Asian, Minority Ethnic (BAME), think about whether or not you could refer to a person or group's heritage or background instead, such as 'South Asian' or 'Black African'.

We know there are many conversations on whether Black, Indigenous, People of Colour (BIPOC), a term used in America and Canada, and BAME, a term used in the UK, are appropriate to use. Some believe that as an 'umbrella' term to bring together groups to communicate topics like anti-racism, it's a relevant term to use. However, in the UK, the government recommended that organizations remove the acronym as it excludes other marginalized groups due to the broad nature of the term 'minority ethnic'. However, in Canada and in the USA, BIPOC is still widely used and is accepted as a general term to describe underrepresented groups. A big challenge with terms like BAME and BIPOC is that they are not understood widely, and it implies that people are one homogeneous group. It also ignores that minority ethnic groups are often a global majority. The term also excludes white minority ethnic groups.

Ultimately, it's not illegal to use the terms but do speak with groups and individuals in your workplace to sense-check their preferences before communicating further.

Reflection points

- A person's skin complexion doesn't define their nationality or cultural background.
- Only use a person's race if it is directly relevant to your point.

TABLE 10.6 Inclusive language to use when communicating about race, religion and ethnicity

Inclusive language	Not inclusive language
Blocklist, allow list	Blacklist, whitelist
Small detail	Nitty gritty
Dual heritage / biracial	Mixed race, mixed
People / person of colour	Coloured people, foreigners, colourblind (in the context of race)
Asylum seeker	Illegal immigrant
Black people	The Blacks
Asian people	The Asians, the Chinese
White people	The Whites / caucasian
Enslaved people	Slaves
First name	Christian name
Antisemitism	Anti-Semitism, Jew (as an adjective or adverb)

- Not all members of religion observe the same practice. We should not make assumptions about individuals based on their religion or belief system. Ask, respectfully, if you're not sure.

Socioeconomic language

Though social mobility is not part of the Equality Act, it's still essential to understand how we talk about this area respectfully. The words you use to describe an area or a community can influence how we view the people that live there and how they see themselves. People who grew up in homes, communities and countries with limited resources can be stigmatized. The way we use language can help prevent blame and help maintain dignity.

Reflection points

- Where possible, use specific metrics such as occupation, income and education and use language that describes what's important to the analysis.
- Avoid generalizing terms such as 'the homeless', 'ghetto', 'poverty-stricken' and instead use specific language such as 'people experiencing homelessness' or 'people who are homeless'.

TABLE 10.7 Inclusive language to use when communicating about social mobility

Inclusive language	Not inclusive language
People who are experiencing homelessness	The homeless
Low-income areas of the city	The ghetto, the inner-city
Under-resourced	Disadvantaged
Communities with high-poverty rates / with access to fewer opportunities	Hard to reach
People with income below the living wage	The poor / low-class people / poor people

- Deficit-based language also focuses on what people lack rather than what they have. So rather than labelling people as 'poorly educated' or 'having little education', provide more specific descriptors such as 'people who don't have a college education or equivalent'.

Removing jargon to cultivate inclusivity

The *Collins Dictionary* describes jargon as 'words and expressions that are used in a special or technical way by particular groups of people, often making the language difficult to understand'. As communication professionals, a crucial part of our role is to translate complicated technical language into terms and phrases that are simple to understand. But when you work in an industry with people with similar characteristics and educational backgrounds, it can be challenging to spot the jargon, and we often distribute information without considering the wider colleague or customer population. Jargon can cause exclusion and disengagement, so we must spend some time and energy understanding where our gaps are.

Jargon not only excludes people from participating but can also be dangerous. Research and studies in health literacy demonstrate that most patient materials are a grade level too high to understand, disadvantaging many patients (Mayer Gloria, 2009). Patients, therefore, struggle to make informed decisions about their healthcare needs. Jargon can also exclude many from applying for job opportunities. Job descriptions are notoriously known to dissuade women, people with disabilities and people of colour from applying due to the language often used to describe the role. Words such as 'dynamic', 'leverage', 'take it to the next level' can intimidate individuals. You could argue that a job description is an opportunity to ensure you're attracting the right talent. However, with so many of our organizations battling for talent from diverse backgrounds, it's essential to recognize how your job descriptions might deter the people you're trying to attract.

Removing jargon in favour of plain language can help build better inclusion and accessibility, helping people feel more engaged, connected and empowered. Think about who you are talking to, their demographic, whether they are specialists in your industry and what they need to know. Towards the end of this chapter, you will find a glossary of terms to help you navigate the complexities of creating an inclusive language guide.

Online accessibility

We've shared some techniques and tips for more traditional communication methods, but it's essential to consider inclusive practices for the online space. There are plenty of tools and resources to help you identify your gaps and understand what areas you need to improve. However, our favourite is by Alexa Heinrich, who has created a free resource called Accessible Social (Heinrich, 2022). It's a hub for digital marketers, communication professionals, content creators and internet users who want to understand how they can make their social media more accessible. The common areas you must be aware of when producing content for social media are:

Captions. All videos should have relevant captions as they can help people with a learning disability and those who are neurodivergent. Captions can also help if the speaker is talking fast, has an accent, is speaking quietly, has poor audio or if the watcher doesn't want to put their sound on. Alexa shares that 69 per cent of people watch videos without sound in public places. There are two types of captions: closed and open. Closed captions can be switched on or off based on what the viewer wants. Open captions are permanently embedded into a video during post-production.

Transcripts. A text description of audio-only or visual information. It's good practice to provide a transcript for any video or audio you produce, as some people can struggle with watching or listening to content for long periods.

Alt text. If someone has a vision disability, then alternative text can help them understand what images are being shared, especially if they use screen readers or text-to-speech programmes to access digital content. If you use any photos on your social platforms, they should be described accurately and give enough context about why that image has been included. Alexa shares three questions: What do people need to know about the photo? What information is going to be written directly in your post? Once the post has been written in alt text, is there any further information missing? It's essential to write in plain English and not over-describe information that isn't visible.

Colour palettes. With the introduction of graphic design tools like Canva, there are many enthusiastic graphic designers creating content for social. If you are responsible for creating graphics, consider colour clashes when developing content. Some colour pairings can be complicated to read, e.g. orange on red or red on green. Also, keep your font simple and size readable. Avoid lots of text on images, as it can be distracting and cause confusion.

Emojis. Overusing emojis in your posts is not recommended as emojis have a pre-determined alt text for screen readers. If you overuse them, it can be difficult for the reader to comprehend what you're trying to say. If you have to use an emoji, use it only if it's relevant. Also, consider what colour emoji you're using to represent the groups you're communicating with.

As we've said throughout this chapter, inclusive language and words can be complex, but it's important to keep learning. You will get things wrong, but we can only learn from mistakes, so don't fear being inclusive. Acknowledge your mistake and improve next time. When we address issues for the minority, the majority of people will always benefit.

KEY TAKEAWAYS

- Language is complicated and subjective, but it's important to understand the power words have and their impact on businesses in terms of reputation.

- Inclusive language isn't a new concept. It's existed for many decades but only recently have people seen the benefits and how it can help organizations thrive.

- It's not only the role of an internal communication professional to communicate using inclusive language. The whole organization needs to be part of the conversations, particularly leaders who have to lead by example.

- Inclusive language guides should be used as a guide and an educational tool. Don't use it to shame others genuinely trying to learn and adapt.

- Avoid jargon and use plain English where possible.

REFLECTIVE QUESTIONS

- Reflecting on the last few months, do you believe your words were as inclusive as possible in your campaigns and messages?
- Are you considering symbols as well as words when you communicate messages across the organization?
- Do you sense-check your language in your messaging to ensure it's accessible?

GLOSSARY OF TERMS

These terms are a selection of common words that you may find helpful.

Ableism Discrimination and social prejudice against people with disabilities.

Ally Someone who supports a specific group with characteristic(s) that differs from their own. An ally will acknowledge the discrimination faced by that group and commit to learning more to strengthen their knowledge whilst attempting to reduce their complicity and raise awareness. Ally should be a verb.

Anti-racist Being anti-racist means believing that racism is everyone's problem and everyone has an active role in stopping it. An action of an anti-racist is actively calling out a comment or an activity rather than disagreeing with it silently.

Colourism This is prejudice against people with a darker skin tone and/or preferential treatment of those of the same race but lighter skin tone.

Cultural appropriation The unacknowledged or inappropriate explorations of other customs, practices or ideas by members of a majority group, often without understanding, acknowledging or respecting its value in the original culture.

Cultural competency The ability to communicate and interact effectively with people regardless of differences. Cultural competence applies to individual behaviours, organizational systems, processes and culture.

Ethnocentrism The belief that one's characteristic(s), group, ethnicity or nationality is superior to others.

Equity This is when you give everyone what they need to succeed, whereas equality treats everyone equally.

Intersectionality A social construct that recognizes the fluid diversity of multiple characteristics that an individual can hold, or identify with, such as gender, race, class, religion, professional status, marital status, socioeconomic status, etc.

Lived experience The knowledge a person gains through direct, firsthand involvement in everyday events rather than representations constructed by others.

Microaggression The verbal, nonverbal and behavioural slights, snubs, insults or actions which communicate hostile, derogatory or harmful messages to an individual that relates to their characteristics or belonging to a particular group.

Misogyny Hatred or contempt for women or girls. It is a form of sexism that keeps women at a lower social status than men.

Privilege A particular advantage or right afforded only to a specific group of people, often without their realization because of ignorance, lack of specific education or cultural bias.

Pronouns Words we use to refer to people's gender in conversation, for example 'he' or 'she'. Some people may prefer others to refer to them in gender-neutral language and use pronouns such as they/their and ze/zir.

Protected characteristics In the UK, specific characteristics are protected by law. It is illegal to discriminate against anyone when, for example, hiring or providing access to services based on nine characteristics: age, disability, ethnicity/race, gender reassignment, marriage/civil partnership, maternity and pregnancy, religion, sex and sexuality.

Safe space An environment where people feel comfortable articulating themselves and participating without fear of attack, ridicule or denial of experience.

Unconscious bias Our brains make swift judgments and assessments of people and situations without us realizing it. Our biases are influenced by our irrational beliefs, which we form from background, cultural environment and personal experiences. Sometimes we may not even be aware of these views and opinions or their full impact and implications. But, we must try to recognize these biases and actively challenge them.

SOURCES National Institute for Health Research, 2021; Institute of Race Relations, 2020; United Nations, 2020; Gov.UK, 2021

Bibliography

Alter, L and Millicent, R (1976) Do the NCTE guidelines on non-sexist use of language serve a positive purpose?, *The English Journal*, 65(9), 10–13

Autistic Advocacy (2019) Identity-first language, ASAN, autisticadvocacy.org/about-asan/identity-first-language/ (archived at https://perma.cc/T2TP-HDCC)

Bailey-King, E (2022, 31 May) Want to be inclusive? You need anti-oppressive content, fightingtalk.uk/thoughts/anti-oppressive-content (archived at https://perma.cc/D7HN-RDJK)

Boffey, D (2021, 30 November) EU advice on inclusive language withdrawn after rightwing outcry, *The Guardian* (Brussels), theguardian.com/world/2021/nov/30/eu-advice-on-inclusive-language-withdrawn-after-rightwing-outcry (archived at https://perma.cc/G5XM-8CCN)

CIPD (2019) Sexual orientation, gender identity and gender reassignment, cipd.co.uk/news-views/viewpoint/sexual-orientation-gender-identity (archived at https://perma.cc/GH77-KK5V)

City of West Hollywood (2018) *Pronouns Can Work*. Los Angeles, City of West Hollywood

Deloitte (2021) 2023 Global Human Capital Trends, deloitte.com/us/en/insights/focus/human-capital-trends.html (archived at https://perma.cc/E9DU-N72E)

Gov.UK (2021, 15 March) Inclusive language: Words to use and avoid when writing about disability, gov.uk/government/publications/inclusive-communication/inclusive-language-words-to-use-and-avoid-when-writing-about-disability (archived at https://perma.cc/6SDQ-FJV5)

Heinrich, A (2022) Accessible Social, accessible-social.com/ (archived at https://perma.cc/M6XY-SY46)

Humanity & Inclusion (2022) Disability: The global picture, humanity-inclusion.org.uk/en/action/disability-the-global-picture#:~:text=Disability%3A%20The%20global%20picture,15%25%20of%20the%20global%20population (archived at https://perma.cc/ZT86-HGPY)

Institute of Race Relations (2020) Definitions, irr.org.uk/research/statistics/definitions/ (archived at https://perma.cc/G3DP-5WJF)

ITV News (2022, 26 September) Hartlepool disability campaigner forced to drag herself to plane toilet makes plea for change, itv.com/news/tyne-tees/2022-09-26/disabled-woman-humiliated-after-being-forced-to-drag-herself-to-plane-toilet (archived at https://perma.cc/UUJ6-Z824)

Learn English (2019) Singular They – Wrong or Right?, learngrammar.net/english-grammar/singular-they-wrong-or-right (archived at https://perma.cc/N8P8-2JRT)

Mayer Gloria, V M (2009) Enhancing written communications to address health literacy, *The Online Journal of Issues in Nursing*, 14(3)

Miller, C and Kate, S (2000) *The Handbook for Nonsexist Writing for Writers, Editors and Speakers*. 2 ed. Lincoln, Lippincott & Crowell

National Institute for Health Research (2021) A guide to creating inclusive content and language, learningforinvolvement.org.uk/wp-content/uploads/2021/09/A-guide-to-creating-inclusive-content-and-language.pdf (archived at https://perma.cc/8VT4-J6BN)

Scope (2020) Social model of disability, scope.org.uk/about-us/social-model-of-disability/ (archived at https://perma.cc/AH55-BJXU)

Stonewall (2018) *LGBT Britain Work Report*. London, Stonewall

Toynbee, P (2022, 25 November) Call these voter ID laws what they really are: voter suppression and an attack on young people, *The Guardian*, theguardian.com/commentisfree/2022/nov/25/voter-id-laws-what-they-really-are-voter-suppression-and-an-attack-on-young-people (archived at https://perma.cc/N2F4-6GKT)

United Nations (2020) Guidelines for gender-inclusive language in English, un.org/en/gender-inclusive-language/guidelines.shtml (archived at https://perma.cc/6EZK-U3NC)

Wichter, Z (2021) This traveler's wheelchair was left in the rain with no guarantee that it won't happen again, USA Today Travel, eu.usatoday.com/story/travel/airline-news/2022/11/11/disabled-travelers-say-airlines-damage-wheelchairs-too-often/8291964001/ (archived at https://perma.cc/39Z7-QM22)

WHO (World Health Organization) (2021, 18 March) Ageism is a global challenge, who.int/news/item/18-03-2021-ageism-is-a-global-challenge-un (archived at https://perma.cc/EV7E-QZA3)

11

How to build an inclusive engagement plan for DEI

This chapter helps you create an inclusive engagement plan for DEI that ties operational initiatives to communication. We introduce you to the Inner Strength Engagement Model created by Priya in 2012 that helps you create engagement goals and specifies areas of focus in order to identify opportunities and challenges.

Let's talk engagement, specifically employee engagement (we can also refer to it as colleague engagement, but employee engagement is the more commonly used term). When organizations and leaders reach out to us for consulting support, they have acknowledged the need for DEI, they have often done their research, have hired or appointed someone in the organization to lead the DEI effort and have created a DEI strategy and plan.

This plan provides clarity on where the organization is today, measures on where it wants to be in the future and sets the goals that the organization aspires to reach along specified timelines. In some cases, the organizations have consulted with leaders, resource groups and colleagues who are invested in the success of DEI efforts, since they are either directly impacted by changes or passionate about justice they hope can be resolved through a commitment to DEI. As we mentioned, this journey has often taken a year or two. It's at this point that organizations start wondering about next steps. Clients often ask themselves 'How do we translate the promise of the plan into action, experience and performance?' and 'How do we manage the resistance and fear being displayed?' This is common in an emotional environment with passionate colleagues on all sides of the debate.

This is when the conversation around engagement comes up. Many think of engagement as being part and parcel of the Gallup Q12 questions that are placed on the annual colleague survey and are benchmarked against other global organizations and competitors (Gallup, 2022):

1   I know what is expected of me at work.

2   I have the materials and equipment I need to do my work right.

3   At work, I have the opportunity to do what I do best every day.

4   In the last seven days, I have received recognition or praise for doing good work.

5   My supervisor, or someone at work, seems to care about me as a person.

6   There is someone at work who encourages my development.

7   At work, my opinions seem to count.

8   The mission or purpose of my company makes me feel my job is important.

9   My associates or fellow colleagues are committed to doing quality work.

10   I have a best friend at work.

11   In the last six months, someone at work has talked to me about my progress.

12   This last year, I have had opportunities at work to learn and grow.

SOURCE Gallup, 2022

Here is what we believe. The answers to the Gallup Q12 that identify engagement scores give us an outcome measure of the relationship the organization already has, based on past behaviours and experiences of their colleagues. They do not, however, provide concrete solutions for improvement. Many HR and communication professionals forget that the survey is the first step for listening and then acting on feedback. Instead, many of the organizations we've worked with focus on the score, prioritize low-cost initiatives and often ignore issues that involve time and resources. This can leave colleagues feeling unheard, resulting in fatigue and frustration.

When we are talking about engagement in this book we are intent on specifically bringing the DEI initiatives and plans to life. The next chapter will expand on internal communication activities and plans. This chapter, however, will really focus on the collaboration that needs to take place to connect plans and strategies to behaviours and beliefs.

Engagement and DEI

As we mentioned, the Gallup Q12 does provide a unique score of general employee engagement in your organization. It also provides benchmarked data, since most engagement surveys ask similar question, so your organization can be compared with other organizations and competitors globally.

There has also been a lot of work done to correlate engagement with business results. In fact, 71 per cent of executives say that employee engagement is critical to their company's success. In a hybrid working world where leaders are concerned with productivity, disengaged colleagues cost organizations around $450–550 billion each year in the US alone. According to Gallup's meta-analysis, organizations that scored highest on employee engagement showed 21 per cent higher levels of profitability and 17 per cent higher on productivity (Gallup, 2022).

But what is the relationship between engagement and DEI? Studies have shown that colleagues who are satisfied with their organization's commitment to diversity and inclusion are twice as engaged as dissatisfied colleagues (Fullilove, 2019). In the UK, according to Changeboard research, companies with diverse leaders generate twice the revenue and profit compared to those without. Colleagues also worked 12 per cent harder, are 19 per cent more likely to stay longer and collaborate up to 57 per cent more effectively with peers (Jouany and Mäkipää, 2022).

You may be surprised to know that a 'good' engagement score is 50+ and engagement market leaders fall above 67 (Barker, 2022).

With many organizations being proactive about self-identification at the recruitment stage, we would not be surprised if organizations begin looking at disparities in engagement scores between diverse groups. One rare study conducted by the British Columbia (BC) Public Service in 2015 (Martin, 2015) found that:

- Persons with disabilities were less engaged than those without disabilities.
- Men were less engaged than women.
- Visible minorities were less engaged than those who were not a member of a visible minority group.
- Aboriginal peoples were as equally engaged as non-Aboriginal peoples.

It is important to remember that a less engaged group does not reflect on the skills, intelligence or work ethic of a group. It may reveal cultural issues that impact a sense of belonging since engagement scores measure whether an individual plans to stay with the organization, says good things about the organization and strives to go above and beyond (Aon Hewitt, 2015). The key to identifying disparities is further research on answering why the disparities exist versus taking them at face value.

As organizations explore challenges with recruitment and retention of colleagues as part of DEI efforts, we're expecting more research specific to diverse groups.

Inner Strength Engagement Model

When it comes to DEI, what organizations are looking for will not be solved by an annual survey that provides a general score. What organizations and leaders are looking for when it comes to engagement is more action-oriented. It's about turning strategies into results and promises into customer and colleague experiences.

That's why Priya created the Inner Strength Engagement Model (ISEM) in 2012 to set goals specific to engagement and connect them to operational plans. We think this model is a good one to identify gaps, what's working and what isn't in your organization. The ISEM encourages organizations to set proactive engagement goals and then connect them to operational and communication activities.

FIGURE 11.1 The Inner Strength Engagement Model

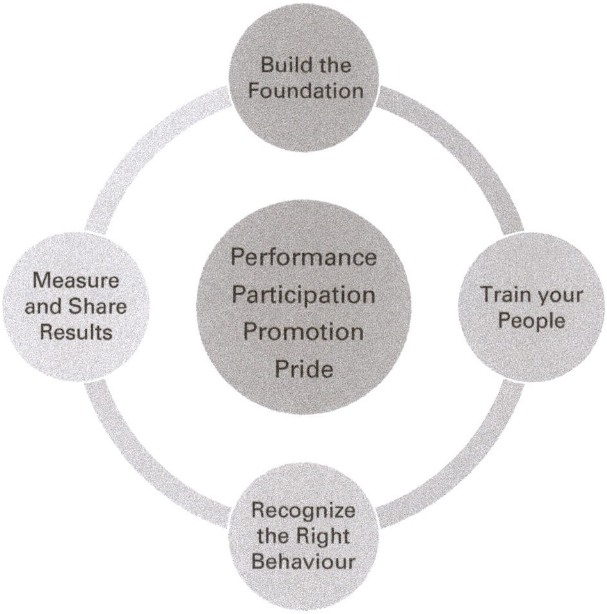

SOURCE Inner Strength Communication Inc.

Setting engagement goals

In the ISEM, we start by setting engagement goals to support performance, participation, promotion and pride. Goals can be aspirational and strategic and they can also be more specific and tactical as a problem-solving technique on a specific activity.

Performance

A performance goal refers to what success looks like for the organization. Here, we are specifically looking for organizational impacts that are likely to be articulated in the DEI plan and are connected to the R's we introduced you to in Chapter 1.

Here are some examples of performance goals linked to a DEI plan.

Representation:

- 45 per cent women in leadership positions by 2025.
- Increase diverse suppliers by 10 per cent in one year.
- Our colleague diversity is representative of our patient diversity by 2025.

Recruitment:

- Increase job applications from diverse candidates by 20 per cent in 2023.
- Create partnerships with 20 colleges and universities to identify high potential students.
- Reduce bias in the recruiting process by training all recruiters on new processes in 2022.

Retention:

- Racialized groups stay with the organization at the same rates as the whole organization.
- Reduce turnover of women by 10 per cent to be in line with the men by 2025.

Reputation:

- Recognized as a top employer of choice by 2025.
- Recognized as a leader in DEI by receiving an award in the community.
- Fewer negative incidents reported online with our organization.
- 10 per cent more positive comment on Glassdoor in 2023.

Results:

- Expand product lines to enter new markets and grow the business by 10 per cent
- Increase productivity by 5 per cent year on year.

Other goals may be more holistic:

- Increase engagement scores by 10 per cent overall.
- Introduce employee resources groups (ERGs) to create a community where colleagues feel they belong.
- Ensure our leaders and colleagues demonstrate our value of respect in their everyday dealings with peers and customers.

Participation

Participation goals clearly articulate what a colleague must do or do differently in order to achieve an organization's performance goals.

So many organizations create overarching statements and strategies and then expect colleagues to automatically understand how those words translate into behaviours, but that's where things tend to go wrong. We create a set of values that are aspirational, we put them on our website, put words and posters on our walls and leaders repeat them often, yet we never clearly articulate what the words mean or what they look like or feel like.

Think of the word **respect** as a value. If not connected to clearly articulated behaviours, respect can mean many things. It can mean we are all equals so we must show respect to each other regardless of age, disability, gender, race, religion, sexual orientation, or title and role. On the other hand, respect may be hierarchical, for example, we always show respect to those ranked higher or older than ourselves. These are two drastically different meanings.

When we're talking about participation goals, we are connecting the dots between intention and action.

If our performance goal is to increase diversity in recruitment, our participation goal can be:

- HR to launch a new recruitment process and hiring managers to use the new process when finding talent.

- Company recruiters to review language and requirements in job descriptions that may unfairly exclude qualified candidates.
- Encourage diverse interview panels to meet with potential candidates.

Promotion

Promotion goals focus on what you want colleagues to say about your organization to customers, partners, peers, ther, friends, families, neighbours and their social networks. Colleagues can be your greatest advocates or toughest critics.

What do we want them sharing about the organization and its DEI efforts?

Thinking about promotion goals in advance will also go a long way to help you solidify the messaging.

Here are some examples of promotion goals:

- 10 per cent more colleagues to refer a friend to work for our organization year over year.
- Colleagues in our ERGs to present at ten local, national and industry conferences this year about our work and accomplishments in DEI.
- 20 per cent more positive reviews on Glassdoor.

In this space, you may even want to think about what you don't want them to say to plan your own messaging to counter the negative narratives that may occur.

Pride

Pride is about how you want colleagues to feel. This goal is always a little harder to measure but must be part of the proactive conversation in order to drive your engagement and communication plan.

When we get DEI right, colleagues should be proud of:

- Working in a positive culture where everyone has an opportunity for growth.
- Being part of an organization that cares and wants to be a good corporate citizen.
- An organization that serves its communities and customers through shared perspectives.
- An organization where they can thrive and grow.

Once goals have been set, it's time to take a look at how to incorporate the goals into the organization's operations.

Using the model

Build the foundation

The first operational area we look at is the organization's foundations. The foundations are what hold the organization together. Foundations answer the questions:

- Who are we?
- What do we stand for?
- How do we do things around here?
- What are our plans?

The foundation is the base or starting point of any programme. It's the words, direction and guidelines that we constantly come back to that determine if we are making the right decisions and going in the right direction.

Let's take a look at some of the foundations that are important for DEI.

VALUES

Values describe who we are as an organization. Many colleagues make these values the centre of the culture and personality of an organization, and are looking for those values to form a connection with their own personal values when they choose the organizations they want to work for.

Brené Brown has a list of values that she shares on her website which is pretty comprehensive (Brown, 2022). Words like excellence, accountability, respect and inclusion are ones we see often.

Let's take a look at the following values:

Coca-Cola (Coca-Cola, 2015):

- **Leadership:** The courage to shape a better future.
- **Collaboration:** Leverage collective genius.
- **Integrity:** Be real.
- **Accountability:** If it is to be, it's up to me.

- **Passion:** Committed in heart and mind.
- **Diversity:** As inclusive as our brands.
- **Quality:** What we do, we do well.

NHS (NHS, 2022):

- **Working together for patients:** Patients come first in everything we do.
- **Respect and dignity:** We value every person – whether patient, their families or carers, or staff – as an individual, respect their aspirations and commitments in life, and seek to understand their priorities, needs, abilities and limits.
- **Commitment to quality of care:** We earn the trust placed in us by insisting on quality and striving to get the basics of quality of care – safety, effectiveness and patient experience right every time.
- **Compassion:** We ensure that compassion is central to the care we provide and respond with humanity and kindness to each person's pain, distress, anxiety or need.
- **Improving lives:** We strive to improve health and wellbeing and people's experiences of the NHS.
- **Everyone counts:** We maximize our resources for the benefit of the whole community, and make sure nobody is excluded, discriminated against or left behind.

Harvard Business School (Harvard Business School, 2022):

- **Respect for the rights, differences, and dignity of others.**
- **Honesty and integrity** in dealing with all members of the community.
- **Accountability** for personal behaviour.

It's not unusual today to have organizations that have words like respect, dignity, integrity, community, inclusion and diversity in their values statement. It remains for you to understand if your values are reflected in diversity efforts, priorities, leader and colleague behaviours.

VISION/MISSION/PURPOSE

Does your organization have a vision, mission and/or purpose? It's important that you have these aspirations in front of you as you plan for engagement.

We like the following definition from Jen Croneberger:

Vision: defines where the organization is going or what the future looks like when the organization is successful.

Mission: defines what the company does, and who it serves and why.

Purpose: defines how the company shows up every day.

To give you an idea of how each one is unique, 'Vision is the picture. Mission is the road map to get there. Purpose is the feeling that everyone, from the CEO to the janitor, has when you accomplish what you set out to do' (Croneberger, 2020).

Other similar foundations like brand promises, employer value propositions (EVPs) and unique selling propositions (USPs) are also important foundations you can rely on to help define your organization and connect them to the why of the DEI strategy.

Ask yourself if there is concrete and inspirational language in mission, value and purpose that can provide support to your DEI plan.

CODE OF CONDUCT AND OTHER POLICIES

A code of conduct, code of ethics and other policies are usually established to protect an organization from liability. We get colleagues or members to sign a document (usually full of legalese) to simply say, 'We told you our expectations, you signed on the dotted line or clicked a box saying you understand', so that when you don't follow the rules, we can take action.

In recent years, there has been a mission afoot to make codes of conduct simpler and more understandable and when understood, they form important foundations on what organizations expect in the words, behaviours and actions of their colleagues and the consequences of breaking the rules.

Ask yourself if language and guidance in codes of conduct and policies support your DEI strategy. If there are disconnects, it may be important to highlight discrepancies or inconsistencies in policies and the DEI efforts.

STRATEGIES

As discussed in our previous chapters, when it comes to DEI, we're looking for a business strategy and DEI strategies and more importantly clear connections between them. A strategy outlines an organization's goals, priorities, key performance indicators (KPIs) and success metrics.

It is critical that the overarching business strategy has references to social and community programmes like corporate social responsibility (CSR), environment social governance (ESG) and/or DEI.

As mentioned previously, it's also important that an actionable DEI strategy has been created as a foundational document for DEI efforts.

When strategies do not exist, there is simply no direction and the result is usually throwing darts randomly and hoping they stick somewhere without having a clear target to aim for.

If a strategy exists, use it as a foundation for building the engagement plan. If it doesn't then help the organization create one.

COLLEAGUE PROGRAMMES

Colleague programmes like health and wellness benefits, remote and flexible working, parental leave, and professional development and learning can provide important foundations when it comes to DEI programmes. They also provide proof and action points.

It's important to understand these people programmes and build relationships with HR teams so that everyone is creating connections with how the organization demonstrates commitment to DEI and offers opportunities fairly.

GLOSSARY OF TERMS

Recently, we've seen many organizations refer to a glossary of terms filled with words that are appropriate and sometimes inappropriate as the DEI conversation evolves. This can be an important foundation. It's important that our language is respectful and appropriate. It's also important to make sure these glossaries are accessible to everyone, and set expectations that they will continue to be updated as we learn.

We've covered some terms and shared some resources in Chapter 10 on inclusive language.

TOOLS AND TECHNOLOGY

Tools and technology are important foundations for some of your DEI goals. They are the foundations that may make some of your plans easier to achieve.

Do you have stock imagery or your own image library that showcases diversity? Do you have software that ensures that communication is accessible? Are there resources available for accessibility? Are your buildings built with accessible design standards? Do you use recruiting software that embeds anti-bias into its efforts?

Questions for internal communication:

- When you consider your engagement goals, what foundations exist in your organization today?
- If they do not exist, do they need to be created?
- If they do exist, can they be improved or updated to include DEI language?
- Are the foundations accessible and easy to understand?
- Does the organization use any tools or technology that can help?
- Can you use the foundations to explain and demonstrate the organization's commitment to DEI?

Train your people

As consultants, we are often amazed when organizations with good intentions and solid foundations are frustrated when colleagues are simply not aware that programmes and plans exist to demonstrate commitment. I'm sure many of you have experienced the following:

- Benefits and colleague programmes are available, yet very few are aware of them, or struggle to know how to access them.
- A strategy is in place, yet very few do what they need to do in order to deliver the results.
- Managers are inconsistent with messaging and can't answer questions.
- Colleagues regularly exhibit behaviour that seems to fly in the face of the values we espouse and the promises we make.

So many organizations and individuals are doing their best, with good intent, yet there tends to be a gap in understanding and action from colleagues.

One of Priya's favourite movies is *Field of Dreams* starring Kevin Costner (Robinson, 1989). In it, Ray Kinsella, Costner's character, builds a baseball diamond in the middle of a corn field, because he keeps hearing a mysterious voice say, 'If you build it, they will come.' They, in this quote. refer to ghosts of his father and some famous baseball players. Priya often uses the quote to describe some activities in the organizations she has worked with. There is the belief that if we create an intranet, people will magically appear without us ever telling them about it. A strategy is in place and has been talked about for years, yet no one explained the need for the strategy to colleagues. A DEI plan is in place, yet we've only talked to those implementing processes, but not to the colleagues who will have to work differently.

That's why we have to connect the dots and teach colleagues through training and communication. So, once you have a foundation to share, what does training and communication look like?

LEARNING AND DEVELOPMENT

Training through your organization's learning and development initiatives is a great way to train your people. There are many options available to your organization:

- Live training or workshops delivered in person or online.
- Online courses delivered through your learning management system or through an external organization.
- Certificate, degree and diploma programmes delivered through colleges and universities.
- Conferences you send your colleagues to in specific areas of interest.

It's important to ensure that any training considers maintenance and sustainability of the learning. For instance, if workshops are done on systemic bias once per year, is it good enough for new colleagues who join after the training is complete to wait one year to learn? Another example is if someone signed off on a code of conduct training at the beginning of employment and has been with your organization for 25 years; is that good enough to influence understanding and behaviour?

When talking about training, think about what needs to be taught and how to maintain knowledge in the long term. The other thing to consider is whether training that was created five years ago is incorrect or inappropriate today.

When looking at training, also think about the colleague life cycle. What do colleagues need to know when they join your organization? What do they need to know when they get promoted to managing people? Is there anything that is important when they are exiting the organization? Also consider how often they must refresh their knowledge, for example when it comes to codes of conduct many of the organizations we've worked with ask employees to take training on an annual basis to refresh and update knowledge.

PERFORMANCE PLANNING AND REVIEW

Another education opportunity is part of the performance management process. In many organizations, foundations like strategy and values are reinforced through performance management processes. This is a key learning opportunity for colleagues.

Many organizations we've worked for or with have leaders, departments, teams and colleagues set annual performance goals that are aligned with the overall strategy and values. It helps to create alignment with the priorities. This encourages proactive conversations and checkpoints to discuss results, actions and behaviours on at least an annual basis. Some organizations also encourage check-in conversations on a monthly or quarterly basis.

From a DEI perspective, perhaps there is an opportunity to connect values and strategies to every day behaviour and business results achieved.

MANAGER COMMUNICATION

In the Gallagher State of the Sector report (Gallagher, 2022) which annually measures the state of internal communication globally, enhancing people-manager communication was one of the top five priorities identified for 2022. Enhancing people-manager communication has always been an important opportunity, especially when the manager/supervisor has regular contact with colleagues. Whether your teams work onsite in retail, distribution, manufacturing or office facilities or in a remote and hybrid way, the relationship between manager and colleague may be the most important contact to connect the strategy with delivery.

When we're delivering programmes for clients, managers are a key group that need to be prepared to communicate and support business initiatives. In order for them to be successful and consistent with the organization's messaging, they need training and support materials. In DEI programmes, managers need to understand what has been planned enough to be able to explain the impacts of the programme on their own decisions and actions and that of their teams.

A few things to consider when it comes to inclusive manager communication:

- Managers will benefit from communication training to build confidence in their work and how they communicate inclusive practices to their teams (for example, how to manage inclusive team meetings).
- Managers should receive organizational information in advance, if possible, or at the very least at the same time as public announcements are

made which are sensitive in nature or require confidentiality for legal reasons.

- Managers need fact sheets to understand what is changing, when things will happen and why decisions were made. They also need to understand specific impacts to their team's processes, procedures and programmes.
- Managers will benefit from having clear messaging that they have permission to share, especially if the messaging is sensitive.
- They also require a thorough set of questions and answers (Q&As) to have the facts and correct answers at their fingertips to drive consistency.
- Finally, ensure you give managers a list of who to reach out to should they or their team members have any further questions.

The more prepared managers are, the better they are in creating consistency and reinforcement of the messages being shared.

In DEI, it may also be appropriate to train managers on what is not appropriate and on what may undermine the organization, against the code of conduct or values. These are the conversations that we are sometimes afraid to have, yet having conversations in the open about what good looks like and what it doesn't look like creates a clear line in the sand of what the organization deems as appropriate or inappropriate. The 'unsaid' often allows people to make up what they believe are exceptions to the rules.

INTERNAL COMMUNICATION

Internal communication is an integral way to make colleagues aware of programmes, understand why decisions were made, do the right things and believe in the cause.

We believe the power of internal communication is not only to communicate on behalf of the organization but to influence how the organization, its leader and colleagues, communicate. Although we covered internal communication planning and best practices in Chapter 5, there are a few things to think about when using internal communication.

Use internal communication practices to launch programmes through campaigns, create consistency through messages and reinforce learning with soundbites and stories. Internal communication also keeps colleagues informed of changes, new programmes and updates.

Many internal communication professionals also function as advisers to executives to help them lead through words and actions.

Questions for internal communication:

- Now that you have a plan or foundations built, how do colleagues learn about them?
- Does the training need to be formally incorporated in learning and development or performance management? Can you deliver through internal communication channels and processes or through supporting manager conversations?
- Do you have a set of key messages that connect the dots between the foundations and the organizational impacts you are looking for?
- Do you need to create a new training/learning opportunity, or can it be incorporated into a programme or training that already exists like the orientation programme or a module in the online training system?
- Is the organization clearly articulating or demonstrating what appropriate and inappropriate actions/behaviours look like?

Recognize the right behaviour

The third part of the Inner Strength Engagement Model is to recognize the right behaviour with a big emphasis on the word **right**.

When it comes to engagement, there is nothing worse than recognizing the wrong behaviour to teach your colleagues what the culture is really like and what the organization and its leaders truly value. We tell our story based on who we promote and who we overlook. Our culture is made up of moments where we herald the hero who swept in to fix an avoidable crisis versus the team that did the work proactively to ensure that the crisis never happened in the first place.

The world is full of examples of performative gestures and empty words and promises. It's probably what causes a lot of frustration when it comes to DEI.

WORDS VERSUS ACTION

An important way to recognize the right behaviour is to match words with actions. What did we say versus what did we do. It's great when we see promises come to life and real work done in order to drive change.

When organizations talk about being committed to DEI, you only have to search for the images of the executive team or board of directors to see a lack of diversity on display, at least visibly. When organizations talk about their commitment to accessibility, one visit will tell you if they have accessible venues and tools.

One of the most interesting demonstrations about the disconnect between words and actions happened recently on International Day of People with Disabilities, December 3 2022 – a United Nations sanctioned day that is observed internationally to raise awareness to build an accessible and equitable world for people with disabilities. As organizations were raising awareness of the work they are doing to support this day, an accessibility twitter bot @GAADbot retweeted tweets of images used that were not accessible, e.g. no alt text.

When looking at engagement, take a good look at what the organization is saying internally and externally, and identify the actions that either support the words as proof that we mean what we said or highlight discrepancies that could create disengagement.

WHAT WE SEE IS WHAT WE BELIEVE

We've noticed an interesting trend lately. Organizations are choosing not to post photographs of their board, their management team or their conference speakers. This usually tends to happen when they don't want a discrepancy to be highlighted or on display on their websites.

When we started A Leader Like Me in 2020, it was to help women of colour so that they could lead the way, show up and be visible in order to help others see what was possible.

Think of the stories that are shared in your organizations. Are the stories and highlights on websites and intranets talking about the leadership team alone? Do we tend to focus on one department, region or country more often than others? Do we talk more often about work at the head office versus what is happening in front of customers. Are we more focused on the products we sell, versus the problems the products solve for the customer and the people behind the innovation.

Colleagues (and customers) are asking if they are part of the stories or treated as outsiders looking into an inner circle.

There is an opportunity to truly try and see from another perspective and use imagery and video to tell the stories that matter to ensure people feel like they belong.

We do, however, need to be authentic in our portrayal. We may show advertising of the diverse teams serving customers but the reality is vastly different when you walk into your reception area or store location. It's okay to be aspirational but we need to be careful not to be completely disconnected from reality.

SHOWCASE WHAT GOOD LOOKS LIKE

There is a real opportunity to show what good practice looks like. Share the values, strategy, mission and vision in action. Storytelling is an incredible way to recognize the right behaviour.

Highlight when a goal has been met and a commitment to diversity has been demonstrated. But here is something to keep in mind. Recognize skill, experience and expertise versus simply putting someone out in front to check a box.

For example, with the increased focus on DEI in the past few years, plenty of diverse speakers were brought in internally and externally to talk about DEI or their lived experience, but we need to ensure we're provided a platform to showcase their knowledge, expertise, innovative way of thinking and the results of their work or advice. For instance, although we are women of colour who provide communication in the DEI space, we've had long careers in internal communication with organizations going through transformational change. We can be hired to help with mergers and acquisitions, programme launches, confidence training and our experience working in complex environments.

FORMAL RECOGNITION PROGRAMMES

Take a look at the recognition programmes in the organization and ask if they have the potential to reinforce the goals and foundations that exist. Some of the best recognition programmes are usually values-based. What if respect was a value and colleagues received recognition for being respectful and inclusive? What if we recognized teams and innovation that have brought new thinking to the organization? What if DEI goals set by teams were actually highlighted and rewarded for meeting goals?

PEER RECOGNITION

There is always an opportunity to encourage peer recognition and storytelling along with customer stories on a positive experience. We often hear the negative voices the loudest but fail to talk about what is working and when things go right. Engaging colleagues and customers to tell their stories of the everyday moments that matter to them are an opportunity to provide a balanced narrative or one that is more positive than you thought. Just be careful of trying to spin messages to be positive when the culture feels like the opposite is true. Also be careful of dominant groups centring themselves and patting themselves on the back versus getting the authentic stories of those colleagues who have had positive experiences. Be careful about compliments that are really microaggressions in disguise, like telling an individual with an accent how good you believe their English is, when they've been speaking English, along with several other languages, their entire lives. What you are looking for are the opportunities to tell the inspiring stories that reinforce the objectives.

Questions for internal communication:

- How does your organization recognize the appropriate behaviour?
- Does the organization recognize the inappropriate behaviour? If yes, are you comfortable highlighting or calling out the discrepancy?
- Do leaders' actions match their words?
- Are the stories you tell and the heroes you highlight representative of the organization, its colleagues, customers and community?

Measure and share results

The final part of the Inner Strength Engagement Model is measuring and sharing results. Colleagues want proof and they want to see progress. They also want to know that the changes being made are leading to the outcomes and organizational impact that were promised. We introduced a conversation on measurement in Chapter 5.

COMMUNICATING GOALS AND MILESTONES

Just like with business strategies, it is important for an organization to share DEI goals and measure results and progress against the KPIs identified. This works even better when those KPIs are embedded into the business strategy and are part of a regular update on progress during town halls and quarterly results reporting.

Many companies share a report card on an annual basis whether it is part of their CSR, ESG, DEI or annual report.

NETFLIX

Netflix published its first diversity report in January 2021 although it had been sharing diversity data on their jobs site since 2013 (Myers, 2021). They published a follow-up report one year later to showcase progress against their goals:

- Women now make up 51.7 per cent of the global workforce.
- They grew to 16 colleague resource groups.

- They conducted their annual pay equity review.
- They continued to offer inclusive benefits, including gender-inclusive parental leave, transgender and non-binary care in our US health plans, and family-forming support for colleagues regardless of marital status, gender or sexual orientation.
- They are also taking a good look at on-screen inclusivity in programming.

SOURCE Netflix, 2022

AUTHENTIC CONVERSATIONS TO SHARE SUCCESS AND FAILURE

In sharing results, organizations will benefit from providing balanced reporting. Many organizations try to keep colleagues motivated through rose-tinted glasses, always painting the positive picture. It's important to keep in mind that trust is built with authenticity and vulnerability.

Make sure you share the successes and the failures. If there is slower progress on specific goals and initiatives, explain why the struggles exist. Explain what the organization and individuals need to do to overcome challenges. Reinforce why it's important to stay the course. Also be ready to explain when the organization needs to course-correct and share changes based on feedback and updated education.

There are also conversations around psychological safety that encourage people to unlearn thinking and behaviour, giving them permission to make mistakes along the way. Of course, there will be situations that will warrant tough and necessary action, A good recent example is advertisers, sponsors and social media outlets who have ended relationships with Kanye West (who has legally changed his name to 'Ye') after antisemitic remarks (Bowen, 2022).

We know that there are things that are simply inappropriate today that would have been accepted only a few years ago. That's why it's important to take context into consideration when talking about the past. The discussion that needs to happen in your organization or with your clients is where lines are drawn when it comes to identifying opportunities to drive change or action that needs to be taken.

From an internal communication perspective, ensure that leaders are transparent about issues and try to talk about them openly. What happened and why? Why was action taken or not taken? What is the plan to ensure it never happens again? What did we learn?

CONTINUOUS IMPROVEMENT

It is okay – in fact it is encouraged – to share soundbites of progress as they are achieved. Announcing new hires. Celebrating new programmes and products. Exploring new markets. Highlighting success. We often say that relationships with colleagues are built through conversations not campaigns. Although people may remember the big milestone celebrations, there is an opportunity to build momentum through the little steps forward along the way. Don't wait for the big moment if you've got progress to share.

Note that when announcing new hires or changes to diversity statistics, the emphasis should be on skills, experience and what individuals have or will add to the organization with links to results and accomplishments.

OUTCOMES AND ORGANIZATIONAL IMPACTS

The data has consistently told us that DEI is linked to business results. Make sure you articulate your goals and link them to the business results colleagues and leaders care about. Has the organization grown? Did it become an employer of choice? Has engagement improved? What does retention and recruitment look like? Are you receiving more applications and interest? What innovation has happened as a result of improving belonging?

Highlighting accomplishments provides proof that strategies are working and having an impact on areas all employees care about including success, stability and sustainability of the organization itself.

FEEDBACK AND ACTION

The final piece on measuring and sharing results focuses on colleague feedback. Many organizations ask colleagues for feedback through colleague surveys, focus groups, polls and pulses. Many complain about the fear of survey fatigue but we've often heard that colleagues are keen to share their feedback as long as they felt leaders were both listening and acting on results. When asking for feedback, it's really important that the organization comes back with results of what they heard, the priorities that will be addressed (and why, since you won't act on everything) and the resulting actions delivered.

Questions for internal communication:

- Do you share DEI progress on a regular basis?
- Do you have authentic conversations to share both success and failure?
- Are goals measurable?

- Do colleagues see progress?
- Do they connect the dots between DEI and business results?
- Does the organization act on feedback and share action plans?

Bringing it all together

Here is a micro-example based on one piece of the DEI plan. What you'll notice is when possible, engagement is simply embedded into existing processes. That's the goal. That DEI is not something that is worked on at the side of the desk and the DEI manager's job, but that it is simply part of how we do things around here.

TABLE 11.1 A high-level example of the ISEM in action

Goals	Build the foundation	Train your people	Recognize the right behavior	Measure and share success
Performance Increase retention by 10%	Business strategy	Communicate strategy	Bonus programme for managers	Quarterly results shared Retention KPI
Participation Colleagues need to be respectful of one another and create a culture of belonging	Code of conduct Values	Orientation inclusion and culture training Code of conduct training Manager training	Manager of the year award which includes colleague recognition awards	Engagement scores
Promotion Colleagues say this is a great place to work	Colleague referral programme Strong benefits programme	Key messages Regular communication of benefits	Peer recognition Colleagues nominate managers	Recognition as employer of choice
Pride Colleagues love working for the organization	Mission Vision Purpose	Feature proud colleagues and why they love to work here	Highlight colleagues and managers making a difference	External promotion of why organization is a great place to work

KEY TAKEAWAYS

- Although the engagement score measured through the Gallup Q12 is the traditional way to measure engagement, we believe the score provides an outcome of work already done versus direction.

- The Inner Strength Engagement Model helps you create engagement goals and identify operational ways to evaluate your work and improve connections.

- Set goals against performance, participation, promotion and pride to create clarity around what success looks like from an organizational perspective and what you want colleagues to do and say and how you want them to feel.

- Foundations including vision, mission, purpose, values, strategies, policies and tools must exist as an anchor for future work to be done.

- It's important to train your people formally through education and training and informally through communication to ensure they are aware, understand, act and believe.

- We must recognize the right behaviours in order to gain trust and credibility.

- Measuring and sharing success regularly provides proof that strategies are working and goals are being achieved.

REFLECTIVE QUESTIONS

- Do I understand clearly what success looks like when communicating the DEI strategy?

- Do I understand how I can use the power of communication to create performance, participation, promotion and pride?

- Am I comfortable pointing out disconnects that are hurting progress in DEI for the organization?

- Do I have the relationships in the organization to make DEI an organization-wide effort, not just the job of one department or individual?

Bibliography

Aon Hewitt (2015, June) Say, Stay, or Strive, aon.com/attachments/human-capital-consulting/2015-Drivers-of-Say-Stay-Strive.pdf (archived at https://perma.cc/4KC9-NGLQ)

Barker, L (2022, 21 July) How to calculate employee engagement score, Kona, heykona.com/blog/how-to-calculate-employee-engagement-score (archived at https://perma.cc/AWQ6-VJ88)

Bowen, C (2022, 25 October) All of the celebrities and brands vowing to boycott Kanye following antisemitism remarks, *Cosmopolitan*, cosmopolitan.com/uk/reports/a41764688/kanye-cancelled-yeezy-adidas/ (archived at https://perma.cc/XR8E-6MZF)

Breen, A (2022, 15 March) It's equal pay day, and this Twitter bot is calling out companies that pay men more than women, Entrepreneur, entrepreneur.com/business-news/its-equal-pay-day-and-this-twitter-bot-is-calling-out/422096 (archived at https://perma.cc/683V-2V5N)

Brown, B (2022, 5 November) Dare to lead list of values, brenebrown.com/resources/dare-to-lead-list-of-values/ (archived at https://perma.cc/ND5C-W2GS)

Coca-Cola (2015, 11 December) Mission, vision, values, coca-cola.co.za/working-at-coke/our-values/mision-vision-values (archived at https://perma.cc/P399-R25R)

Croneberger, J (2020, 4 March) Vision, mission and purpose: The difference, Forbes, forbes.com/sites/forbescoachescouncil/2020/03/04/vision-mission-and-purpose-the-difference/?sh=70d9e0f2280e (archived at https://perma.cc/WF6R-UQ53)

Fullilove, C (2019, June) Improving the employee experience through diversity, ADP, adp.com/spark/articles/2019/06/improving-the-employee-experience-through-diversity.aspx#:~:text=By%20providing%20diverse%20employees%20with,to%20share%20ideas%20and%20grow (archived at https://perma.cc/L3BR-YNKW)

Gallagher (2022) *State of the Sector 2021/22*. Chicago, Gallagher

Gallup (2022, 29n October) Gallup's Employee Engagement Survey: Ask the Right questions with the Q12® Survey, gallup.com/workplace/356063/gallup-q12-employee-engagement-survey.aspx (archived at https://perma.cc/WMC6-M2HH)

Harvard Business School (2022, 6 December) Community values, hbs.edu/about/campus-and-culture/Pages/community-values.aspx (archived at https://perma.cc/F7UF-G385)

Martin, J (2015, 7 December) Keeping diversity and inclusion at the top of the agenda, Changeboard, changeboard.com/article-details/15981/keeping-diversity-and-inclusion-at-the-top-of-the-agenda/ (archived at https://perma.cc/P23P-KEGD)

Matheson, S Y (2016, May) How much does engagement vary among diversity groups, www2.gov.bc.ca/assets/gov/data/statistics/government/wes/driver-topics/how_much_does_engagement_vary.pdf (archived at https://perma.cc/5V4N-7HRZ)

Myers, V (2021, 13 January) Inclusion takes root at Netflix: Our first report, Netflix, about.netflix.com/en/news/netflix-inclusion-report-2021 (archived at https://perma.cc/6976-RGMU)

Myers, V (2022, 10 February) Our progress on inclusion: 2021 update, Netflix, about.netflix.com/en/news/our-progress-on-inclusion-2021-update (archived at https://perma.cc/XPU9-J85K)

Netflix (2022) Inclusion & Diversity, Netflix, about.netflix.com/en/inclusion (archived at https://perma.cc/5BLW-M3SC)

NHS (2022) The NHS values, healthcareers.nhs.uk/working-health/working-nhs/nhs-constitution (archived at https://perma.cc/B3ZS-AGYT)

Robinson, P A (Director) (1989) *Field of Dreams* [Motion Picture]

Jouany, V and Mäkipää, M (2022, 30 October) 8 employee engagement statistics you need to know in 2022, Haiilo, haiilo.com/blog/employee-engagement-8-statistics-you-need-to-know/ (archived at https://perma.cc/BCJ7-T8P2)

12

Best practices to develop and communicate your DEI strategy

Inclusive internal communication enables powerful connections, demonstrates curiosity and cultivates belonging through two-way engagement. This results in trusted, clear and effective communication, allowing people to thrive in their work and impact organizational performance.

As we enter the final chapter of this book, we hope we've made a case for the vital role of internal communication in supporting the DEI strategy in organizations we help. In this final chapter, we will fine tune and talk about some of the best practices we've seen through our work and our research with organizations around the world. We'll also share some of our reflections on the state of the work and what it means to work on the DEI focus for your organization or client.

It's been interesting for both of us, two brown women, from different generations, working across two continents (Priya is part of Generation X while Advita is a Millennial). Priya immigrated to Toronto, Canada, while Advita was born and raised in Manchester, UK. We should have different experiences, yet the similarities we share have been a source of surprise and connection.

Our work in internal communication has been well received. It's where we run successful agencies: Advita with CommsRebel and Priya with Inner Strength Communication. We are well regarded in our respective communication associations and have both earned fellowships – Advita with the Chartered Institute of Public Relations (CIPR) and Priya with the International Association of Business Communicators (IABC).

The work we do in internal communication is our passion and expertise. Although it has its challenges when we're helping organizations through transformational change, we find the work relatively easy. On the other hand, the work we do in the DEI space can feel like an uphill struggle to a peak we cannot see. It's especially hard in this age of chaos full of stoked divisions, a fight against woke and the rise of white supremacy and right-wing activism. We're surrounded by messages that create us-and-them scenarios centred around scarcity complex and the fear that when someone else benefits, the rest are left behind. We often wonder if the light is fading on DEI or whether many will give up because of the hardship and trauma involved in the work.

Yet, let's take this opportunity to remember that there are signs of progress:

- Investors are waking up to the marketing potential of DEI with the Principles of Responsible Investment (PRI) urging investors to integrate DEI into investment and ownership decisions (Chiu, 2022).

- We are seeing more diversity in governments and organizations as women and ethnic representation begins increasing at all levels worldwide.

- Large multinationals report on diversity figures and actions on an annual basis.

- All around us, we're seeing movies, entertainment, music, awards recipients and advertising (to name a few) changing to be more representative and reaping the rewards of doing what they previously thought would be too difficult.

- DEI is front and centre in the public discourse, whatever side you're on.

- And research continues to find correlations between embracing diversity and bottom-line results.

Our work at the intersection of both internal communication and DEI allows us to see possibilities and progress. We believe that conversations need to continue for us to navigate change until inclusion is valued and simply becomes the expected and foundational. We strongly believe, and the data has consistently proven, that inclusive cultures create innovative and successful organizations that can better serve their publics. We also believe that internal communication connects the dots between words and actions; values and behaviours; strategy and results; and brand promises with colleague and customer experiences. The hard work that focuses on the long term will make a real difference to organizations. So, stay the course. Focus on doing a few things well and make the case to move forward, even if it feels like one step ahead and two steps back some days. So here are a few things to remember as you navigate your path forward.

Acknowledge history

It's simple to believe that the DEI conversation that seems loud and active today is based on recent events. The murder of George Floyd in 2020 was a catalyst for a conversation that has aided acceleration. Yet the fight for human rights has been going on for centuries. That's why only talking about what's happening in the 2020s without acknowledging the atrocities of the past and the progress made by activists over generations will diminish history and perspectives. Acknowledgement tells people we see you and understand the systems and history that have brought you to the present.

Ask yourself:

- When highlighting a cause, do you understand the history and effects on the group impacted?

- Is there an individual in your organization or your inner circle who can share their perspectives (with permission)?

- Are the stories you tell from a dominant culture perspective or are they fairly representative?

Expect flashlights, mirrors and beacons

Understand that people will take DEI plans, language and actions personally. They will look for themselves to see if they can see they are represented. They will be faced with truths that highlight privilege and their past behaviours, beliefs and biases. They may not like what they see. They will look for guiding lights that create hope and warning lights that create fear. Lead with hope.

TABLE 12.1 Flashlights, mirrors, beacons

Flashlights	Mirrors	Beacons
• Looking for yourself	• Looking at yourself	• Looking for direction
• Feeling included or excluded based on what you find	• Liking or not liking what you see	• Guiding light or warning light?
• Will you keep searching to find your role and share the spotlight?	• Feeling attacked or uncomfortable	• Will you choose hope or fear?
	• Will you look closer and reflect or turn away?	• Will you choose the past, present or future?

Remember that we, as a human race, have much more in common with each other than we believe. Create conversations that allow people to express their hopes and fears safely.

Ask yourself:

- Do you create empathy by allowing colleagues to see perspectives they can relate to?
- Do you ensure everyone is represented and can see themselves in the plans and the progress?
- Are you clearly articulating the 'what's in it for me' to all colleagues?
- Are you ensuring that you are focused on both the hopes and addressing the fears?

Focus on representation

Review existing data or research to understand what representation looks like for your organization. A robust stakeholder analysis in the DEI space asks you to truly understand the demographics of your colleagues at different levels, your potential colleagues, your customers, your future customers, your suppliers, your communities and your countries or regions. What do you need to understand about disability, age, education, gender, race, religion, sexual orientation, socio-economic status when planning your communication?

The bottom line is people are looking for inclusion. They want to know that they matter to the organization and want to see themselves reflected in the stories told. Beyond demographics, do you really understand attitudes, opinions and beliefs? Also remember that when trying to represent, it needs to be realistic.

Ask yourself:

- Do you have a clear picture of who your stakeholders are?
- When colleagues read your strategy and stories, and see your videos, do they see themselves included in the narrative?
- Do you tend to tell stories closer to you or in a hierarchical fashion? More stories about head office than frontline? More about leaders versus teams? Do you focus on a variety of departments or just talk about sales and HR?

- Do you have real images or are you forced to use stock photography? When choosing stock, does it reflect what it looks like walking into your offices or places of work?

Articulate the DEI – why

Clearly articulate your and/or your organization's why. There are many reasons for focusing on DEI, and the more that it can be tied to your organization's business, the more successful you will be. The DEI – why is your anchor that holds everything together and creates a solid foundation for the work your organization needs to do.

There are plenty of reasons for why: the fight for human rights, to drive more representation, to impact recruitment and retention, to protect our reputation and to drive results.

We also need to articulate the DEI – why from the colleague point of view – connect it with purpose, help them buy in to progress, tie results to performance, centre the why around people and make it personal.

Ask yourself:

- Has your organization articulated why DEI is important for the organization and connected it to the business?
- Have you articulated why DEI is important to colleagues and creating an environment and culture where everyone belongs and is treated fairly?
- Can you create a manifesto or statement that connects the dots between brand promises and colleague and customer experiences?

Identify foundations

It can be an eye-opening practice to identify and take a good look at the organizations foundations including mission, vision, values, codes of conduct, policies and strategy. In most cases, you will find words and promises that can easily be connected to DEI efforts. Words like global, respect, diversity, community and customer often seem to have an element of DEI intuitively connected.

On the other hand, you may look at some foundations and see language and terms that are clearly disconnected to the DEI strategy. If this is the case, it is important to point out the disconnects in order to create clarity and update language to create consistency.

Ask yourself:

- What foundations exist that can be tied to the DEI strategy?
- Are there foundations that are disconnected?
- Are there new foundations that must be built in order to create clarity?

It's all about trust

Effective communication is one of the cornerstones of building trust in an organization. We often say that in the absence of communication, people tend to make up their own stories. Now imagine DEI strategies that involve operational changes that no one is warned about without any context of why, when and how. It's sure to drive fear and scepticism.

Our role is to ensure colleagues are aware, understand, act and believe. That doesn't happen by accident. Internal communication must be proactive and intentional in order to create the alignment and trust we're hoping for.

For internal communication, there are plenty of trust pitfalls you can fall into:

- Not allowing an opportunity for feedback.
- Irrelevant messaging.
- Inaccurate communications.
- Making assumptions.
- Limited representation within channels.
- Lack of information.
- Not coaching line managers in communication skills.
- Inconsistent cadence.
- No time to respond to the information shared.
- Lack of action fatigue.

Ask yourself:

- How can your DEI communication strategy build trust?
- What are the connections that are consistent and credible?
- Where are there disconnects between what you say and what you do?
- Is your environment and/or culture psychologically safe?
- Are you empathetic to the needs of your colleagues?

Leaders must lead

C-suite/executive leaders who are accountable for delivering the business strategy and making decisions on budget must be actively involved and accountable for DEI plan delivery as well. Colleagues take their cues from leaders' words and actions.

When it comes to DEI, CEOs/executives must:

- Be visible in support of DEI efforts.
- Ensure the business strategy has DEI embedded.
- Provide investment into communication resources and budget.
- Ensure actions and decisions match words and commitments.
- Be accessible to those leading the DEI and communication efforts.
- Be accountable for and report on results.

Ask yourself:

- Do your c-suite and top leaders lead communication of DEI for your organization, or is it simply seen as the DEI or HR leader's job?
- Have you created clear messaging that ties the organization's values, mission, vision and strategy to DEI so that leaders are consistent and comfortable?
- Are you comfortable telling leaders when their actions are in conflict with their promises and words?
- Do you have a direct connection to advise leaders on their communication approach or is there an influencer who can help?
- Do leaders need training in this space to deal with resistance, fear and anger with empathy?

Managers need support

In office, shop-floor, manufacturing, hybrid and remote workplaces, managers and supervisors are the frontline to our colleagues. Just like in any change project, they need support in order to help organizations bring the DEI strategy to life on the ground.

This becomes even more important if changes impact how they make decisions about who gets hired, fired, selected and promoted. HR and operations will make the decisions on changes, and we need to ensure that managers understand how these changes impact their actions and words. Without clarity, we risk inconsistency from managers.

Ask yourself:

- Is there a plan to brief managers on the DEI strategy?
- Can you clearly help them understand what processes stop, start and continue as a result of the plan.
- Do managers need training in order to change processes and behaviours?
- Do they need training to communicate effectively?
- Have you provided managers with answers to frequently asked questions?
- Do managers know who to ask if they have questions?

Establish clear connections

There is a correct order to this work, and connections must be made. They cannot exist in a vacuum or silo. Our focus is from the inside-out versus the outside-in. If we focus on reputation first without thinking about what we are doing inside the organization to prove our support and commitment, it will lead to anger and resentment. You can't have black boxes, rainbows and statements of support without the work to understand why DEI is important to the organization, colleagues, customers and communities.

Ask yourself:

- How is DEI connected to the vision, mission, purpose, values and strategy?
- Is there a DEI strategy supported by the business and or is there a communication strategy supporting DEI? If it's the latter, you need to influence leaders to consider the former.

- Has money been identified to invest in communication resources and programmes needed to truly move the needle forward?
- What is the role strategic communication can play to bring the plan to life and engage colleagues?

Have a clear sense of the present state

Always begin with research. A focus on understanding the present state will give you a clear starting point and help you plan the next steps, advice and counsel. It will help you set expectations on what the organization wants and needs to do to get there. It will also help identify and explain any barriers and challenges you may have along the way.

As with most audits, you may need to work with someone external to provide an unbiased opinion and recommendations to your leadership. The only exceptions are when a new DEI or communication leader joins the organization. They are often impartial enough at the beginning of the process to have credibility with both leaders and colleagues, especially since they have been hired specifically with this purpose in mind.

Ask yourself:

- When it comes to DEI, where is the organization today?
- Can you use the DEI E-volution to see where the organization and individuals are along the six stages – exist, enter, educate, embrace, engage, embed?
- Can we use one of the models and frameworks to identify our present state?
- Does it make sense to have a third party brought in to help assess present state?

Mind your bias

Understand how bias can play a role in your communication plans. We all need to acknowledge that we all have bias. Bias is our comfort zone designed to help us make unconscious decisions quickly every day. They are largely impacted by nurture versus nature. We've learned them over time to keep us safe and secure. What we often don't realize is that these biases have been informed by how we've been taught by our families, communities, educational and religious institutions and the media we interact with.

Use the SPARK framework to create conversation and address biases:

- Seek out information and find evidence.
- Powerful questions can get you to dig deeper to understand why.
- Adjust your mindset based on what you have learned.
- Revise your thinking around viewpoints and opinions.
- Kindness is critical when exploring with curiosity and confidence.

Ask yourself:

- Do I really understand my audience?
- Do I have a diverse group of colleagues that can influence plans and messaging?
- Does my team represent the publics that we serve?
- Is my plan built for people like me or does it feel like it includes everyone?
- Do I surround myself with people who think like me or do I bring different perspectives to the table?

Curiosity versus judgment

Having a growth mindset is critical for DEI work. It's important you have a mindset where you approach what is working and isn't with curiosity versus judgment. Mistakes will happen. Biases will reveal themselves. We're stepping into new territory so if we are committed to going on a learning journey and correcting as we go, we are more likely to stay the course for the long term.

When things go wrong, ask yourself why and what can you learn or do differently next time. There is also an opportunity to ensure that we position our DEI journey in the same way. We often say progress not perfect. Don't be so hard on yourself. This work is for the brave and you have the courage to want to make a difference even when the road is full of twists and turns and may be a little bumpy.

Ask yourself:

- When something goes wrong, are you hard on yourself or can you quickly move into a growth mindset?

- Do you ask yourself why and are you committed to continuous improvement?
- Are you hard on others or do you support them in staying the course through helping them learn and evolve?

Set clear goals and objectives

Best practice internal communication starts with business goals and then moves to communication objectives that are SMART – specific, measurable, achievable, realistic and time-bound. Ensure your organization's business goals are tied to the DEI goals that are then connected to the communication objectives.

The ultimate goal for internal communication is to use the power of communication to bring the business goals to life through real impact and stories. By helping the organization set clear goals, you can then set measurable objectives yourself.

Ask yourself:

- Do you ask leaders what success looks like from a business impact perspective?
- Do you ensure goals and objectives set are clear and measurable?
- Do you understand why the organization prioritized these goals versus others?
- If a colleague asks, can you clearly articulate why the goals are the goals?

Clearly define your stakeholders

One of our most important practices is to create a clear stakeholder map of who we are trying to communicate with. Our challenge with internal communication happens when we create one-size-fits-all messaging and programmes that we feel are the same for everyone. Your DEI strategy will create goals and identify processes and procedures that need to change and systems that need to be dismantled in order to create a more inclusive organization and culture. It may even identify behaviours that require changing or questioning.

As a communication professional, you need to ask who needs to be aware, understand, respond and believe. Does everyone need the same information or must it be personalized or tailored based on level, role, demographic and responsibility?

Also be conscious that different groups of individuals may have various attitudes, opinions and beliefs depending on how they perceive the changes will impact how they operate professionally and personally. Stakeholder maps give us demographic information yet also provide us with psychographic information that may impact our messaging and approach.

Ask yourself:

- Who are your colleagues now? Who are they in a more inclusive world?
- Is your communication plan tailored and personalized to address the different demographics in your organization?
- What do we need to do differently in order to engage colleagues to implement the plan?
- Are there specific departments or roles impacted by changes more than others?
- What DEI questions are going to be asked? Do we have the answers?

Incorporate listening

In our work, listening exercises are critical in planning, delivering and evaluating communication and DEI strategies. By using surveys, pulses, polls and focus groups, you have an opportunity to both test your ideas and messaging and slowly help stakeholders through the change process.

We've seen some of our clients lock themselves into a room and create a DEI strategy and subsequently a communication plan independently without consultation. In some cases, they have been working and reworking plans for months. Then when they are ready to launch, they press send or announce the strategy as a celebration expecting to receive pats on the back and kudos, only to be greeted with shock and anger.

One of the ways to acclimatize colleagues to changes is to announce that you are working on a plan. Ask them for ideas on how it is best to communicate with them. Participate in conversations about what they are afraid of or excited about. And answer questions along the way. Once launched, ask colleagues what they like about the strategy and what they think needs to be improved. The key here is to ensure colleagues feel heard and safe expressing their concerns so that you can address them with facts.

It's also important to proactively seek out diverse perspectives if your team lacks diversity or representation.

Ask yourself:

- Do colleagues know that a DEI plan is in the works?
- Do colleagues understand the core objectives of the DEI plan?
- Do they have a chance to express their concerns and have questions answered?
- Can they provide feedback along the way?
- Do you have a place where frequently asked questions can be archived and answered?

Focus on the conversation not the campaign

It's not unusual for internal communication professionals to see DEI communication as a series of campaigns. Let's host celebrations every week or month. Let's create posters that show diversity no one sees in real life and advertising that identifies a future state disconnected with the present state.

The real opportunity in internal communication is to drive conversations that link the strategy to actions and results. Instead of talking about what we're doing wrong, perhaps we talk about where we are, where we want to go and what needs to change to get there.

Ask yourself:

- Where can you create conversations that matter?
- Do you challenge campaigns that are superficial or disconnected from reality?
- Where conversations are happening that you are not aware of?
- Can you bring colleagues together to work on solutions?
- Do you have a strong relationship with the DEI leader?

Make sure you are ready to manage change

Remember that DEI strategies are change plans that are personal. It is okay for humans to react with shock, denial, frustration, anger and resistance before they move to acceptance, adoption and commitment. For organizations who have been successful and comfortable in the present state, the thought of change is incredibly uncomfortable. They are grieving what was and are afraid of what is required of them in order to step into an unknown future.

By acknowledging people's human reaction to change, we can create personalized messages that paint a picture of a future that they can buy into.

Ask yourself:

- What is the organization's readiness for change?
- Where are individuals and groups on the change curve or cycle?
- What information do you need to communicate to help them be aware, understand, act and believe?
- Create desire, focus on knowledge, build ability and reinforce messages (ADKAR).

Measure results

Make sure you measure results and track progress along the way. Use the AMEC Integrated Evaluation Framework to identify outputs, outtakes, outcomes and organizational impacts in order to truly connect the communication work to business results:

- Outputs are all of the things you need to deliver.
- Outtakes are the consumption of what you've delivered. Did people read the email and attend training? Did they click to the new policy?
- Outcomes are behaviour-based. Did they change their behaviour as a result of the training. Did they understand the new code of conduct? Did they hire a more diverse team?
- Organizational impact is the impact on the business as a result of changes. Are we seeing changes to customer experience or innovation? Did new ideas emerge? Did the organization find new markets that have grown sales?

Colleagues are going to be looking for proof that DEI strategies are working. This applies evenly to those excited about DEI efforts and those sceptical about them.

Ask yourself:

- What did you deliver? How did you make colleagues aware? What changes did you see that could be measured?
- Do you tell the success stories linked to DEI efforts?
- Do you also share stories of failures and what you learned to do better next time?

Create a scorecard

Many organizations create DEI scorecards to identify where they are making progress and where they are experiencing challenges. Some simply showcase changes: a plus sign (+) to identify improvement, an equal sign (=) to identify no change and a minus sign (-) to explain that we have gone backwards. Other organizations use green for completion, yellow for progress and red to explain lack of action or a programme that has not yet started or is stalled. Some other organizations simply identify measurable targets and provide annual numbers-based updates on progress toward the target.

Whatever you use, a report card tends to be a simple way to provide updates to internal and external stakeholders. Some organizations measure progress annually, while others provide quarterly or more frequent updates.

Ask yourself:

- Does it make sense to create a report card to showcase DEI initiatives and progress?
- Can you make it visual and easy to understand?
- Can you create a regular process for updates?

Highlight milestones achieved along the way

Outside of scorecards and annual reviews, make sure you highlight milestones achieved. Celebrate success. Highlight innovation. Explain the benefits of the strategy. What people want to see is progress along the way.

In other words, they want to see the values, strategy, vision and mission in action.

Remember to close the loop. Here is what was planned. Here is what we did and accomplished. Here is the impact on the business.

Ask yourself:

- What are the milestones identified and promises made in the business and DEI plan?
- Are there smaller achievable steps to highlight along the way?
- Can you create clear connections to achieving DEI milestones and the subsequent impact to the business?

Share stories

There is a real opportunity to encourage storytelling both formally and informally. What we've learnt is that there is so much inspiration out there when people are allowed to share their success and what it took to get there. There is also an opportunity to use storytelling to help leaders and colleagues to connect with their similarities.

There is a chance for both leaders and peers to share their lived experiences and break down barriers by being authentic and perhaps vulnerable if they are comfortable doing so.

A recent article on sharing stories to build inclusion in the *Harvard Business Review* (Gordon and Rezvani, 2021) highlighted that when people hear stories that feel representative, it creates a vehicle for nuanced conversations that can truly drive change. In her book *Stories for Work*, Gabrielle Dolan (Dolan, 2017) talks about the four types of stories you need in business. They are stories of:

- Triumph – Moments you are proud of.
- Tragedy – Moments when you felt regret or when something negative happened to you.
- Tension – Moments that may have compromised your values.
- Transition – Moments where you faced a choice or significant change.

The key to storytelling, according to Dolan, is that the story must be authentic/true and it must be linked to purpose or a business objective. We believe that from an inclusion perspective, the story may simply be used to create connection, awareness and understanding.

Ask yourself:

- Can you encourage leaders and colleagues to tell their stories?
- How can you help to build confidence in others so that a diverse range of stories can be shared to connect people?
- Can we use a story to show humanity and vulnerability to create connection?

Embed DEI into operations

The goal with DEI programmes is to change systems of bias and operations that were previously consciously or unconsciously used to discriminate. A sign of success, over time, involves what was a new and uncomfortable process or system simply becoming the way we do things around here without a second thought. That's why it's so important that DEI is not seen as an arm's length initiative that functions in a vacuum and is one leader's or team's responsibility.

From a communication perspective, there is an opportunity to look at your own operations when it comes to DEI. Is your team representative of your customers, communities and colleagues? Do you have the perspectives needed to tell stories accurately? What changes need to be made to accurately advise leaders on DEI?

Ask yourself:

- Where can we embed DEI into our own operations?
- Are our actions aligning with our words and promises?
- Are there disconnects between what we say and what we do that could harm our credibility?

Enable, engage and empower

We believe that the role of internal communication is to:

Enable – Give colleagues the information they need.

Engage – Encourage colleagues to get involved and make a difference.

Empower – Provide clear direction so that colleagues make the right decisions and exhibit the right behaviours when no one is watching.

This does not happen by accident or osmosis. People do not magically know what is expected of them and until they receive clear direction, they simply do their best and make up their own actions and stories. It's a best-guess scenario in most cases.

By proactively creating an inclusive internal communication plan, colleagues can become aware, understand, act and believe they belong and can thrive in our organizations. Our role is to create connection between the words said and the promises made to the actions and experiences delivered inside and outside the organization.

Ask yourself:

- Do colleagues have the information they need?
- Can colleagues get involved in the DEI strategy in development, during launch or in sustainable programmes?
- Do colleagues have what they need to impact words, decisions and behaviours?

Relationships are key

Progress on any initiative requires collaboration and teamwork. This is especially important with DEI work. We require engagement from the top down. Internal communication professionals must work closely with leadership, DEI professionals, HR professionals and operational teams. You will need to rely on diverse perspectives to ensure you address hopes and fears. The role of internal communication is to use communication expertise to solve business problems. By understanding pain points and people, you have a better chance of bringing their perspectives to decision makers.

Ask yourself:

- Do we have a trusted relationship with all leaders needed for DEI to succeed?
- Do we know ERG advocates and ambassadors?
- Do we foster collaboration to drive success?

Ask for help

As internal communication professionals, we are more powerful not when we are communicating on behalf of our organization and leaders but when we are influencing how our organizations, their leaders and colleagues communicate.

It's important that you do not do this work alone. DEI success is when everyone in the organization has a role to play in creating inclusive cultures. If your bandwidth is limited, ask for resources or bring in a third party to assist. There is expertise out there that you can rely on to evaluate present state, create strategies and deliver results.

Ask yourself:

- Do you have the resources you need to drive culture change?
- Are there others in your organization who can help?
- Can you bring in temporary support to fill in gaps and provide expertise?

Build confidence

We've often said that the challenges that face internal communication professionals from being more strategic are not capabilities and capacity but more about courage and confidence. Use the models and frameworks to identify present state. Say 'no' to the busy work that has the communication team running in circles checking boxes and make the case for the work that will drive change and impact culture. The risk is attrition, disengagement and apathy.

Work with leaders and colleagues to identify priorities that will really make a difference.

Ask yourself:

- What work takes a lot of time and has no relevance on DEI progress or improving culture?
- What are the few things you can do to drive change?
- What are the priorities most important to the organization connected to DEI?

Conclusion

In a recent study by Lever (Schwantes, 2021) major misalignments between employers and colleagues were discovered that were hindering DEI efforts. One interesting finding was the fact that nearly all employers reported that they had introduced inclusion measures in the past year, while a quarter of organizations reported that their colleagues had not introduced new measures. What is clear is there is a lack of awareness.

We believe that internal communication is an integral enabler of business success and helps connect the dots. We can choose to believe that just because we've built a diversity plan and have good intentions for a fair and just organization, colleagues will automatically know what to do. Unfortunately, it doesn't work this way.

The role of internal communication is to fill the gaps, create clarity, reinforce action and encourage conversations that build trust over time. It's also our privilege to influence others – their words and behaviours – and use the power of communication to help leaders and colleagues understand what good practice looks like.

Our role in creating inclusive cultures enables powerful connections. We use our expertise in communication and our understanding of people to solve business problems, in this case, progress on DEI. By bringing DEI plans to life and understanding the nuances of how people react professionally and personally to change, we have the potential to allow people to thrive in their work and impact organizational performance.

Bibliography

Chiu, B (2022, 1 March) Investors are waking up to market potential of diversity, equity and inclusion, Forbes, forbes.com/sites/bonniechiu/2022/03/01/investors-are-waking-up-to-market-potential-of-diversity-equity-and-inclusion/?sh=6b148e5d5597 (archived at https://perma.cc/A5GB-NP67)

Dolan, G (2017) *Stories for Work: The essential guide to business storytelling.* Melbourne, Wiley

Gordon, S A and Rezvani, S (2021, 1 November) How sharing our stories builds inclusion, *Harvard Business Review*, hbr.org/2021/11/how-sharing-our-stories-builds-inclusion (archived at https://perma.cc/L9EZ-99KZ)

Poppulo (2022) Resources, poppulo.com/resources (archived at https://perma.cc/WD47-WC3X)

Schwantes, M (2021, 5 October) Study: What companies are doing (and not doing) to make the workplace more diverse, Inc., inc.com/marcel-schwantes/study-what-companies-are-doing-and-not-doing-to-make-workplace-more-diverse.html (archived at https://perma.cc/H2EA-ZWWE)

INDEX

NB: page numbers in *italic* indicate figures or tables

4A Framework, the 2–3, 137–59, *138*, 228
  accountability 154–57
    dashboards 157, *158*
    organizational impact 156
    outtakes, outcomes and outputs 155
  acknowledgement 139–45
    of bias 140–41
    defining 139
    of diversity 144
    of effort 144–45
    of existence 139–40
    of history 141–42
    of importance 140
    of pain 143–44
    of systems 142–43
  action 149–54
    action plans, your 150–51
    focus areas 151
  apologizing 157–59
  awareness 145–49
    listening exercises 148
    surveys 147–48
    where we are 145–46
    where we want to be 147

abbreviations 3–4
Accessible Social 243
accuracy, in comms 54
Adidas 191
affirmative action 198
age 14, *15*, 84, 212–13
  inclusive language around 233–34, *234*
Ahmed-Omer, Dahabo 74
AIDE (accessibility, inclusion, diversity,
    equity) 4
Airbnb 38
allyship, understanding 190, 245
AMEC Integrated Evaluation
    Framework 155, 287
anchoring bias 86, 87
Anna Delvey Foundation 81
Anthony, Susan B 207
anti-bias training 140–41, 174
antisemitism 18

Arbery, Ahmaud 188
Asana 26
assumptions, making 54
AT&T 27
authority bias 97
availability heuristic 87
awareness days 193–94

Baby Boomers 14
Bailey-King, Ettie 223
bandwagon effect 87, 187
Barnes, Bob 142
beacons *see* flashlights, mirrors and beacons
belonging 8
Benson, Buster 86
Berry, Jennie 235
bias 80–99, 282–83
  acknowledging 140–41
  anti-bias training 140–41, 174
  Cognitive Bias Codex 86
  common biases *87–88*
  and curiosity 87, 89–92
    humility, intellectual 90–91
    SPARK framework 91–92, 95
  decisions, making 82–83
  defining 81–82
  internal communication, role of 92–95
  stereotypes 84
  and trust 80–81
  unconscious bias 84–86, 246–47
Bill of Rights, US Constitution 9
Black, Asian, Minority Ethnic (BAME) 240
Blackburn, David 152, 154
Black History Month 69, 195
Black, Indigenous, People of Colour
    (BIPOC) 240
Black Lives Matter movement 18, 187–89
Blacknorth Initiative 74
Botsman, Rachel 37
brand promises 258
BRAVING framework 44–45
Breakfast Culture 175
BrewDog 36–37
British monarchy, the 89–90

Brown, Brené 44
burnout 21, 36
Business Case for Equity, The 175

Camhi, Sarah 191
Campbell, Andrew B 179
Canadian Association of University Teachers
          (CAUT) 147
candidate evaluation tools 22
Carpenter, Mary 207
Center for Culturally Proficient Education
          Practice 179
Centre for Global Inclusion 165
Chan, Arthur 198
change, managing 287
     Cycle for Change, the 161–65, *162*
     leadership, role of 74–77, 165
          belief 75–76
          communication leader 76
          desired state, the 76–77
          enablement 77
          follow-up 77
          participation 75
Cherry, Don 158, 159
Coca-Cola 27, 256–57
'cognitive bias' 82
     Cognitive Bias Codex 86
cognitive dissonance 88
cognitive diversity 95–98
colleague programmes 259
Combahee River Collective 207
confirmation bias 88, 96, 97
Coty 27
Courtaulds Plant 107
Covey, Stephen 34, 39, 42–43, 45
Covid-19 pandemic 1, 16, 21, 36, 102, 111
credibility *40*, 41
Crenshaw, Kimberlé Williams 205–06,
          207, 216
Croneberger, Jen 258
cultural appropriation 245
Cultural Competence Continuum *178*,
          179–81
cultural competency 245
curiosity 87, 89–92, 231, 283–84
     humility, intellectual 90–91
     SPARK framework 91–92, 95
Cycle for Change, the 161–65, *162*
     internal communication, role of 164,
          165, *166*

Dare To Lead 44
Darrell, Jefferson 175
dashboards 157, *158*

DeBruine, Lisa 81
DeGaffernreid v General Motors 206
DEIB (diversity, equity, inclusion,
          belonging) 4
DEI E-volution *68*, 282
     Educate 70–71
     Embed 73–74
     Embrace 71–72
     Engage 72–73
     Enter 69–70
     Exist 68–69
dignity 8
disability 14–15, 84
     ableism 245
     inclusive language around 235, *236*
     social model of disability 235
     #Wethe15 15
disinformation 39
'diversity of thought' *see* cognitive diversity
diversity targets 198–99
Dolan, Gabrielle 289
Drucker, Peter 114

eBay 38
Edelman Trust Barometer 38, 62
EDI (equality/equity, diversity,
          inclusion) 3–4
Edmondson, Amy 49
Elections Act 2022 233
Elizabeth II, Queen of England 89–90
employee engagement 36, 249–71
     Gallup Q12 249–50
     Inner Strength Engagement Model
          (ISEM) *252*, 252–71, *270*
          foundations, organizational 256–60
          goals, setting 253–56
          results, measuring and
               sharing 267–70
          right behaviour, recognizing
               the 264–67
          training 260–64
employee resource groups (ERGs) 18, 69,
          70, 148
     and intersectionality 208–10
employee value proposition (EVP) 108, 258
English Bill of Rights 9
Equality Act 2010 (UK) 198, 237, 241
Equality Act, US 198
Equity Continuum 175–78, *176*
equity vs equality 19–20, 246
ethnicity
     diversity, impact on results 24
     ethnocentrism 245
     inclusive language around 240–41, *241*

Etsy 38
European Commission 226
Everyone Belongs CRIAW-ICREF's
        Intersectionality Wheel 210–11
Expedia 27

Facebook 62, 108, 153
    Facebook Marketplace 38
Farley, Harriet 104
Fawcett, Millicent 207
Fearless Organization, The 49
feedback, gathering 53–54, 269–70
Field, Jenni 113
Field of Dreams 260
Financial Services Compensation Scheme
        (FSCS) 152–54
flashlights, mirrors and beacons 10–11, *12*,
        276, 276–77
Fleishmanhillard 231–32
Floyd, George 1–2, 9, 18, 83, 143, 188, 276
foundations, organizational 278–79
Fulani, Ngozi 85, 86

Gallup Q12 249–50
gender 16, 84
    gender pay gaps 16, 93
    inclusive language around 236–37,
        237–38
    misogyny 246
Generation X 14
Generation Z 14, 27
Glassdoor 38, 108
Global Diversity, Equity and Inclusion
        Benchmarks (GDEIB) Model 165,
        167–75, *169*
    benchmarks summary 168–69
    internal communication, role of 170–75
    levels in 170
glossary, organizational 259
'Great Resignation, The' 21, 65
groupthink 87, 96, 97
growth mindset 111
'gut feeling' 89

Hall, Wes 74
halo effect 88
Handbook of Nonsexist Writing, The 225
Harvard Business School 257
Heinrich, Alexa 243
Heron, Alexander R 104–05
Hiatt, Jeff 195
Hierarchy of Needs theory 61
history, acknowledging 276
history of DEI 9–10

Holocaust, the 141
Hooman, Daniel 183
Human Side of Enterprise, The 105
Humphrey, John 9
Hussey, Susan 85
Hyde, Cheryle and Hopkins, Karen 181

iceberg model of culture *114*
    artefacts 115
    assumptions, basic 116–17
    values, shared 115–16
IDEA (inclusion, diversity, equity,
        accessibility) 4
identity-first language 4, 231
Ifill, Gwen 207
Inclusion on Purpose 2
inconsistency, in comms 55
influencers 37, 66, 197
Influential Internal Communication 113
information overload, avoiding 55–56
Inner Strength Engagement Model
        (ISEM) *252*, 252–71, *270*
    foundations, organizational 256–60
    goals, setting 253–56
    results, measuring and sharing 267–70
    right behaviour, recognizing the 264–67
    training 260–64
Inner Strength i5 framework 118–30
    impact 129–30
    implementation 119
    influence 128–29
    integration 127–28
    interaction 119, 127
Institute of Internal Communication
        (IoIC) 105, 113
    Profession Map Framework 109, 112
Intel 27
internal communication 102–31
    and bias 92–95
    and change 164, 165, *166*
    communication channels for 119,
        120–26
    Cycle for Change, the 164, 165, *166*
    defining 113
    employee engagement 263–64
    enable, engage and empower 290–91
    Global Diversity, Equity and Inclusion
        Benchmarks (GDEIB)
        Model 170–75
    employee value proposition
        (EVP) 108
    'house organs' 105
    social media 108
    history of 103–08

internal communication (*Continued*)
   iceberg model of culture *114*
      artefacts 115
      assumptions, basic 116–17
      values, shared 115–16
   inclusive behaviours 117, *118*
   influential people for *129*
   Inner Strength i5 framework 118–30
      impact 129–30
      implementation 119
      influence 128–29
      integration 127–28
      interaction 119, 127
   outtakes, outcomes and
      outputs 130
   performative actions 192–93
   relationships, building 291
   research methods for *126*
   skills for *112*
      active listening 109–10
      adaptability 111
      analysis 110
      challenging 112
      creativity 110–11
      curiosity 112
      empathy 110
      empowering others 111
      tenacity 110
      trustworthiness 111
   and trust 45–49, 52–56
      pitfalls in 53–56
International Bill of Human Rights 10
International Day of People with
      Disabilities 195, 265
International Women's Day 62, 69, 93, 189,
      195, 208
intersectionality 205–21, 246
   defining 205–08
   employee resource groups
      (ERGs) 208–10
   Everyone Belongs CRIAW-ICREF's
      Intersectionality Wheel 210–11
   inclusion, steps to 213–15
   internal communication, role
      of 216–17
   'Missing White Woman Syndrome' 207
   'Oppression Olympics' 209, 215
   and personalization 218–21
      technology, using 219
   Privilege Pyramid *211*, 211–12
intimacy *40*, 41
Inventing Anna 81
'invisible army syndrome' 86, 89
Islamophobia 18

jargon, removing 242–43
JEDI (justice, equity, diversity, inclusion) 4
Jet Blue 26
Johnson, Kevin 23
Just Billingham 105
justice 8

Kahneman, Daniel 82–83
Kashyap, Deepak 12
Khan, Maria 232
King, Martin Luther 29
Klein, Mike 128
Klotz, Anthony 21
Koh-i-Noor diamond 90
Krais, Howard, Pounsford, Mike and Ruck,
      Kevin 200
Kübler-Ross Grief Cycle 161–62

'lack of action fatigue' 56
language, inclusive 223–47
   accessibility, online 243–44
   age 233–34, *234*
   change, in language over time 225, 227
   defining 224
   disability 235, *236*
   discriminatory language 233
   ethnicity 240–41, *241*
   gender 236–37, *237–38*
   glossary 245–47
   history of 225–27
   jargon, removing 242–43
   mental health 238, *239*
   mindset, your 227–29
   mistakes, making 231
   neurodiversity 238–40, *240*
   principles of 229–31
   race 240–41, *241*
   religion 240–41, *241*
   sexual orientation 236–37, *237–38*
   social mobility 241–42, *241*
leadership 280
   and change 74–77, 165
      belief 75–76
      communication leader 76
      desired state, the 76–77
      enablement 77
      follow-up 77
      participation 75
   cognitive diversity, fostering 96–98
   importance of 60–61
   inclusive behaviours 117, *118*
   and representation 140, 182–83
   shared values, modelling 116
   Theory X and Theory Y 105–06

and trust 41–43, 46–49, 53, 55, 61–62
    communication leader 64–65
    C-suite / executive 62–63
    DEI leader 63–64
    individual contributor 67
    influencer 66
    people manager 65–66
    types 60
LGBTQ+ people see sexual orientation
LinkedIn 26, 38, 153
listening 285–86
    active listening 109–10, 199–202
    listening exercises 148
lived experience 246
LIZZO 158, 159
Loden, Marilyn and Rosener, Judy 210
Lowell Offering 103–04, 109
Lululemon 177–78

Maclean, Ron 158
Magna Carta 9
Make America Great Again 11
managers, supporting 281
Manoogian III, John (JM3) 86
Maslow, Abraham 61
Mastercard 27
McGregor, Douglas 105–06
Menopause Workplace Pledge 153
mental health 209
    inclusive language around 238, 239
'MeToo' movement 143
microaggressions 85, 246, 267–68
    apologizing for 157–59
Millennials 14, 27
Miller, Casey and Swift, Kate 225
'Minoritised NHS Manager™' 189
mirrors see flashlights, mirrors and
        beacons
misinformation 39
misogyny 246
'Missing White Woman Syndrome' 207
mission, organizational 257–58, 282
Myers, Verna and Juday, Daniel 96

National Coal Board 107
National Council of Teachers of English 225
National Front 106
National Health Service (NHS) 257
Netflix 267–68
net promoter score (NPS) 196
    employee net promoter score (eNPS) 126
neurodiversity 200–01, 243
    inclusive language around 238–40, 240
Nike 26, 27, 149, 149

observer effect 86
O'Mara, Julie and Richter, Alan 167
On Death and Dying 161
'Oppression Olympics' 209, 215
Organizational Diversity Climate
        Continuum 181–83, 182
outtakes, outcomes and outputs 130,
        155, 287

Parnes, Rachel 29
peer reviews 38
people-first language 4, 231
people-manager communication 262–63
PepsiCo 24–25
performative actions 187–202, 264
    active listening, importance of 199–202
    allyship, understanding 190, 245
    awareness days 193–94
    diversity targets 198–99
    internal communication, role of 192–93
    process, proper 195–97
PESTLE analysis 47
Pfizer 27
Planned Parenthood 198
policies, organizational 258
positive action 198
Pride Awareness Month 189, 195
Principles of Responsible Investment
        (PRI) 275
Privilege Pyramid 211, 211–12
privilege, understanding your 85–86, 246
'progress not perfect' 3, 138, 156
pronouns 225, 246
Prosci 195
protected characteristics 198, 211, 246
psychological safety 49–51, 50
purpose, organizational 257–58, 282

race 16, 17, 17–18
    anti-racism 245
    Black History Month 69, 195
    Black Lives Matter movement 18,
        187–89
    colourism 245
    inclusive language around 240–41, 241
    progress in the 1960s 106–07
    systemic racism 142
    white supremacy 11, 61, 207, 275
Race Relations Act 1965 106
RACI charts 150–51
'rainbow-washing' 189
Ravishankar, Raskshita Arni 85
Rebel Ideas 97
recognition programmes 266

Reddit 38
Refugee613 158
Reinemund, Steven 25
relevance, in comms 54
reliability *40*, 41
religion 18
    inclusive language around 240–41, *241*
representation 20, 54, 277–78
residential schools, Canada 18, 143
Reynolds, Alison and Lewis, David 97
Rice, David 14
Roosevelt, Eleanor 9
Ruck, Kevin 113

safe spaces 44, 49, 50, 97–98, 118, 144,
        199, 246
Schein, Edgar 114
scorecards, using 288
self-identification 147–48, 230–31, 251
self-orientation *40*, 41
sexual orientation 18–19
    inclusive language around 236–37,
        237–38
    'rainbow-washing' 189
Shapiro, Ben 215
Sharing Information with Employees 104
Silverman, David 141
Sinek, Simon 7
    Golden Circle 25
SMART goals, setting 76, 150, 193, 284
social mobility
    inclusive language around 241–42, *241*
social model of disability 235
Sorokin, Anna 81–82
SPARK framework 91–92, 95, 110, 283
Speed of Trust, The 34, 42
Sportsnet 158
stakeholders, your 119, 173, 284–85
Starbucks 23
stereotypes 84
Stories for Work 289
storytelling 116, 266, 289–90
strategies, organizational 258–59, 281–82
success, celebrating 288–89
surveys 147–48, 200
SWOT analysis 47
Syed, Matthew 97
System 1 and System 2 thinking 82–83, 96

Taylor, Breonna 188
technology, organizational 259–60
Thanksgiving 141
Theory X and Theory Y 105–06
Thinking, Fast and Slow 82

This Land is Their Land 141
Thomas, Jamila and Agyemang, Brianna 188
Thornhurst, Sara 13
TikTok 38
tokenism 181, 187–89
toxic productivity 36
Traditionalists 14
Transport and General Workers Union
        (TGWU) 107
TripAdvisor 38
Truss, Liz 95–96
trust 34–57, 279–80
    and bias 80–81
    distributed trust 37–38
    employee engagement 36
    institutional trust 37
    internal communication, role of 45–49,
        52–56
        pitfalls in 53–56
    in leadership 41–43, 46–49, 53, 55,
        61–62
    local trust 37
    organizational values 51–52
    psychological safety 49–51, *50*
    reputation 36–37
    and self-identification 147–48
    'trust gap', the 51
    trustworthiness behaviours *40*, 53
    Trustworthiness Equation 39, *40*, 81
    and vulnerability 44–45
Tulshyan, Ruchika 2
Turchin, Peter 61
Tversky, Amos and Kahneman, Daniel 82
Twitter 38, 108, 153, 189
    bots on 189, 265

UN Commission on Human Rights 9
unconscious bias 84–86, 246–47
'Uncovering Belonging' 12
unique selling propositions (USPs) 258
United Airlines 27
Universal Declaration of Human Rights
        (UDHR) 9, 10
UN Sustainable Development Goals 172
US Airlines 235

vagueness, in comms 55
values, corporate 256–57
vision, organizational 257–58, 282

'warrior mentality' 12–13
Weinstein, Harvey 143
Westfall, Chris 139
#Wethe15 15

white supremacy 11, 61, 207, 275
why? of DEI 278
    for employees
        people 28
        performance 28
        personal 29
        progress 27
        purpose 26–27
    for employers
        recruitment 22–23
        representation 20
        reputation 23
        results 24

retention 21–22
rights 19–20
William and the Werewolf 225
Wilson, Chip 177
Wilson, Trevor 175
'worth' 8

Ye (Kanye West) 191, 268
YouTube 108

Zak, Paul J 46, 48
Zhao, Chloé 29
Zuckerberg, Mark 62